FILMMAKERS SERIES

edited by
ANTHONY SLIDE

In Preparation

TWENTIETH CENTURY-FOX:

A Corporate and Financial History

by

AUBREY SOLOMON

Filmmakers, No. 20

THE SCARECROW PRESS, INC.
METUCHEN, N.J., & LONDON
1988

Permission has been granted by the following for the publication of extracts from an oral history and previously published material: Philip Dunne, Stanley Hough, Michael Nolin, Tom Stempel (for his participation in the Dunne oral history), and <u>American Cinematographer</u> for the article "Cinemascope--What it is; How it Works," Vol. 34, No. 3, March 1953, p. 112.

British Library Cataloguing-in-Publication data available

Library of Congress Cataloging-in-Publication Data

Solomon, Aubrey.
   Twentieth Century-Fox : a corporate and financial history / by Aubrey Solomon.
      p.   cm. -- (Filmmakers ; no. 20)
   Bibliography: p.
   Includes index.
   ISBN 0-8108-2147-8
   1. Twentieth Century-Fox Film Corporation--History. 2. Twentieth Century-Fox Film Corporation--Finance. I. Title. II. Series: Filmmakers series ; no. 20.
PN1999.T8S55   1988
384'.8'0979494--dc19   88-18403

■ CONTENTS ■

▪ TABLES ▪

■ EDITOR'S FOREWORD ■

Although there have been many book-length histories of individual studios, these studies tend to concentrate on the product and the personalities behind the films. This is the first volume to offer a corporate and financial study of a specific studio from its beginnings to the present. The studio here is Twentieth Century-Fox, but the book serves as a valuable textbook for the workings of any major studio. That it is Twentieth Century-Fox is important in that it is one of the few extant studios (the only other two are Paramount and Universal) which have been powerful entities within the film industry from the teen years into the eighties. The surviving studios from the early years of the motion picture industry were all dominated by strong, often ruthless men, and the powerful individuality of the central figures in the history of Twentieth Century-Fox is apparent throughout this study.

Aubrey Solomon is a professional film producer and screenwriter--he was involved in the popular Twentieth Century-Fox television series That's Hollywood. He is also coauthor of the standard volume on The Films of Twentieth Century-Fox (currently available in a revised 1985 edition). This present book makes a perfect companion piece to the earlier study. It also breaks new ground for the Filmmakers series, being the first book to examine the role of a company, rather than an individual, as a filmmaker.

Anthony Slide

Darryl F. Zanuck

■ AUTHOR'S NOTE ■

Much has already been written about Twentieth Century-Fox, its movies, and the talent it created and nurtured. Darryl Zanuck, in particular, has been the subject of several (some very good) biographies. This volume is not intended to be a complete history of the studio and its movies. Instead, it covers a general overview of the finances (in laymen's terms, not accountants') and corporate practices in producing and releasing the studio's output. As well, it tries to present a clear development of the movie business and audience trends, charting a path to the crazy quilt of financing and producing patterns in today's market.

The terms "box office gross," "net receipts," "gross rentals," and "distributor's gross" have been simplified for the purpose of this volume. "Box office gross" or "gross" refers to the dollars which come into the theater. "Film rentals" are the amount remitted to the distributor after the theater takes its percentage (usually figured on a sliding scale depending on the weekly take). "Domestic rentals" refer to the United States and Canadian (English-speaking only) markets, while "foreign rentals" cover all other markets and French-speaking Canada. "Negative cost" usually refers to the total amount a studio pays (including interest) to get a picture into release, excluding advertising, print, and distribution costs. Under the studio system, it is impossible to figure out whether figures on older movies had interest charged to their total costs, so for the purpose of this study, "negative cost" will, for all intents and purposes, represent the actual cost of the movie, excluding interest.

It has always been taken for granted in Hollywood that the figures given out on motion picture costs varied depending on who was releasing the information or what purpose it was to serve. After a great deal of research, in and around the Fox studio, the figures reported here are, to the best of anyone's abilities, accurate. This does not mean there cannot be errors in judgment or information. However, for the most part, over the past decade, the information seems to have been held up and has been confirmed with various cross-checks. Grosses and rentals are a little more difficult. Again, research has indicated that the reports published in Variety are relatively accurate. Since they began publishing rental figures only in 1946, a reconstruction was necessary to provide the Fox figures from 1935 onward. This has been done using another periodical which gauged results, Boxoffice magazine. Comparing the Boxoffice percentage of average business figures to grosses in post-1946 years, it was possible to construct a corresponding set of dollar results. This serves as the basis for Appendix A on Fox's domestic rentals.

This project began as an American Film Institute Research Associateship under the Louis B. Mayer Foundation. Gratitude is extended for their contribution towards laying the groundwork for this final work. Also, thanks are extended to the late Nunnally Johnson, Delmer Daves, Sol Lesser, and Samuel G. Engel, and the still-active Philip Dunne, Stanley Hough, and Michael Nolin for the time they gave for interviews. Tom Stempel's set of oral histories for the Louis B. Mayer Foundation was also an incalculable help, and Bob Knutson of the U.S.C. Special Collections of the Doheny Library graciously made Philip Dunne's collection of scripts and memos available. Also, thanks go to Gina, Gabriel, and Eden. Last but certainly most important, my gratitude is acknowledged to Jack Haley, Jr., whose offer of employment at Twentieth Century-Fox ultimately made the verification of much financial research possible.

Aubrey Solomon
No. Hollywood, CA
June 1987

▪ INTRODUCTION ▪

In June 1981, Marvin Davis, a Denver oil wildcatter, purchased Twentieth Century-Fox. For the first time since the
heady days of Hollywood, an individual owned a major motion
picture studio. It was yet another milestone in the tumul-
tuous history of probably one of the most high-profile corporations in the world. Movies and television programs are
mass-market products in the supreme glamour industry. A
business sometimes runs on whim and gargantuan egos; it
offers fame and wealth by selling adventure, beauty, and
dreams.

The history of Twentieth Century-Fox encompasses virtually the entire life of the movies and it remains one of the
few major studios to survive and prosper after seventy years.
R.K.O. and M-G-M have been ruthlessly dismantled; Paramount was taken over by Gulf + Western; Columbia by Coca-
Cola; Warner Bros. by Kinney, then spun off as Warner
Communications; United Artists became a part of the Transamerica conglomerate, then was married to M-G-M and di-
vorced shortly after. Only Disney and Universal, which itself
became a part of the giant Music Corporation of America,
exist in relative autonomy within their own realms. Fox,
recently absorbed into the Rupert Murdoch media conglomerate,
is now the fairly autonomous cornerstone of a production and
broadcasting empire being developed by the Australian publishing magnate.

Because of the personality-driven nature of the motion
picture business, the current studio is a result of a compo-
site blend of strong-willed creative people who joined together to promote one of the greatest forms of mass entertainment in modern times.

In its seventy years, Fox Films and Twentieth Century-

Fox have given the world an indelible stream of entertainment and images. It has helped society weather some hard times--the Depression, World War II, and the political upheaval of the postwar years, providing much-needed escapism. It has also contributed to the visual legacy of an entire culture and helped shape the soul of several generations.

However artful some of its releases may be, there is a fact of life. Twentieth Century-Fox, like any other corporation, is a business and a business can function only with a cash flow--which brings up the subject of money. Whether one approaches filmmaking as an art or an industry, its final product is indisputably very expensive.

In the golden years of Hollywood, when Twentieth Century-Fox, as well as the other studios, owned its own theater chains, the entire business was a closed circle. Only studio bookkeepers knew for certain whether a picture made or lost money and even then they were never sure. The more money a movie grossed, the more overhead a studio lopped off that gross. With such practices, most movies never showed more than meager profits. However, the money was going from one area of the company, exhibition, to another, distribution, then back to its origin, production. The only monies paid out were to the government, and that was a mighty strong reason to show as little profit as possible.

Things have changed. The entire financing structure of the motion picture industry has been radically altered over the years. Public investment is now steadily finding its way into film financing, talents are sharing in grosses or profits, and the sale of stock in all companies makes it imperative for companies to explain their expenditures.

This new source of financial information along with the regular reportage of Daily Variety and The Hollywood Reporter, industry trade papers, has led to a greater awareness of what exactly is at stake when a studio like Fox decides to earmark $20 million for a movie. In addition to the negative costs, there are the staggering advertising and distribution expenses which can add $10 million to get an initial $20 million investment played off. The odds against making back that amount are just as staggering. If a film of that cost is only moderately successful at the box office, it will gross $50 million. Whereas that figure may once have been tantamount to a blockbuster, today's economics conspire to make it a studio disaster. Probably half that amount would be kept by the theaters. After distribution costs of 35 percent on the remaining $25 million, there is only $16.25 million returning to the producer--assuming the star does not have 10 percent of the gross up to $20 million. Otherwise, a further $5 million disappear into a performer's pocket, leaving an $11.25 million return to the production department on an outlay of $30 million. The loss is $18.75 million, not including interest which has been charged to the production.

That said, it is easy to understand why money plays such a heavy-handed part in why a movie is made. A bankable star like Tom Cruise, a white-hot director like Steven Spielberg, or a script so uniquely commercial as RAIDERS OF THE LOST ARK is enough reason to make a movie. Without an overview, one would think that it wasn't always this way. If so, how did sensitive, controversial, artistic movies get made? The answer was always the same--money. Industry has fostered filmmaking, not art.

Today, with budgets and grosses more familiarly discussed by critics and television commentators, a movie's cost has become another production statistic--like cast or credits. Reviewers are ready to chastise Michael Cimino not only for making an unsatisfactory HEAVEN'S GATE, but for spending $42 million to do so. HOWARD THE DUCK is noted for its lack of the entertainment quotient despite its production cost of $35 million. It has also become "newsworthy" for entertainment reporters to state grosses on a hit like TOP GUN or the likelihood of losses on Columbia's $40 million comedy, ISHTAR.

More than ever, the public is attuned to the cost and success of a motion picture. For many years, when the studios were efficiently run factories, such information was never released unless an ad carried a catchline, "Five years and five million dollars in the making." There was no reason to give out the cost or gross of a movie. Before the 1960's participation in profits was uncommon, and with talent under contract, no studio wanted performers to realize their true value, especially when it came time to renegotiate a contract. Only in recent years, with megamillion-dollar budgets, has the overall cloak of secrecy been lifted from movie costs.

xiii

Studios are a little more liberal with information relating to past administrations' financial successes and blunders, allowing more studies of fiscal results. Will these eliminate future disasters? Probably not. The entertainment industry changes too rapidly for rules. Many producers have called the film/TV business a "crap shoot" with odds longer than in Las Vegas. That too is true. But the industry, like Las Vegas, is crass, glamorous, exciting--and gives rise to a vibrant history.

Twentieth Century-Fox Studios, Beverly Hills

CHAPTER 1

■ THE MOVIES BECOME AN INDUSTRY ■

In the beginning, Edison perfected the camera and the pro-
jector, but the industry was without form and void. Films
had not yet flickered across the screens. From such negligible beginnings, the motion picture industry, only three
decades later in 1926, had become one of America's top 10
industries. The phenomenal fortunes made by a handful of
movie pioneers--William Fox, Carl Laemmle, Louis B. Mayer,
Samuel Goldwyn, the Warner brothers, and Adolph Zukor--
were a result of the public's overwhelming acceptance of
moving pictures. No matter how crude they initially were,
their novelty created an industry and an art. Even with
public enthusiasm for movies, the business proceeded because
of the visionary and sometimes power-hungry, egomaniacal
personalities who propelled the dream factories known as
studios. Theirs were personalities forged from the struggle
for survival, and as such were never complacent. Fear or
caution could not obstruct their ambitious quest to provide
glamorous dream fulfillment to generations of audiences.

One of those pioneers, William Fox, went to work as a
coat liner for S. Cohen and Son of New York in 1900.
Thirty years later he would head a $300 million film empire.
Saving whatever possible from his weekly salary of $25,
Fox's greatest asset, as his name coincidentally implies, was
a shrewd and irrepressible business instinct.

A Jewish emigrant from Europe, the 21-year-old Fox developed many talents which would help him build his corporation.
Even at this young age, he realized that to advance in business he needed capital. Depriving himself and his wife of
anything more than the bare necessities, William Fox was able

1

to save enough money to start his own business. The Knickerbocker Cloth Examining and Shrinking Company did exactly what its lengthy name described, and in its second year managed to show a profit of $10,000. The untiring Fox worked long, hard hours to give his business the needed momentum. His arduous efforts finally led to profits of $50,000 in 1904, when he sold the company.

It is no coincidence that men who had been in the garment industry were able to survive in the film business. Samuel Goldfish had been a glove salesman before he became Samuel Goldwyn, motion picture producer. Both Adolph Zukor and Marcus Loew had been furriers. The same kind of tenacity, hard-sell techniques, and inventiveness were the prerequisites of both industries. With similar, extremely narrow margins for error and cutthroat competition, Fox, Zukor, and Goldwyn were able to carve out empires where none had been before.

In 1904, with the profits realized from his cloth business, William Fox bought a common show, which was a store remodelled for the exhibition of motion pictures. (The term "common show" was a legal phrase for places with fewer than 299 seats, which were not required to follow the fire regulations of larger theaters.)

Because their price of admission was five cents, common shows were referred to more colloquially as nickelodeons. From the very first day of business, Fox believed that there was a great future in such places of entertainment, even though his initial receipts were not encouraging. To bolster audience attendance, he hired a magician to stand in front of the theater. The magic worked and once again William Fox was at the helm of a profitable business. Not one to stagnate, Fox immediately parlayed his profits from the first store show into a second, and then a third. Soon he owned 25 such establishments.

Before the advent of the nickelodeon, films had been exhibited in "peep shows," where an individual customer could select the film of choice on an upright viewing machine. When projection facilities made it possible to run movies for larger audiences simultaneously, there was a greater need for change of program. Rather than destroying a print to make way for a new bill, films were routed to other exhibitors.

This was the very beginning of film distribution. In 1902, a San Francisco exhibitor named Harry Miles set up the first "exchange" by purchasing films from producers and then leasing them to exhibitors for one-week runs. The idea caught on and within five years there were almost 150 such exchanges. Paying producers a flat fee of ten cents a foot, exchanges then tacked on a surcharge and rented the films to nickelodeon owners.

The production of motion pictures was not quite as open as distribution. In 1909, a group of production companies, along with Thomas Edison, set up the Motion Picture Patents Company. They alone owned the equipment and film for production and anyone else would have to pay royalities for such materials. Through the General Film Company, their distribution subsidiary, they regulated the length of films and the rentals exhibitors would pay. Other distributors were either bought out or forced out of business by not having a supply of film. The General Film Company had nationwide exclusivity setting up fifty-two exchange branches across the country.

William Fox was the only owner of an exchange who remained independent, and even though the monopoly cut off his supply of films, he was determined to fight them. He quickly opened up a studio and began production on his own. Although Fox had been offered $75,000 for his exchange by General, he openly antagonized them by demanding $750,000. Finally, Fox brought a suit against the combine for $6 million in damages for violation of the Sherman Anti-Trust Act. Victory came in 1912 when the courts ruled against the monopoly and put an end to the stranglehold placed on the industry by Pathé, Biograph, Kalem, Essanay, Selig, Edison, and Vitagraph. No longer were producers, distributors, and exhibitors under the regimentation of these few. The film business was a free and open industry.

Under the restrictions of the combine, producers had been limited to single reels of film. Audiences and theater-owners, however, were clamoring for longer films. In 1912, Adolph Zukor's Famous Players Company successfully imported Sarah Bernhardt's four-reel portrayal of Queen Elizabeth from France. More "full-length" features were produced by Zukor, Carl Laemmle's Universal Pictures, the Loew's Corporation, and Box Office Attractions Film Rental Company, which later became Fox Films and Fox Theaters.

The longer films resulted in immediately rising production costs. Whereas the average negative cost in 1909 was $1,000, Famous Players' 1913 version of THE PRISONER OF ZENDA cost $20,000. With audiences on the increase, though, these costs were absorbed by grosses which rose to $100,000-$125,000 for such films. ("Gross" was then defined as the amount remitted to the distributor by the theater. Theater remittances were later to be referred to as "rentals.") More patrons prompted a greater number of films to be produced and theaters to change their shows three to four times weekly rather than twice.

While William Fox was filming subjects in New York and New Jersey in 1913, the Los Angeles Chamber of Commerce was promoting its city as a center for production. Fox, along with Zukor and Laemmle, decided that the temperate climate might more easily facilitate year-round filmmaking. After a brief production stint in Florida, he inaugurated studio facilities in 1916 at the corner of Sunset and Western in Hollywood. This became the headquarters of the Fox picture-making organization. Although production soon moved entirely to Los Angeles, distribution and corporate head offices would remain centered in New York for nearly 60 years.

Along with the increasing popularity of motion pictures came the ascendancy of the star system. Those actors or actresses who were popular with the public commanded higher salaries. Producers quickly realized that if audiences wanted to see these luminaries, their tremendous salaries were well worth paying. William Fox discovered many stars who became popular in his films--William Farnum, Theda Bara, Tom Mix, and Gladys Brockwell. Many of these personalities became veritable gold mines for Fox Films, endowing the studio with profits as well as prestige. Theda Bara's screen success resulted in one film a month from 1915 to 1919, and a salary of $4,000 a week. Tom Mix began his screen career at Fox as a horse trainer at $350 a week, but ended his contract in 1928 at $17,000. On the average, the gross of a Tom Mix five-reeler was between $600,000 and $800,000, and his films earned him nearly $4 million in his 10 years with Fox. To the studio he brought that amount many times over.

Four- to eight-reel pictures were, around 1915, getting theater rentals of $100 to $150, with almost daily program

changes. This brought in about $100,000 for the average
picture. Returns were divided as follows:

Rentals $100,000

Distribution   less   35,000

Negative cost   less   25,000

Prints and advertising   less   10,000

Profit to producer $ 30,000

With an average of $30,000 per picture, at 52 pictures yearly,
producers could show overall profits of $1.5 million. Motion
pictures were, by now, big business and were continuously
expanding.

New markets were sought for motion pictures and William
Fox quickly recognized that Europe had great potential. In
1919, after World War I hostilities ended, he set up his own
distribution offices in every major European city. Not only
did he get maximum rentals, avoiding continental middlemen,
but he also had a headquarters for filming Fox newsreels.

The Fox Corporation kept growing, led by a man with
an almost compulsive desire to dominate the industry. By
1920, he sold his 25 store shows, remodelled existing vaude-
ville houses, and built up a chain of 12 theaters in the four
largest boroughs of New York. In only 10 years, this chain
grew into the Fox Metropolitan circuit of 175 houses. Nation-
ally, William Fox held a network of over 1,000 theaters by
1927.

Production was quick to respond to the tastes of the
public, which demanded better stories, more lavish sets and
costumes, and bigger casts. This led to a rising cost of the
average film from $25,000 in 1915 to $150,000 by 1920. A
large part of this increase was due to the six-figure salaries
of such stars as Charles Chaplin, Mary Pickford, and Douglas
Fairbanks. The studios were willing to give in to these exorbitant star salaries because their films could gross in the
millions. The lure of those golden millions was too hard for
producers to resist, creating a budgetary extravagance
for which Hollywood would always be known. Some examples

TABLE I

EXAMPLES OF COSTS AND GROSSES

PICTURE AND COMPANY	COST	GROSS
Over The Hill to the Poor House (Fox, 1920)	$ 100,000	$ 3,000,000
Robin Hood (U.A., 1921)	700,000	3,000,000
The Thief of Bagdad (U.A., 1922)	2,000,000	1,500,000*
The Ten Commandments (DeMille, 1923)	1,476,000	5,000,000*
The Covered Wagon (Para., 1923)	800,000	4,000,000
The Big Parade (M/G/M, 1925)	200,000	5,500,000
The Phantom of the Opera (Univ., 1925)	1,000,000	2,000,000*
The Black Pirate (U.A., 1926)	1,500,000	2,000,000
Old Ironsides (Para., 1926)	1,500,000	1,500,000*
The Cohens and the Kellys (Univ., 1926)	150,000	2,000,000
Uncle Tom's Cabin (Univ., 1927)	2,000,000	500,000*
Ben-Hur (M/G/M, 1927)	4,500,000	9,386,000
The King of Kings (DeMille, 1927)	2,500,000	3,000,000*

*denotes approximation

of the costs and grosses during this expansionary period are as shown on Table I (above).

At the Fox organization, William Fox was aided by his attorney, Saul E. Rogers, and Winfield Sheehan, an assistant and general manager who is credited with building the company's distribution arm. Together, these men had to cope with various setbacks, one of which Benjamin B. Hampton describes in A History of the Movies.

> After that memorable milestone, Armistice Day, when a new generation suddenly asserted its power and remade the movies to suit current desires, the closely-knit Fox film family began to feel the pressure of the changed order. Young people considered Fox stars out of date, and Fox pictures began to slip behind in public favor. (Fox's) corporations continued to make money, but for a while they were dangerously near standing still, and in the film industry a lack of progress, or hesitation for a short time, had usually meant retrogression and defeat. While the changing tastes of the box office were diminishing his earnings, and the increasing costs of pictures were sending studio expense-sheets to the sky, Zukor, Loew, Mastbaum, and First National were hammering away at Fox's theater position. Fox had been expanding steadily, but not at a pace sufficient to keep abreast of Zukor and Loew, and in many cities they had gone ahead of him by acquiring or building new houses that threw his own into the second class. [1]

Suddenly, Fox realized that his organization was slipping and began to restructure his operation. He sent Winfield Sheehan to Los Angeles to take charge of the studio and revitalize his production arm. For strength in exhibition, he moved A.C. Blumenthal from the west coast to New York to increase purchases of existing theaters and land where new ones could be built.

During this period, Fox bought controlling interest in what was to be the Roxy Theater for $5 million. This 1925 acquisition gave him the distinction of controlling, and later owning, the largest theater in the world, with seating capacity for 6,200 persons, built at a cost of $12 million.

There were necessary changes to be made in casting Fox pictures. The "vamp," Theda Bara, had lost her following

to other exotic screen personalities like Greta Garbo and
Pola Negri. William Farnum left the screen in ill health.
Gladys Brockwell, no longer a leading lady, became a character actress, and Tom Mix left Fox in 1928. As well, other
studios had been treating audiences to star-studded films,
so that only one top-name performer was not enough to carry
a feature. Fox, at the time, found it lacked the star-power
needed to make profitable movies.

Winfield Sheehan set out to correct these ills. "Some-
where in his career as reporter, Manhattan police-department
official, and general handy man for William Fox, Sheehan had
acquired an uncanny understanding of the popular mind and
a sure hand in devising entertainment that would please it.
Fox pictures again leaped into the first rank of popularity,
and his profits increased half a million to a million dollars
a year."²

Sheehan, rather than depending on stars, turned towards
better story material, and in the process of producing successful films, developed some new popular talent. Alma
Rubens and Edmund Lowe starred in EAST LYNNE (1925),
which grossed $1.1 million. In the following year he teamed
Lowe with Victor McLaglen in WHAT PRICE GLORY?, which
not only took in $2 million, but also began a string of popular
films for the pair. Raoul Walsh, director of WHAT PRICE
GLORY?, was also on his way to becoming one of the most
prolific and profitable of Hollywood directors.

Under Sheehan's administration, many other directors
started their careers, or continued them. Among them were
John Ford, William K. Howard, Howard Hawks, Irving Cummings, Lewis Seiler, Alfred Santell, Henry King, John Bly-
stone, Leo McCarey, and Frank Borzage. Borzage started
his extremely successful Fox career with LAZYBONES in 1925,
but it was not until 1927 with 7th HEAVEN that he initiated
a series of highly successful romantic melodramas. 7th
HEAVEN also launched the very popular team of Janet Gaynor
and Charles Farrell, who both stayed at Fox for the next
decade.

By 1926 the prospect of sound was on the horizon, but
most major producers rejected the idea of intruding on an
audience's enjoyment with mere "talking." William Fox was
one exception. By 1925 he had already encouraged engineer

Theodore Case to experiment with the possibilities of sound-on-film. The near-bankrupt Warner Bros. were another. Raising $800,000 to invest in sound, they placed the future of their shaky company on that invention. Warners soon joined forces with the Bell Telephone Company, which had managed to synchronize pictures with discs. This became the Vitaphone process, widely adopted by theaters.

Fox, however, was involved in a more practical process that "worked on the principle of the sound being recorded directly on the film. The sound waves, picked up by the microphone, were transferred into electrical vibrations which, in turn, were changed into light variations that were 'photo-graphed' on the edge of the film. When the film was projected, the process was reversed and the re-created sound waves were transmitted to the audience from amplified speakers behind the screen. The Fox-Case system was given an intriguing name: Movietone." [3] To protect his ownership of Movietone, Fox bought the patents to a process known as Tri-Ergon, a similar invention developed in Europe. With these patents, Fox wanted to establish Movietone as the only sound process and therefore control the industry through his patents.

Warner Vitaphone and Fox Movietone appeared to the public in the late spring and summer of 1926 in comedy short subjects and newsreels. At the time, there was no great importance attached to the new processes.

Attendance, by 1926, was placed at approximately 100 million customers a week, with total annual volume between $1 billion and $1.24 billion. There was a gigantic audience for Hollywood to satisfy and it soon became obvious that the masses wanted sound. Fox first used a Movietone musi-cal soundtrack added to WHAT PRICE GLORY? on January 21, 1927. If there was still any doubt in other producers' minds, October 1927 made everything very clear.

THE JAZZ SINGER opened to all-time record business in October, and because many theaters had been equipped for Vitaphone short subjects, Warner Bros. had the edge over Fox. On a $500,000 negative cost, Warners took in $2.5 million. Their dramatic gamble in sound later made up for losses between 1926 and 1928, and led to profits of $17 mil-lion in 1929. From a $16 million corporation in 1928, Warners became, through the acquisition of theaters and with help from Vitaphone, a company with assets of $230 million by 1930.

Sound threw Hollywood into one of its periods of vast reorganization and revitalization. Production was slowed until the overall effect of sound could be evaluated. When it was determined that sound had arrived permanently, producers were saddled with large inventories of silent films.

They had to be salvaged some way. As a result, many silent films at Fox ended up with Movietone sound prologues or epilogues. Effects and musical scores were added whenever possible. Into this hybrid category fell many of the studio's important releases for 1928, such as Frank Borzage's STREET ANGEL, John Ford's FOUR SONS, and Raoul Walsh's THE RED DANCE. Each of these had some elements of sound, either through added "talkie" sequences, or effects and music. Either way, the grosses of these films were not hurt by Movietone. Each of them took in an average of $1.5 million.

Silent films in 1926 required eight to ten weeks of shooting on major productions, but sound films took only two to six weeks. Due to the limitations of an enclosed camera, sequences were played mainly in long shots, so "talkies" involved fewer camera set-ups, shortening shooting schedules. It also momentarily impeded strides made by the silents in photographic fluidity. Since the advent of the extravagant budget, producers had wanted longer playing times for their pictures to earn back costs. This was not possible if they continued to grind out 700 features annually. Production output on the new sound films was voluntarily held at 400–500 features a year. That way, good films would not be pushed aside by a steady flow of incoming product. Producers also found that sound films returned their investments in about one quarter of the time it took to recoup on the silents. Many sound films made over $1 million, and the $2 million figure was no longer a rarity. With a new and more prestigious commodity, theaters were able to raise their admission prices to 50 cents and $1 from the original 10 cents and 25 cents.

The tremendous popularity and widespread acceptance of the talkies made 1929 a year of huge profits for Fox. SUNNY SIDE UP, a musical starring Janet Gaynor and Charles Farrell, showed domestic rentals of $3.5 million, a record for the company. A sequel to WHAT PRICE GLORY?, again pairing McLaglen and Lowe, THE COCK-EYED WORLD, earned

$2.7 million, outgrossing the original with the added attraction of sound. IN OLD ARIZONA brought in $1.3 million and initiated a series of Cisco Kid films for Warner Baxter. This slate of releases was bolstered by other strong products, such as HAPPY DAYS, an elaborate all-star musical; FOX MOVIETONE FOLLIES OF 1929; SALUTE, directed by John Ford; and a Will Rogers film, THEY HAD TO SEE PARIS. Profits hit a record-breaking $9.5 million for the year.

Amidst the coming of sound, William Fox was not one to be satisfied only with "talkies." He produced HAPPY DAYS in 70mm., a film gauge twice as wide as the normal 35 mm., and projected it onto a much larger screen. Mordaunt Hall of the New York Times mentioned the new "Grandeur" process in his review of the film:

> William Fox's first Grandeur audible picture has the studio advantages of special settings and illumination, is now at the Roxy, which, besides being the largest cinema theater in the world, can for the time being also boast of having the largest screen ever constructed. It is 42 feet wide and 20 feet high, the standard screen being 24 feet by 18 feet. The single Grandeur film frame is twice that of the standard picture and a trifle higher. An additional advantage of the Grandeur film is that it permits the sound track to be three times as wide as that of the standard film. [4]

In 1930, Fox also released his epic western, THE BIG TRAIL, costing $1.9 million, in 70mm., but the large image did not catch on. Many producers argued that audiences were too involved with sound to discover another "novelty." William Fox had been lucky in having Paramount, Universal, Metro-Goldwyn-Mayer, and Columbia use his Movietone system, but his luck ran out when it came to Grandeur. Had Fox been able to devote more time to his production unit, he might have been able to save the giant-screen process. However, events were conspiring to keep him occupied with his own financial survival.

Fox had always dreamed of dominating the motion picture industry, and he formulated a plan of attack. First, his theater chain was 1,000-strong, and was supplied by equally powerful production and distribution arm. He held the Tri-Ergon and Movietone process of sound reproduction and kept

his theaters out of American Telephone Company control.
He also built a modern 100-acre production facility lavishly
dubbed Movietone City on Pico Boulevard to provide sound
stages for talkies. This strength produced enemies which
Fox was not aware of. Other producers feared that his further expansion would produce a monopolistic threat to the entire industry. There were also many businessmen, bankers,
and investment consultants who viewed William Fox as a plum
to be picked. Unfortunately, Fox played right into their hands.

On one of his campaigns to expand, Fox overstepped his
financial limits. With a $15 million loan from the Telephone
Company and a similar loan from Halsey, Stuart and Company
of New York, Fox intended a three-way expansion. The one
element which caused the most animosity was the acquisition
of a controlling block of Loew's stock. In early 1929, Fox
let it be known that he was interested in acquiring the more
powerful Metro-Goldwyn-Mayer and its parent, Loew's Corporation. President Louis B. Mayer never imagined that Fox
could get control of his vast company. Nevertheless, Fox
offered to buy all the holdings of the Shubert and Loew
families, as well as those of Vice-President Nicholas Schenck
and Treasurer David Bernstein. Schenck admitted wanting
to make a grand profit on the deal, but he thought Fox was
bluffing when he offered over-market prices. Fox was not
bluffing, and in a surprise transaction, he acquired 53 percent of Loew's stock for $50 million. Louis B. Mayer, who
had been out of town, returned to find himself an employee
in the mighty Fox empire. In fact, when Mayer's contract
expired, he would have to ask Fox for a raise in salary.
Fox would refuse. This did not develop any fondness between the two moguls.

Fox also paid $20 million for the Poli theater circuit in
New England, and bought up half the voting stock of the
holding company which controlled Gaumont-British. At this
point, Fox claimed to have a fortune of $100 million and a
company worth three times that amount. To keep his company solvent, Fox would issue stock to refinance his loans
and service the interest payments. However, he had extended his credit beyond its limit.

When the company's loans became due in late 1929 and
early 1930, William Fox began to feel the full animosity of the
persons he had been dealing with. Halsey Stuart, the

Telephone Company, and Harley Clarke, president of General
Theatres Equipment Corp., all wanted Fox dethroned so they
could divide up his kingdom. Halsey Stuart represented the
Chase Manhattan Bank and various other individuals who
felt they could make an easy profit by acquiring the Fox
Corporation. Harley Clarke had publicly craved control of
the Fox empire as a huge market for his theater supply
company. American Telephone wanted to install their sound
systems in Fox theaters. When the stock market collapsed,
Fox was unable to refinance his bank loans. His creditors
maliciously managed to turn any possible source of money
away from him. Any friends he might have had abandoned
him, and he spent six unfruitful months locked in a personal
struggle, fighting desperately for the financial survival of
his company.

Finally, with no alternatives, Fox was forced to sell off
his important holdings to raise capital, and then shares in
the company he had built up from such a modest beginning.
Everyone else got what they wanted, including Harley Clarke,
who bought his way into the presidency for $18 million worth
of shares. Fox's situation was further complicated by an anti-
trust suit brought against the company for the proposed
merger with Loew's. The Loew's shares were then sold
back to M-G-M, now out of harm's way. Everything which
William Fox had done was about to be undone.

And so, began the first looting of a Hollywood studio.
A handful of investors made many millions from the stock
and financial transactions which followed. The American
Telephone Company acquired complete control to all the sound
recording and reproduction patents necessary for motion
picture production, and Harley Clarke had all Fox houses
order equipment from his General Theatres Equipment Corp.
Clarke was more concerned with imposing minimum orders on
theaters for new seats or marquees than with running his
company profitably. The Fox Film Corporation managed to
show $9.5 million profits in 1930, a carryover from William
Fox's presidency, but in 1931, with Clarke's wasteful habits,
the company showed $5,560,305 in red ink and 1932 followed
with a staggering loss of $19,964,498. Harley Clarke would
not last long as Fox's president.

CHAPTER 2

■ FOX STARTS AGAIN ■

In the wake of the looters, the Fox Film Corporation was left
as a shell of its previous dynamic and aggressive self.
William Fox was deposed and even though he had offered to
participate in running the company at no cost, he was never
consulted.

With business increasing even after the stock market
crash, industry sages who concluded that film was a
depression-proof business were ultimately proven wrong.
Box-office receipts did decline for various reasons. Admission prices had been on the rise in the last years of the
silents and the early months of the "talkies." Sound had
begun to wear thin as a novelty and audiences were increasingly selective in the types of pictures they wanted to see.
Radio had been introduced and provided a less expensive form
of entertainment. When 1931 rolled around, many theaters
were suffering losses and some were forced to close down,
producing a reduction in earnings for the studios. Whenever there was money to be made in the film business, producers were ready to backroll higher-priced films, but
when reductions in earnings occurred, it was common sense
to pull back. Budgets for 1931 dropped markedly. Program pictures (those done on quick schedules with lesser-
known actors) were set at between $100,000 and $150,000.
The higher-class films ranged between $300,000 and $500,000.
The million and multimillion dollar budget was much less
common than in the apex years of the silents.

Theater owners quickly realized that audiences were dropping and attempted new policies to lure back patrons. The
theaters, which had pretty much all been classed similarly,

14

were now more strikingly divided. First-rate houses would charge top rates for lush interiors and the finest in projection facilities. Reserved seats were also available in these cinemas, and admissions could reach $1-$2 or higher. Next came the large, centrally-located theaters that could play lesser films at 50 cents to $1. Finally, there were the older theaters playing the second or third run of a film charging 15 cents to 50 cents.

What the ailing Fox Corporation needed in 1932 was a new president. Sidney R. Kent had worked his way up from salesman to vice-president and general manager at Paramount-Publix. Therefore, he was more equipped to cope with the needs of a distribution unit than Harley Clarke. While Kent provided solid managment of the company's finances and theaters until his death in 1942, he never managed to arrange a more-than-adequate working relationship with Winfield Sheehan, still the production chief in Hollywood. This prevented Kent from being as effective a president as William Fox.

Winfield Sheehan, apparently was losing some of the "know-how" which had helped Fox to a string of hits. Even though five of the films he produced in 1931 grossed over $1 million each, he was not able to produce a single winner in 1932. Fox was clearly losing its talent edge to other studios, and some of the company's best directors were only doing one or two films annually for Fox compared to multiples in previous years. Raoul Walsh only did one film for Fox in 1932, ME AND MY GAL with Spencer Tracy and Joan Bennett. Frank Borzage finished his last two films for Fox, AFTER TOMORROW and YOUNG AMERICA, but neither was very successful. In that same year, Borzage went to Paramount and directed the smash success, A FAREWELL TO ARMS, starring Helen Hayes and Gary Cooper. Fox's only newly added star power came from purveyor of homespun humor, Will Rogers, who starred in four films yearly. Sheehan continued to produce Janet Gaynor films, Charles Farrell films, McLaglen and Lowe sequels to WHAT PRICE GLORY?; and he occasionally would switch team partners, combining Warner Baxter and Edmund Lowe, Janet Gaynor and Warner Baxter, or Warner Baxter and James Dunn. However, the policy was not very successful. There was even a futile attempt to bring a faded Clara Bow back to the screen in CALL HER SAVAGE and HOOPLA.

If 1932 was a bad year for film companies, 1933 looked even worse. When the banks closed in the spring, and a new monetary policy was introduced, business was below 1932 by 20 percent and grosses would be $100 million lower for the year. However, this disheartening news was followed by the beginning of a turnaround in the late summer, and there was a hint of optimism. Variety reported, "A good sign always is when distributors foment talk about increased rentals from exhibitors." [1] Indeed it was, for Fox edged into the black again with satisfactory profits of $1,674,353.

Even though 1933 promised the end of the movies' economic slump, some financial problems surfaced at Fox due to its previous administration. Fox West Coast theaters was forced into receivership on a note for $410,000 which had been signed by William Fox several years earlier. Charles Skouras, a successful theater man himself, was appointed receiver of Wesco and became responsible for its finances. Along with Skouras came his two younger brothers, George and Spyros, the latter a future president of Twentieth Century-Fox.

Aside from the occasional hit, the 1933-1934 season for Sheehan's production unit was not altogether heartening. CAVALCADE, which had production costs of $1 million, brought in $3 million domestically, a welcome windfall for Fox, and the company's highest-grossing film for the period. CAVALCADE also won three Adademy Awards for Best Picture, Best Director, and Best Art Director, a notable amount of prestige. Also that year, Fox released STATE FAIR with Will Rogers, which was the first motion picture from the studio to open at Radio City Music Hall in New York. It was a hit, earning a healthy $1.5 million domestically.

The most nagging problem with Fox's production slate was that the majority of releases were following the patterns of previous pictures. Fox had made a fairly successful series of James Dunn romantic dramas which had initially pleased audiences, but by 1933, were bringing complaints about the repetition of stories. The same complaint was registered in a review for the Victor McLaglen-Edmund Lowe film UNDER PRESSURE (1935). As a result audiences became more wary of Fox films.

Dull characters, mediocre performances and sluggish

pacing plagued the Fox slate of product. Forgettable movies like BROADWAY BAD, THE WORST WOMAN IN PARIS, and SIX HOURS TO LIVE helped to propel Fox's reputation in 1933 into the critical and commercial cellar. Even the occasional anomaly like THE POWER AND THE GLORY and ZOO IN BUDAPEST, which both received good notices, failed to attract audiences.

With the reorganization of theater chains, only certain houses would play top product, and studios would compete to get their films played in the most prestigious of movie palaces. The remaining houses of a chain were forced to play lowercase products and soon such smaller budget "B" pictures were being made in great numbers for these situations. More and more, the "B" category of films were produced at Fox. Their series were the ultimate in rehashing of tried-and-true formulas, designed for this market. The Cisco Kid, introduced in the high-budget IN OLD ARIZONA, reappeared in films of lower cost and standards.

James Dunn's series, as mentioned, was on its way downhill. Warner Baxter and Edmund Lowe, who had been top stars, found their films dropping in quality and returns. Fox's poor showing in 1931 and 1932 forced the company to cut budgets to $300,000 for the average film of 1933-1934. Since it was also obvious that Winfield Sheehan was no longer as astute a judge of material, Fox signed deals with various independent producers to make pictures for the company to release. Jesse Lasky made two or three films a year for Fox. Sol Lesser made a series of George O'Brien westerns as a continuation of the Fox program. Lesser recounts how the deal came about:

> Fox was making a series of westerns with George O'Brien. The Fox people on a national basis were grossing $250,000 to $300,000 per picture. But it was costing Fox $200,000 to produce that picture. And so, with the distribution costs added, Fox was making nothing on it, and decided to discontinue the sale of these pictures. I think they were making four or six a year.
> Now, I heard about it and George O'Brien was available. So I made a proposal to George O'Brien that I'd like to make a series of pictures with him. I'd give him a very nominal salary and give him a

> percentage of the profits, if I could get a release through Fox.
> So, I went to Sidney Kent, who polled the exchanges to find out, if they made a deal with me, would the exchanges like to have these pictures? And a hundred per cent of them wired back affirmatively, at the same price, the same terms, whether Fox made them or Sol Lesser made them, it made no difference.
> I made four pictures a year with George O'Brien and they cost me $90,000 and they had an equivalent quality of a studio-made picture that had cost Fox a quarter of a million.
> I delivered the picture without an advance; they distributed it for 35%. They got 35% of a quarter of a million and I got the difference against my cost. [2]

Since sound had come in, other major studios were refining their product and building up either star or story power. Fox was clearly lagging behind in these areas. In the period between 1930 and 1935, Warner Bros. boasted such films as LITTLE CAESAR, PUBLIC ENEMY, I AM A FUGITIVE FROM A CHAIN GANG, GOLD DIGGERS OF 1933, FORTY SECOND STREET, CAPTAIN BLOOD, and elevated such names as James Cagney, Edward G. Robinson, Ruby Keeler, Dick Powell, Ginger Rogers, and Errol Flynn to public prominence.

Paramount had introduced audiences to Mae West, the Marx Brothers, Marlene Dietrich, Gary Cooper, and Maurice Chevalier in films such as THE LOVE PARADE, MONKEY BUSINESS, MOROCCO, I'M NO ANGEL, and LOVE ME TONIGHT. As well, Paramount had made vast artistic strides with directors like Ernst Lubitsch, Josef von Sternberg, and Rouben Mamoulian.

R.K.O. had such popular films as CIMARRON, KING KONG, THE LOST PATROL, LITTLE WOMEN, OF HUMAN BONDAGE, BILL OF DIVORCEMENT, FLYING DOWN TO RIO, and the first three-strip Technicolor feature, BECKY SHARP.

Needless to say, Metro-Goldwyn-Mayer was gathering all the stars in the heavens and neighboring regions. Greta Garbo graced ANNA CHRISTIE, SUSAN LENOX, THE PAINTED

VEIL, GRAND HOTEL and Rouben Mamoulian's QUEEN CHRISTINA with her presence and box-office appeal. DINNER AT EIGHT, THE CHAMP, RED DUST, THE THIN MAN, A TALE OF TWO CITIES, and MUTINY OF THE BOUNTY displayed the talents of Clark Gable, Jean Harlow, Marie Dressler, Wallace Beery, John Barrymore, Lionel Barrymore, Ronald Colman, Charles Laughton, Myrna Loy, William Powell, and Jackie Cooper.

In addition to the majors was a fledgling company headed by the president of United Artists, Joseph M. Schenck and the ex-production head at Warner Bros., Darryl F. Zanuck, who released their films through United Artists. Zanuck had started his career at Warners as a writer in the early 1920's. He worked his way through the ranks from RIN-TIN-TIN features to produce top Warners products. Prolific and ambitious, the young Zanuck had a flair for action and adventure in his stories. From writing scripts, he became a story editor and chose projects for production, becoming heavily involved in the casting of films. Zanuck was responsible for launching the careers of Edward G. Robinson, James Cagney, and Paul Muni by starring them in such notable films as LITTLE CAESAR, PUBLIC ENEMY, and I AM A FUGITIVE FROM A CHAIN GANG.

Because Zanuck was the vice-president in charge of production, he had been nominated by the Warners to tell producers, directors, and salaried executives of austerity cuts in the weekly paychecks. Zanuck agreed, but when the Warners decided to extend the salary cut two weeks longer than had been agreed upon, they raised his hackles and their thirty-one-year-old production chief left his $5,000-a-week job on April 15, 1933.

Joseph and Nicholas Schenck, like all the other Hollywood moguls, had come into film from various other enterprises. They, too, were emigrants, from Russia, and became eminently successful in motion pictures. Nicholas took over the presidency of the Loew's Corporation after the death of Marcus Loew in 1927, and Joseph had gone into independent production, but eventually wound up as president of United Artists, which was merely a releasing firm for Douglas Fairbanks, Mary Pickford, Charles Chaplin and Sam Goldwyn.

Three days after he left Warners, Zanuck met with Joseph

Schenck who proposed the formation of a new company.
With William B. Goetz, Louis B. Mayer's son-in-law, Schenck
raised $1.2 million; another $750,000 came from Consolidated
Film Industries, a processing laboratory. The major sum,
however, was put up by Bank of America which arranged
a $3 million loan. Schenck and Zanuck soon were forming
their new production unit. Samuel G. Engel, Zanuck's
assistant at the time recalled:

> They hadn't yet a name for the company and they
> were eager to sign George Arliss, whose contract
> was then expiring with Warner Bros. Zanuck knew
> that. And so, it was that week, I believe, when
> we had just gotten going over at the Goldwyn lot,
> and he said he wanted a name for the company.
> I said, "I'll give you a name that's good for 67 years."
> He said, "What is it?" I said, "Twentieth Century
> Pictures." And that's how the name came about. 3

Since Twentieth Century Pictures did not own a studio,
they rented space at the Samuel Goldwyn lot. Staff was
pretty much at a minimum, as Sam Engel recounts:

> At Twentieth, I served as a story editor and as
> an assistant to Zanuck. As we only made a limited
> number of pictures there, I could do everything and
> anything because it was a very, very small group of
> people. As a matter of fact, I worked as an assistant
> director, a second assistant, I shot second unit stuff--
> I did everything. 4

Zanuck agreed to make twelve movies a year for Twentieth Century.

> Starting with THE BOWERY, he produced a suc-
> cession of the virile, melodramatic films that he under-
> stood best. And to balance them, he scheduled one
> ambitious production for George Arliss: THE HOUSE
> OF ROTHSCHILD. His other pictures were success-
> ful. But THE HOUSE OF ROTHSCHILD was an out-
> standing hit of the year. By September, 1934 (the
> end of its first schedule year), Twentieth Century
> had spent $4,500,000 on its twelve productions. The
> first four had cost $1,500,000, and had already earned
> their cost. And miscellaneous receipts totalling

$1,500,000 had come in, to be applied against the $3,000,000 cost of the remaining eight. With "... more than enough receipts to pay for the rest in the offing, Darryl Zanuck could congratulate himself on his debut." [5]

Halfway through his second year, Zanuck had eighteen features completed and seventeen released. BORN TO BE BAD was the only failure of the group, costing $250,000 and resulting in a $50,000 loss. Zanuck elevated himself into the world of "A" producers and away from the sensational melodramas he had started out making. All of his major productions, including THE HOUSE OF ROTHSCHILD, CARDINAL RICHELIEU, THE AFFAIRS OF CELLINI, and LES MISERABLES were hits. CLIVE OF INDIA did not perform as well as the others in the United States, but foreign receipts would propel it to a successful return.

BORN TO BE BAD was acknowledged as a flop even though it starred Loretta Young and Cary Grant, because it ran into problems with the Hays Office and had to be drastically cut and reshot, eviscerating a good deal of the story. Zanuck's other successes were attributable to his ability to give the public fast-moving and popular entertainment. His skill in casting was given a boost with Louis B. Mayer's son-in-law as a partner. Able to borrow Clark Gable from M-G-M for CALL OF THE WILD added inestimable star value to the final result. Zanuck also knew how to use a performer to his best advantage. While filming FOLIES BERGERE, a Zanuck replication of the Busby Berkeley movies he had popularized at Warners, he realized Maurice Chevalier's enormous box-office potential in France and shot a separate French version simultaneously. The French responded favorably to Chevalier's actually speaking his native language rather than being dubbed.

Zanuck was also lucky to have started Twentieth Century Pictures when business was beginning its upward climb. By 1935, business was again up, this time 12 percent over 1934, and distributors were once again hoping to equal rentals they had gotten in 1929.

However, at the Fox Film Corporation, the situation was still verging on catastrophe. The Sunset-Western studio in Hollywood, and the large Pico lot gave filmmakers the potential for grand-scale productions. Distribution was also covered by one of the most comprehensive setups in the business. Yet, for a $36 million corporation, Fox had an annual earning power of only $1.8 million in 1935. Zanuck's company had no studio and no distribution arm and was without theaters, but on a net worth of $4 million it could produce an annual return of $1.7 million. Therefore, the earning power of both corporations was almost equal and facilitated the talk of a merger. Sidney Kent knew that Fox needed a dynamic studio head, and Zanuck needed sound stages and a better distribution organization to expand his program of pictures.

At first, Kent felt Twentieth Century could be bought out to supply his theaters with better films, but Zanuck and Schenck would not agree. A merger was eventually announced on May 29, 1935. Joseph Schenck became chairman of the board and resigned his presidency at United Artists, but stayed on with their theater circuit. Schenck would be paid $130,000 a year by Fox. Sidney Kent continued on as president at $180,000, and a guarantee of an additional $25,000 as president of National Theaters Corporation, a Fox affiliate.

Darryl Zanuck had been the main reason for the merger, and his salary made that obvious. Zanuck was made vice-president at $260,000 annually. Although he had earned the same salary at Warners, he was now given 10 percent of the gross of his films as well. At the time of the merger he received a bonus of enough stock in the new company to bring him at least $500,000 annually.

To make sure that Schenck, Zanuck, and Goetz did not dilute their investment when the merger took place, shares in the new company were divided evenly, 613,264 each, between the Fox shareholders and the Twentieth Century triumvirate. Whereas the Fox company had many shareholders to divide this amount, Schenck and Goetz each received 214,642 shares and Zanuck 183,979 shares.

> As an additional safeguard to Fox, it was provided that the preferred stock should be convertible into common (one and one quarter shares for one) so that if the company were prospering greatly and a disproportionate share of the earnings were being drawn out in big dividends on the common, the Fox stockholders

could join in by acquiring more common.

To insure stability of control, voting as on a cumulative basis whereby each stockholder is entitled to as many votes as shall equal the number of his shares multiplied by the number of directors to be elected. Since the officers are important stockholders of their representatives, it is to be expected that the dividend policy of the company would be both steady and generous within the limits of the company earnings. 6

At both Fox lots, all work stopped on screenplays and on films which were to go into production, those under Winfield Sheehan's aegis. He was the only person on the lot who was not going to be swayed by the dramatic presence of Darryl F. Zanuck. Until Zanuck arrived at the studio, other Fox employees pondered the future of their jobs. They did not have to wonder for long, for when Zanuck arrived it was obvious he had one objective, which he would carry out ruthlessly if necessary. That was to get his studio to the top.

CHAPTER 3

■ FOX ON THE MARCH ■

Darryl F. Zanuck was faced with two immediate problems when he became vice-president at the newly-merged Twentieth Century and Fox--the reorganization of the studio production team, and the weak product it was turning out. Production itself had various subdivided obstacles and one of these was named Winfield Sheehan. He had been with William Fox for 18 years and then with the Clarke and Kent administrations for another five. Sheehan was also accustomed to being the vice-president in charge of production. Both he and Zanuck knew that there could not be two production heads, and that one would eventually force the other out.

Sheehan realized that Zanuck had the advantage of being younger and more aggressive, with a recent record of success. On July 23, 1935, Sheehan departed with a settlement of $360,000. This left Zanuck to run the studio by himself, much to the satisfaction of Sidney Kent.

Given a free hand, Zanuck began replacing the Fox people with his own the day after Sheehan's departure. Many of the Twentieth Century executives left their rented suites at the Goldwyn lot for the more permanent quarters at the Pico Boulevard studio. Lew Schreiber became casting director; Harry Brand, head of the publicity department; Alfred Newman, head of the music department; and Julian Johnson, story editor. As well, Zanuck brought with him writers, directors, and producers, all of whom he considered part of his team. In the early days of Twentieth Century, Zanuck established the policy of working with people he knew and respected. This respect had to be mutual though, because the studio boss was aware that there had to be an understanding based on trust in the making of motion pictures.

24

From that point, those who accepted Zanuck's word as law stayed and prospered. Those who did not, went to other studios.

The only Fox executive of note kept on after the merger was Sol Wurtzel, who had produced many successful films for Fox, including BRIGHT EYES with Shirley Temple, LIFE BEGINS AT 40 with Will Rogers, and Rogers' STEAMBOAT ROUND THE BEND, the company's biggest hit of 1935. Zanuck "rewarded" Wurtzel with the cloak of executive producer of all "B" pictures and designated the Sunset-Western lot for their production. Wurtzel would continue to produce the Charlie Chans, the Jane Withers films, and other productions budgeted between $75,000 and $200,000.

Wurtzel had been brought out from New York as a book-keeper by William Fox. He eventually worked his way up the production ladder to producer. Recognizing the value of an iron-clad contract early on, he was protected by his agreement with the company during the merger. Sam Engel remembered him as "a very complicated, uneducated, and highly-opinionated man." [1]

> Off and away from the studio, he had this Italian marble palace on Stone Canyon road in Bel-Air... He had two Rolls Royces and in those days he was making big money--I think $3,500 weekly.... He wore very expensive clothing but was still in un-attractive man. Ostentatious to all get-out. [2]

However, Engel claimed, Wurtzel did have the absolute power to control all production on the Western lot.

> He got involved to the extent that he would approve or disapprove. He never contributed anything. Per-haps he thought he did, but no one else thought so... Whenever he did say anything it was usually, "More menace." I guess what he really meant was he wanted more conflict or action. Wurtzel badgered some writer so much that he walked out. This made Wurtzel angry and he said, "I asked you to find some menace. Can't you find some?" The writer answered, "The only menace I can find is right here." And he pointed to Wurtzel then walked off the assignment.
> I don't really care to remember those awful days

because you really and truly had to conform to the
certain low standards dictated by the budget. And
as I recall, $75,000 was about right, with 12-14 days
shooting schedule. It was only grinding out a lot
of film, which was all right for Wurtzel and the com-
pany--but it wasn't for those who worked there. [3]

With the announcement of a planned $4.5 million for eight
productions, Zanuck made public his intention to reorganize
the studio machinery. He would institute the producer system at his studio, assigning one producer to each film, but
he would supervise all production, in addition to personally
producing six films in 1935-1936. Every script would be
written with Zanuck's strict instructions regarding pacing,
character, and action. Story conferences would be held with
all writers at various intervals in the creation of the screenplay. Then producers and directors would be advised regarding the casting of these scripts. Once a film was in
production, Zanuck would watch the daily screenings of
rushes with the directors. Upon completion of production,
he would supervise the cutting of every film.

Although it might have seemed like a one-man operation
to some, the amount Zanuck controlled a production depended
on the amount of trust he had in the individual. Nunnally
Johnson, one of Zanuck's favorite co-workers, remembers
good cooperation. "He never interfered with me more than
I wanted him to interfere with me. I thought of him as a
collaborator. It was a joy for him because he'd hand me a
story and in effect say, 'I hope I'll see you again in two
months.' He didn't bother me and ask how many pages I'd
done. This was fine for him because he had a dozen other
producers and writers he did have to keep after."

At the Westwood lot, Zanuck reread all the scripts which
had been prepared for production before the merger. He
changed some and cancelled others. Properties which he had
developed at Twentieth Century were brought in to replace
the cancellations. On the lot, the presence of agents was
restricted. Zanuck emphasized that if agents were to come
on the lot, they would have to make appointments for lunch-
hour meetings only. There would be no meetings during
production hours and absolutely no soliciting on the Fox lots.
As well, there would no longer be guests on the lot during
production hours.

To keep a firm control over the larger number of productions he would be supervising, Zanuck hired Edward Ebele away from Warner Bros. and made him the studio production manager. Ebele would be responsible for evaluating the estimated production costs and shooting schedules and for paring back when necessary. The average shooting schedule would be cut from almost sixty days as in Fox's expensive DANTE'S INFERNO and WAY DOWN EAST productions to forty days.

The transfusion of new talent seemed to work, for the company once again began to produce films on a regularly scheduled basis. Although the blending of material and talent had worked smoothly in the production end, distribution was still acting as though there never had been a merger. At first, they announced that Twentieth Century's films would be distributed by Fox Films' organization. Then Fox Films took ads in Variety announcing their product for 1935-1936. There was, as well, some confusion over the company name. In some Variety articles it was referred to as Fox-20th, and in others, as 20th-Fox. It was not until September 18, 1935, that a full-page ad announced a new trademark:

20th
Century-
Fox

New As A Trademark

Proven As A Standard

of

Strength * Quality * Leadership

Ballyhooing the recent merger, Fortune magazine devoted a full 14 oversized pages to Twentieth Century-Fox and provided a revealing glimpse behind studio gates.

Handsomest lot in Hollywood is Fox Movietone City, where Zanuck works. There are 96 acres of it (nearly twice as many as M.G.M. requires) on the outskirts of Beverly Hills, littered with house fronts, gardens, bits of synthetic jungle, Manhattan streets, and a replica of Berkeley Square in London. Its value as property is small: $4,000,000 for the land

and all the buildings on it.... But certain outdoor
sets are unique and valuable. There is a section
of an ocean liner which Fox constructed at a cost
of $60,000; the vista of Manhattan, with the elevated
railway at the corner, cost $135,000. These may
be rented out to other studios a dozen times or more
each year. And they bring a good price: the ship
yields from $750 to $1,250 a day when it is in use;
the New York City set brings $2,500. 5

While Movietone City had more sets than it could use,
there was a lack of sound stage space. With only five in
operation, a new one under construction, Zanuck still hoped
to add ten more. But even with sixteen stages on the lot,
he would not be able to produce movies as economically as
Warner Bros., with seventeen stages and six under construction.

At a cost of $125,000, a sound stage would pay for it-
self in less than two years by allowing more pictures to be
shot at the same time, speeding up production and allowing
indoor sets to be saved longer for reuse.

In 1935, Hollywood's output of negative film for exhibition totalled nearly four million feet, costing producers $120
million to produce and bringing in about $650 million at the
box office. Approximately $100 million was spent by the
eight major studios (M-G-M, Twentieth Century-Fox, United
Artists, Warner Bros., Paramount, R.K.O., Columbia,
Universal) and the average picture cost hovered around
$285,000.

Zanuck found himself at Fox with one of the highest
production budgets in town--$20 million. The average cost
of an M-G-M picture was $500,000; Paramount spent $450,000;
Zanuck was allowed $415,000. But it was not as much as
he had been spending at Twentieth Century. At Warners,
he had made movies for an average cost of $225,000. The
first twelve at Twentieth came in at $385,000 and did so
well he increased his budgets to an average of $650,000.
However, Zanuck found a way to stretch his "A" budgets
by assigning only $5 million of his annual total to all of Sol
Wurtzel's "B" pictures. Leaving $15 million for nearly thirty
pictures gave Zanuck M-G-M's level of $500,000.

Once all the corporate and administrative problems had been settled, Zanuck turned his attention to the production schedule. One of the major causes of Fox's lack of important product was a dearth of contract stars. Among a roster of 60 actors and actresses there were only a handful who really had much box-office drawing power. These included Warner Baxter, Will Rogers, Jane Withers, Shirley Temple, Janet Gaynor, Jack Haley, Lew Ayres, and Alice Faye. Although Spencer Tracy had been under contract from 1930 through 1934 he was never given a vehicle in which his talents were commercially exploited. Fox people had somehow never caught on to his star potential as M-G-M did shortly after. Under Winfield Sheehan's administration there had been a tendency to use the more established, though sometimes fading, talents of Janet Gaynor, Warner Baxter, and Rochelle Hudson.

At Twentieth Century, Zanuck had signed a total of twelve contracts, and at least eight had proven to be fruitful. They included George Arliss, Fred Allen, Wallace Beery, Ronald Colman, Fredric March, Loretta Young, and Sophie Tucker. After the merger of Twentieth and Fox, Zanuck signed Victor McLaglen, who had been with Fox for many years.

Out of the 72 contracts with acting talent, two were worth millions for Fox, and then for Twentieth Century-Fox. Shirley Temple's films became box-office bonanzas. Made for between $400,000 and $700,000, they were virtually assured million-dollar-plus grosses in the United States and Canada. Seven-year-old Temple had become another of "America's sweethearts" and the audience romance with her films showed up in the year-end figures.

Will Rogers, the other top contractee, had made many successful films for Winfield Sheehan. Wooing audiences into theaters with his easy-going style, the cowboy turned humorist-actor, had a steady string of hits, ranging from THEY HAD TO SEE PARIS (1929) to STEAMBOAT ROUND THE BEND (1935). In 1935, Fox's top two films of the year both starred Rogers. The next three highest grossing films starred Shirley Temple. Even after Zanuck's arrival, his first releases could not top the returns on Shirley Temple's vehicles.

Unfortunately, Rogers' career was cut short with his untimely death in an airplane crash at age 50. Zanuck

immediately halted the distribution of his previous films
until his two last features were in release. Ironically, these
films proved to be his most popular, leading Fox's returns
for 1935. The studio estimated a loss of $5 million in poten-
tial revenue due to the accident and occasionally forbid air
travel for top talent under contract.

Zanuck's first month of releases came in November 1935.
METROPOLITAN, his debut offering, was a comeback for
singing star Lawrence Tibbett, and although it received good
reviews it did not produce results at the box office. Neither
did the remake of WAY DOWN EAST, starring Henry Fonda,
which had been produced by Sheehan. IN OLD KENTUCKY
did very well due to Will Rogers, and THANKS A MILLION
was helped by Dick Powell and Fred Allen. THE MAN WHO
BROKE THE BANK AT MONTE CARLO featured Ronald
Colman, but was not overly successful either. All in all,
it was a moderately encouraging beginning, for Zanuck in-
curred no major losses for the company. In fact, business
started to take a definite upswing as a continuation of the
general trend out of the depression years.

The next year was to prove that both Zanuck and the
rejuvenated economy were good for Fox. First of all, business was steadily increasing. The slump years of 1931-1933
were well behind now, and theater attendance showed remarkable improvements. When construction was halted in
1933 with the slow years, theaters had been doing 50 percent
to 75 percent business. Now, with renewed interest in
motion pictures, these same theaters were doing SRO (Standing Room Only) business and major chains found themselves
pitifully underseated. There had been no real construction
going on for nearly five years and more prosperous times
brought more people to the movies.

Based on the returns of the average film, it could be
expected that if a film ran as long as 65 weeks and earned
its million dollars, it would have taken $530,000 in the first
13 weeks, $750,000 by 26 weeks, $880,000 by 39 weeks,
$950,000 in one year, and $1 million in 65 weeks. Therefore,
if Fox had to earn $1 million to break even on a budget, it
would generally take over a year to get that money back.
The pictures that failed were those that never lasted one year
in release.

Fortune again provided insight into the profitability of the company.

> Out of fifty pictures produced in a year, such a company as Twentieth Century-Fox may call itself lucky if a dozen are big hits, with receipts of $1,000,000 or more. If as many as thirty earn a good profit, the year's schedule is a success. From fifteen to twenty can usually be counted on to show a loss. Distribution costs (and other expenses of the New York office) average around $10,000,000 a year. Production costs take $20,000,000. For the actual prints--as many as 310 of a popular picture --and for dubbing foreign dialogue or titles on pictures sent abroad, another $5,000,000 is spent. And finally there is about $6,000,000 which goes for participations: royalty payments (ranging from 50 to 80 percent) to various other companies that share in films distributed but not made by Twentieth Century-Fox. Thus, from its total receipts, the company must take in at least $41,000,000 in order to break even. 6

If it was to earn as much as both companies had before the merger, the new Twentieth Century-Fox had to gross $45,000,000 at the box office, which would cover its $41,000,000 nut and provide an after-tax profit of $3,500,000. On a per picture basis, the fifty-three releases would have to earn about $775,000 each for the company--or about twice the average production cost.

The year 1936 may not have been one of particular quality for Darryl Zanuck, but it certainly was remarkable for quantity. Under his leadership, and with the help of Sol Wurtzel's "B" department, the company produced over 50 features and distributed six series of short subjects with one two-reeler every week, over 30 one-reelers, and 26 Terrytoon cartoons.

Zanuck starred most of the major contract talent in the higher-budget films. Warner Baxter played in THE PRISONER OF SHARK ISLAND, which was directed by John Ford and written by Nunnally Johnson, probably Zanuck's most important film of the year. Baxter also starred in KING OF BURLESQUE with Alice Faye, and TO MARY--WITH LOVE.

He was then teamed with Fredric March in THE ROAD TO GLORY, directed by Howard Hawks. Ronald Colman joined Charles Laughton in UNDER TWO FLAGS, and Wallace Beery headed A MESSAGE TO GARCIA.

More important, though, were Zanuck's discoveries involving new talent. If Shirley Temple had captured the nation's hearts, then surely five tiny tots would do this five-fold. Sensing that public interest was at a peak for the Canadian-born Dionne quintuplets, Zanuck sent a camera crew, director Henry King, and star Jean Hersholt to Calendar, Ontario, to film THE COUNTRY DOCTOR. After production had already begun, Zanuck rushed the film through as quickly as possible to take advantage of the event's publicity. Much to Henry King's chagrin, six days were cut from his shooting schedule. Nevertheless, King brought the film in at 28 days and $650,000. Zanuck's anxiety paid off, for THE COUNTRY DOCTOR was a hit and ranked third on the year's Fox hit list. It was flanked by Shirley Temple films, which garnered the number one, two, four, and five positions. That year, the studio's five hit pictures were attributed to children.

Zanuck also made millions for the studio by signing a contract with an ice skater. If anyone doubted his wisdom, they needed only witness the box-office results of ONE IN A MILLION, a very substanial hit. Sonja Henie went on to become the highest paid actress in Hollywood at her peak, earning over $250,000 annually. Zanuck also starred her with Fox's top leading men in THIN ICE, SECOND FIDDLE, SUN VALLEY SERENADE among others.

In this same period, Zanuck had starred a young man named Tyrone Power in a bit part in GIRL'S DORMITORY with Herbert Marshall. Audiences reacted more strongly to Power's appearance than any other part of the picture. The following year, Zanuck made an important decision in casting Power, a virtual unknown, in the lead role of Fox's biggest picture of 1936, LLOYDS OF LONDON. There were other considerations as well. Fredric March, who had been approached to play the part, wanted $150,000, but Power was under contract to Fox for $250 weekly. Zanuck took a risk with Power, and placed an $800,000 "A" picture in his hands. His showman's intuition proved to be right, for the film was a great success and started Power on a 20-year association with the studio.

RAMONA had originally been scheduled as a "B" picture under Sol Wurtzel's supervision, budgeted at $200,000. Then came the idea to shoot it in Technicolor. Audiences had never paid much attention to the old two-color (red and blue) Technicolor process of the mid-Twenties, but in 1935, BECKY SHARP introduced a new, more realistically vivid three-color (red, green, blue) process which added glamor and excitement to motion pictures. Fox had used the new process for a short closing in Shirley Temple's THE LITTLE COLONEL, and Zanuck had used it himself to end THE HOUSE OF ROTHSCHILD. However, neither Zanuck nor Fox had ever used the process for a feature--until RAMONA.

Henry King took his crew on location and filmed Don Ameche and Loretta Young in subdued color tones. It was an experiment which cost $600,000, but even though the film did not become a big success, Zanuck recognized the potential production value of Technicolor and was to use it again often.

The one drawback to Technicolor was the tremendous amount of light needed to get a proper image on the three strips of film. The camera was also very bulky and had to be leased directly from the Technicolor Corporation, which supplied a cameraman in addition to the one used by the studio. Of RAMONA's $600,000 budget, almost 10 percent went for Technicolor costs. The sum of $59,742 paid for all the film stock, equipment, cameraman, and lab work supplied by Technicolor. It was not an unreasonable amount to get such an enhancing effect for a motion picture.

Moving away from total studio dependence on Shirley Temple, Zanuck offered audiences a wider range of stars and stories. LLOYDS OF LONDON was the most popular Fox film of the year. Sonja Henie, Shirley Temple, and Tyrone Power supplied their share of hits. However, to join Henie and the Dionne quintuplets, Zanuck introduced the three Ritz Brothers in LIFE BEGINS IN COLLEGE. Although the Ritzes were never as popular as M-G-M's Marx Brothers, they did manage to attract enough audience attention to appear in subsequent films. Zanuck's taste in this kind of screen novelty led Frank Nugent, reviewer for the New York Times, to call him "the supreme past master of the non-sequitur in entertainment." 7

At the studio, films were written, put into production, and released with ever-increasing ease. There was a marked difference for creative talent, however, depending on whether they were working on the "B" lot or on "Zanuck territory." Sam Engel noted that "with the B's you were condemned to hell, and the A's were the hallowed halls of heaven." [8]

Nevertheless, the films from either the "A" or the "B" unit were produced to supply theaters with films that would bring in admission dollars. The studio's responsibility, and Zanuck's, was to make sure that the product's cost would not exceed its potential gross. Sam Engel was writing a film which he felt could benefit from the use of sets that were already standing.

> I went out on the lot, the main lot in Westwood, and Nunnally Johnson had just produced, and Gregory Ratoff had just directed, one of the biggest bombs we made at the studio, CAFE METROPOLE.... It had a big cast and it cost a lot of money. I know one thing. The sets were tremendous. They were all Parisian sets. And they were still standing. So I went out ... and I rewrote this script (LANCER SPY) to fit the standing sets. I got, at least in those days, a half a million dollars worth of production on a picture that I think was budgeted for a hundred and seventy-five (thousand). [9]

The ingenuity and craftsmanship of studio talent, such as the productive suggestions of Sam Engel, contributed to making the studio an efficient, profit-making venture. With all the talent under contract, it was just a matter of assigning a star or a writer or a director to various projects. All the sound stages, equipment, crews, and administration facilities were provided by the active studio.

It was at the end of the year, however, that Zanuck's policies were translated into a language that both executives and stockholders could understand--profits. Table II (p. 35) shows how Fox ranked in comparison with the other studios. Each feature release is assigned a weight, according to indicated box-office appeal (estimated) and a weighted average for the entire year is computed. A perfect score of 1.000 would result only if every film of each producer were given a "hit" rating.

TABLE II

AN ESTIMATE OF BOX OFFICE STRENGTH
OF FEATURE PICTURES
CLASSIFIED BY COMPANIES [10]

COMPANY	Ratings					
	1933	1934	1935	1936	1937	1938
Columbia	.260	.302	.335	.366	.339	.339
Loew's (M-G-M)	.582	.552	.519	.521	.510	.538
Paramount	.380	.508	.425	.435	.415	.463
R.K.O.	.395	.433	.411	.361	.400	.365
Twentieth Century-Fox*	.368	.446	.427	.466	.508	.515
Warner Bros.	.486	.429	.468	.456	.446	.463
United Artists**	.583	.762	.750	.675	.570	.703
Universal	.362	.366	.366	.378	.351	.395
Industry average	.424	.453	.439	.440	.428	.457

*Fox Film only to and including September 30, 1935.
**Includes Twentieth Century to September 30, 1935.

"The chief value of the specially constructed index in the table [II] above is as a comparison of the producing policies of individual companies." (Standard Trade and Securities, Motion Pictures, Basic Survey, June 1939, Part I.)

As Table II shows, a little over one in every three films was a Fox "hit" in 1933, but Zanuck had raised this figure to over one in every two films. There was a marked difference between a hit, a picture that made more than its money back, and a smash hit, a picture showing profits of $500,000 to $1 million. Each year, Zanuck had more smash hits as well. Very often smash hits which were not too intrinsically American could gross an additional 50 percent in foreign markets.

TABLE III

NEGATIVE COSTS AGAINST WORLD FILM RENTALS

YEAR	NEGATIVE COST	AVERAGE COST	DOMESTIC RENTAL	FOREIGN RENTAL	TOTAL RENTAL
1935	$17,117,000	364,000	23,736,000	11,002,000	34,738,000
1936	$20,219,000	381,000	27,346,000	15,645,000	42,991,000
1937	$20,595,000	420,000	27,165,000	14,404,000	41,570,000
1938	$25,854,000	497,000	30,990,000	14,198,000	45,189,000

From Table III (p. 36), the actual dollar figures can be seen on the annual negative cost against the rental returns, showing the importance of the foreign market.

On rentals of nearly $35 million in 1935, Fox showed operating profits of $3,563,000 (after taxes). Yet, in Zanuck's first full year, in 1936, operating profits rose to $7,924,000 (after taxes). His showing for the next two years proved to be more successful, and profits continued to rise.

Until the outbreak of World War II, Zanuck turned his attention to the spectacular "A" picture. He learned that the big-budget, usually historical film had made the most money at Twentieth Century Pictures, and was now going to apply it to Fox. Zanuck also knew that he could never compete with Metro or Warners when it came to stars, so instead, he made his stories his stars. Action and spectacle would be the drawing elements of his latest films, along with Tyrone Power, who had a considerable box-office name, Don Ameche, Henry Fonda, and Alice Faye.

Budgets were raised to provide the large-scale entertainment Zanuck wished to produce. What followed was a series of highly profitable films, most of them budgeted over the million dollar mark. In 1938, they included ALEXANDER'S RAGTIME BAND, SUEZ, KENTUCKY, and IN OLD CHICAGO. The following year offered JESSE JAMES, DRUMS ALONG THE MOHAWK, THE RAINS CAME, and STANLEY AND LIVINGSTONE. Zanuck had, in these films, dedicated himself to spectacle and went to any expense to get it. For the burning of Chicago in 1938's IN OLD CHICAGO, studio crews had to build a special tank of water beside the set which delayed the shooting schedule and added to the cost. The actual burning of Chicago, including special effects, consumed nearly 10 percent of the entire budget.

JESSE JAMES was also an expensive gamble. To achieve a feeling of authenticity, the film was taken on location where costs escalated. Even with the added time needed for Technicolor shooting and locations, the film cost a reasonable $1,165,242.72; only $26,509.73 over budget. Location shooting in Africa, and a lengthy schedule, brought STANLEY AND LIVINGSTONE up to $1,337,926.69; $42,000 over budget.

With all this lavish spending, Zanuck put Fox much closer to the top than ever before. His pure enthusiasm and energy inspired Nunnally Johnson to call him a "stirring spirit." Zanuck was responsible for all production, and if a film failed, he took the blame. He always considered himself the reason for success, or the bearer of disaster at Fox. There was no disputing the fact that Darryl F. Zanuck was the moving force, and a profit-making one, at Twentieth Century-Fox.

CHAPTER 4

■ DARRYL ZANUCK--MAN OR MOGUL? ■

It would be difficult to separate the policies towards film-making from the person who made them. From the year Darryl Zanuck came to Fox, the studio was his home, his mother, and his mistress. It brought him life, love, and a surrogate "family." Zanuck was the studio and the studio was Zanuck, the two almost inseparable or indistinguishable.

Norman Zierold, in THE MOGULS, described men like Fox, Zukor, Laemmle, and Mayer as highly energetic and possessing a variety of talents, including gall, persistence, imagination, showmanship, and a gambling instinct. "One mogul who carried all these traits and headed policy at a major studio and was non-Jewish was Darryl Zanuck. To a satirical New Yorker profile, Zanuck was an anomaly indeed, for he had not come from the ghettoes of middle Europe, but from Wahoo, Nebraska. Nor was he altogether illiterate, having managed to reach the eighth grade before abandoning his education." [1]

Time described Zanuck as a "wiry, high-domed man," gnawing on a massive cigar as he "paced back and forth, and spewed memoranda in a loud Midwestern twang." [2] At five feet, six-and-a-half inches, Zanuck was a fierce player of polo, and a fearless safari hunter. Physical fitness was very important to him and he prided himself on the fact that he could survive either in the jungles of Africa or in the mountains of British Columbia.

Even in his youth, Zanuck was an adventurer at heart. At the age of 15, he managed to enlist to fight in World War I. By lying about his age, he was able to see the battlefields of Europe. Zanuck was also an avid writer and would grind out his fantasies on paper. From his prolific works, he managed, after the war, to find a sponsor to publish his short stories. When the volume came out, it contained three original stories and a testimonial to Yuccatone hair restorer, within an adventure story, of course. Once he was published, the next step was to take the material to the film studios. With a need for material, the movies bought the volume.

By 1922, Zanuck had been hired by Warner Bros. and was creating stories for Rin-Tin-Tin. This success behind him, he graduated to "serious" feature films. Zanuck turned out so many screenplays that his boss, Jack Warner, demanded he use pseudonyms so the competition would not think Warners could only afford one writer. In one record year, Zanuck was credited, under all his names, with 19 screenplays. Within five years, he was promoted to the head of production at Warner Bros.

After a successful career at Warners, Zanuck continued his meteoric climb with Twentieth Century Pictures and the subsequent merger with Fox. There were many reasons why Zanuck was so successful. Since he had been a writer, he understood the concept of scriptwriting and as Nunnally Johnson points out, "He would read a script and sometimes a geiger counter would go off when he got to some dull stuff. He'd leaf back to the point where this started." 3

In a Saturday Evening Post article called "He's Got Something," the general public was given a very flattering portrait of Zanuck's skills. "Apparently, Zanuck knows instinctively and definitely what he wants. After watching him at work [it's clear that] not only does he know all the successful movie plots and formulas but he has a practical genius for each improvisation of endless combinations and permutations of these formulas to fit all the various kinds of stories that pour through a big studio." 4

"He cut every picture." [Nunnally Johnson recalled] "It was never without cooperation though. There were very few disputes I ever heard of ... and there was no question as to who was the man doing the cutting. That was Zanuck-- and he was a very good cutter." 5 Zanuck possessed an innate sense of pacing and could anticipate an audience's reaction to a film, thereby increasing the odds for success.

Philip Dunne, a writer and director at the studio and a member of the "team" that spent entire careers at Fox, thought of Zanuck as "something of a tyrant and very much an enthusiast. You left his office always feeling that this was the greatest project and would be the finest motion picture ever made." [6]

Sam Engel concurred,

> I would think that Zanuck, at age two, thought he'd be great. I don't think he ever had a doubt in his mind about his own capabilities, or that things were going to move for him. He wasn't just an optimist, he was completely and totally without fear.... I think it's safe to say that Zanuck, in his heyday, excelled any movie star, any royalty, in terms of living the good life. He passed up nothing. He indulged himself to the hilt. But it's important to say, as much as he did that, so did he work. He was the hardest working son-of-a-gun that ever came down the gangplank. He was endowed with great physical strength and good health. And he took care of it. Three times a week, it was (polo). Out he'd go to his place and ride for an hour or two. Every day, the massage and the steam bath. At United Artists, before he could have a stable, he had an enormous wooden cage put on the back lot at Sam Goldwyn's studio, where he could practice polo. He'd sit down on a wooden horse and he'd take his mallet and he'd practice. [7]

At Fox, Zanuck was the tyrant in charge. Everyone answered to him--especially directors. Leonard Mosley, in his revealing 1984 biography said, "He admired directors as a breed and he knew they could make all the difference to the quality of a film, especially in securing a good performance from the actors. But they were his servants and they did what he told them, and he always made it crystal clear that he was their master and arbiter of everything they filmed." [8] Schedules were arranged to fit his, very often upsetting everyone else's arrangements, because Zanuck only got to the studio in the late morning. He would work until mid-afternoon, then take a nap, have dinner, watch the day's rushes and rough cuts of films. Around midnight story conferences might sometimes begin. This usually conflicted with the writers, who were at the studio in the early morning. Nevertheless, concessions were made because there was no other choice.

Zanuck also had an entourage consisting of friends and associates, many of whom were non-film people, to give him a layman's opinion of an idea or a film. His entourage accompanied him to meals at the studio commissary, to the steam bath, and to screenings.

Prizes of former safaris adorned the walls of Zanuck's luxurious office, and story ideas were discussed amidst the "stuffed heads of a water hog and an antelope, the skins of a lion and a jaguar, the sawed-off feet of an elephant and a rhino." [9] In addition to these fond trophies, Zanuck's office would be filled with secretaries and associates during story conferences. Nunnally Johnson recalled those conferences fondly: "There were usually five or six people in the room with us. I had an assistant who complained when Zanuck got very enthusiastic when he'd think of a love scene. My assistant, who happened to be rather pretty, said, 'I wish he would stop casting me as the girl.'" [10]

Zanuck was surrounded by friends even at work, and he was known for being generous when it came to offering a producing or directing job to a close acquaintance. The most obvious of these favors went to those known as the "court jesters," Zanuck's card-playing cronies, George Jessel and Gregory Ratoff. Both had been well-known in the industry, but Zanuck gave them regular employment on his top productions. Jessel had been hired as a writer and producer. Zanuck would assign him to properties which needed a watchdog rather than a top-kick production boss. Ratoff proved to be slightly more than competent as a director, and many of his films could easily have been made by others. Both men stayed with Zanuck through the war years and the latter half of the forties. Raymond Griffith had been a silent screen star, whose career was ruined by the advent of sound. Griffith was installed as a producer of "A" product and turned out some very successful films. In the late 1930's, aside from Zanuck and Kenneth MacGowan, Griffith was the most important producer on the lot. Mal St. Clair had directed Rin-Tin-Tin films at Warners, but when Zanuck learned he would be unemployed, he assigned him to direct Fox's "B" pictures. The relationship lasted for ten years, within which period St. Clair directed over a dozen films for Fox.

Two more unusual acquaintances led to similar situations. Otto Lang had been Zanuck's ski instructor before he was made a producer. Among the films he produced was Joseph Mankiewicz's FIVE FINGERS in 1952. Zanuck's French tutor, Edward Leggewie, was later appointed as an executive of the Fox European organization.

A fact of life to everyone in the film industry was the rampant nepotism running through the studio system. Sidney Kent's brother-in-law, Robert Kane, had been a producer with Fox before the merger. After, he was named vice-president in charge of England's Fox Corporation. Since there was hardly any activity in England at the time, there was little problem. However, as production increased, it became obvious Kane was not doing an outstanding job. Sam Engel had found out about a seemingly ill-fated deal which had been in Kane's hands.

> Joe Schenck had signed a deal with Gracie Fields while he was over in Monte Carlo, and with Monty Banks, who was then a director and Gracie Fields' boyfriend. This deal was most improbable and impractical. Gracie was then at the height of her fame as a music hall star (in England) and they agreed to pay her $250,000 per picture for two pictures per year. And they paid (Banks) $87,500 per picture. That's $337,500 per picture, play or pay. So that's four pictures. And now it's June of the first year. The first picture has not yet been made. [11]

Engel knew that Kane was not developing any material for the films, so he suggested to an upset Darryl Zanuck that "Mae West used to do those gold rush things in Alaska, so why can't we do a gold rush story or a diamond story set in South Africa...? I tell you, practically in 24 hours, I was on a boat for England ... and I made the picture for $500,000." [12]

Even into the 1950's, with more sophisticated production techniques, money was occasionally squandered over friendship. Delmer Daves, in 1954, was assigned to direct LORD

VANITY, which had already been announced as an upcoming release.

> That was a misguided thing right from the start [said Daves], Zanuck had a pet second-unit director working abroad whom he wanted to keep on the payroll. So, he had this man, without any script because Charlie Brackett and Walter Reisch were still working on it, build a budget of way over $1 million of shooting location scenes in Italy, North Africa, Morocco. Darryl gave me all the film to run and I didn't know what to do with it. This guy had lit canals in Venice for 18 blocks, and I asked Darryl what would happen to scenes like this if the story didn't call for them. He said, "Well, make it call for them."
>
> I did tests on Robert Wagner, Clifton Webb, and Joan Collins, who was new at the time, but the minute I saw Bob come down in the powdered wig, I remembered him in PRINCE VALIANT with the page-boy bob. I saw him going from the page-boy to peruke and it was just ridiculous. He was an American boy and didn't have the style to play this young Frenchman. That's basically how the thing ended. It was the kind of thing we hid in the closet to forget about. Darryl's casting instinct was also sometimes less than great. [13]

Testimony to this statement can be pinpointed in several films Zanuck made as showcases for his periodic "romantic interests." Although married since January 24, 1924, Zanuck, by the fifties, was making constant trips to Europe, Paris in particular. There he met Bella Wegier, and after rechristening her Bella Darvi (from Darryl and Virginia), he tried to give the "star buildup" in Hollywood. He handed her a leading part in his 1954 extravaganza, THE EGYPTIAN, a $4 million epic based on Mika Waltari's best-selling novel. Zanuck obviously favored Darvi, constantly referring to her in memos. "I am certainly happy we have Jean Simmons in the picture. She does wonders for [Edmund] Purdom in the earlier part of the story when he needs help but fortunately he also gets amazing help from Bella." [14]

In another, Zanuck was concerned about all the foreign accents among extras in THE EGYPTIAN. "With the exception of Bella Darvi and some of the foreign girls in the Nefer sequence we should not have any other foreign accents in the picture. It will be very confusing. We can excuse Darvi and some of the other girls because it is made clear that they are Babylonians." [15]

In a memo to a writer who was designing a role for Darvi in an upcoming script, Zanuck advised, "We are going to be very careful in our selection of a second role for her. Her present role [as a prostitute] is made to order and we must be careful not to type her." [16]

Zanuck did not really have to worry because Bella Darvi only starred in three Fox films and never caught on with the public or the critics. She returned to Paris where she continued her career on an erratic basis, and later committed suicide.

Darvi's failure did not daunt Zanuck. In 1957, he discovered a popular French singer, Juliette Greco, and starred her in important roles in THE SUN ALSO RISES and THE ROOTS OF HEAVEN. Both were his own personal productions. Again, Greco's Gallic charm never touched the American public. Zanuck starred her in other films, until their relationship ended in 1960. Next came Irina Demick, an attractive woman of Franco-German descent. After Demick followed Genevieve Gilles. Zanuck was persistent, but his taste in European women never proved very successful at the box office.

At Zanuck's peak, however, he was an efficient head of production at Fox. His first five years of output did not produce any major cinematic breakthroughs, and his films were generally hit hard by the critics, but he was most successful at producing mass-audience pictures.

> The characteristic Zanuck picture of that period , [writes Mel Gussow], was a romanticized look at American history; the building of a city, the founding of a religion, the finding of a musical sound, the making of a president, the invention of a telephone. As Zanuck saw America's past, it was the same movie over and over again, one huge, brawling, sprawling, Quirt-and-Flaggian epic, where in the end, usually with the help of mother love, all conflicts are resolved. [17]

When Zanuck hit upon something good, he would very often try to use it again. Gussow described two basic types of pictures at the studio in these years, sequels and remakes. There were also partial remakes, which utilized one of the elements of a popular film. Zanuck's favorite plot device was the "story of two young boys who loved each other ... and then ... parted; one became a famous man and the other became more or less insignificant, but the insignificant one made possible the greatest victory of the famous one." [18] In 1937, Zanuck made LOVE IS NEWS, a comedy starring Tyrone Power and Loretta Young. It was remade as a musical in 1943, SWEET ROSIE O'GRADY with Robert Young and Betty Grable, and then again in 1949 as a straight comedy with Tyrone Power called THAT WONDERFUL URGE. Even though the basic idea of two identical characters who are mistaken for each other goes back to the second century B.C. and the Roman author Plautus, Zanuck managed to revitalize it for modern viewing. The first of the series was made in 1935 starring Maurice Chevalier, FOLIES BER-GERE. From Paris, Zanuck moved the story to Rio de Janeiro and the lead role was played by Don Ameche in THAT NIGHT IN RIO in 1942. Then came Danny Kaye in 1951 in ON THE RIVIERA. "Sometimes the theory of remakes was stretched to ridiculous lengths, on at least one occasion by Bryan Foy, who was in charge of Zanuck's "B" pictures in the Forties. He assigned Henry and Phoebe Ephron to remake TO THE SHORES OF TRIPOLI as RIP GOES TO WAR, with a dog playing the John Payne part." [19]

Over the years, probably the sturdiest of warhorses was the story of three attractive young women searching for wealthy husbands. Zanuck shamelessly reused this plot device in LADIES IN LOVE (1936), SALLY, IRENE, AND MARY (1937), THREE BLIND MICE (1938), MOON OVER MIAMI (1941), THREE LITTLE GIRLS IN BLUE (1946), HOW TO MARRY A MILLIONAIRE (1953), and finally THE PLEASURE SEEKERS (1964).

Because Zanuck loved horseracing, Fox turned out more equine epics than any other studio. Very often, the climax was set at a race track. KENTUCKY (1938), MARYLAND (1940), MY FRIEND FLICKA (1943), HOME IN INDIANA (1944), SMOKY (1946), and THE HOMESTRETCH (1946) are just a few of the titles in this series of commercial releases.

In Fox's favor, Zanuck not only excelled in rehashes but also took great strides in advancing the state of the serious dramatic film. Both he and his board of directors were afraid that the public would not accept THE GRAPES OF WRATH, but he never once considered cancelling the project. John Ford, the director of the film came back to the studio the following year and filmed HOW GREEN WAS MY VALLEY, depicting the lives of downtrodden mine workers in Wales. Both films displayed to the public, and to critics, a new side of Darryl Zanuck.

When war broke out again, Zanuck enlisted in the "Hollywood Corps " to fight for his country by making movies. From 1941 to 1943, Zanuck left the studio business to vice-president William B. Goetz, but made certain enough scripts had his approval for shooting. Although he only made one film for the Armed Forces, AT THE FRONT, he came in contact with a new type of filmmaking. Frank Capra and John Huston were making war documentaries with a new immediacy and frankness. This realistic honesty impressed Zanuck and later affected the type of films he produced when he returned to the studio.

In a series of very bold post-war filmmaking ventures, Zanuck tackled the problems of corruption on a city council in BOOMERANG, anti-Semitism in the United States in GENTLEMAN'S AGREEMENT, race relations and miscegenation in PINKY, and treatment of the mentally ill in THE SNAKE PIT. The latter remained Zanuck's proudest achievement, directly promoting a change in mental institution laws in 26 states.

For these films and many others, Time had good reason to feature Zanuck on their cover in 1950 and state that "...he embodies what may be nature's ultimate effort to equip the species for outstanding success in Hollywood. Producer Zanuck is richly endowed with tough-mindedness, talent, an outsized ego, and a glutton's craving for hard work. These qualities, indulged with endless enthusiasm for a quarter-century, have not only sped him to the top but have somehow left him free of ulcers and in the pink of health." [20]

Producers tended to agree.

I think he had high aspirations, but they weren't on any intellectual levels [Nunnally Johnson reminisced]. He had plenty of courage--all the courage in the world--physical and commercial. He always thought of himself as a writer, which is funny since he wrote some hair tonic ads. He'd always say "we writers," and I guess if you feel you are, you are ... I suppose he had weaknesses, but they were inconsequential.

I remember when my contract at Universal International terminated, L. B. Mayer invited me over to have lunch with him and talk about signing with M-G-M. I was planning to go back to Fox where I'd been for so many years. Mayer mentioned all the stars on the lot, but I still didn't want to sign. He asked me what Fox had that they didn't--and I said "Zanuck." 21

CHAPTER 5

■ THE TAIL THAT WAGGED THE DOG ■

Before the production monopoly imposed by the General Film Company in 1910, theaters had been supplied with films by the independent exchanges. When the General combine invaded their realm, theater owners either lived with the terms of the Film Trust, or they went out of business. William Fox knew there was another way and when he was cut off by the Film Trust, he set up a studio and began to produce his own films.

This was an extremely important development in the motion picture industry, because Fox might have stayed only in the theater business. Very soon he realized the importance of his diversification. Not only did he earn the extra rentals from the films, but he had virtually guaranteed his theaters of a steady supply of films. And there was one undeniable fact--his theaters could not exist without film product. After Fox's court victory over the Trust in 1912, other theater owners began making their own films. This resulted in the establishment of studios by the major theater chains--Loew's, Paramount, Warner Bros., and later, R.K.O.

As the number of theaters and circuits grew in the United States, producers like William Fox realized there were also potential play dates in independent theaters and chains. Not only could a film get exposure through its own studio's exhibition channels, but through others as well. In this way, film production became a more profitable venture. The ascendant majors were those who were making profits on two fronts: successful films brought the acquisition of more theaters, and more theater admissions meant more expenditures on the product. Those producers who did not own theaters were always at a disadvantage because they lacked the financial security theaters provided. As a result, Universal and Columbia very often showed erratic earnings and sometimes losses.

With the growing importance of the major theater chains, "the United States was divided into territories," says Sol Lesser, an independent theater owner at the time.

> There was a New England territory with one or more chains of theater circuits dominating that area. Likewise, Eastern Pennsylvania, Western Pennsylvania, Illinois, the deep South, the Midwest, the Chicago area. California, Nevada, and Arizona. And Utah, Colorado, Wyoming, and New Mexico, and so forth and so on. All 48 states, at that time, had these kinds of divisions, which were dominated by one, or perhaps two, in some cases, three, different large theater circuits.... Now, the circuits were so strong in those days that they dominated the situation. What I mean by dominated is that some of these circuits were owned by the big producing companies. But, by agreement with one another, they agreed to stay out of each other's territory. For example, Paramount was dominant in New England states, and they had an agreement, for instance, with Warner Brothers, who were dominant in Eastern Pennsylvania. If they didn't go into Eastern Pennsylvania, Warners wouldn't go into New England. And these kinds of internal and external agreements were very general throughout the motion picture industry. [1]

There were other agreements as well.

> The studio operations, if they had theaters, wouldn't have theaters in every city.... A Paramount picture, if they had no Paramount theater to play in Philadelphia, they had to book to the Warner Brothers. Well, if they exacted high terms from Warner Brothers, Philadelphia, when Warners had a big picture for New England, they would reciprocate by asking high terms for New England. [2]

This type of reciprocity was carried out by the majors in many ways. To keep a theater chain in good standing with

the other majors, Fox, for example, had to produce a fair
amount of successful films, because it would therefore be
"owed" another company's successful films for the first-run
playdates. Production again became an important factor in
the industry. Certainly, when the first-run theaters were
separated more sharply from neighborhood houses by the
price of admission, top product became increasingly valuable.
Each studio could only produce a certain number of "A" pictures, not enough to keep film on all its screens, so, ultimately, one major would depend on another for product. By
the late thirties, with the annual production output in steep
decline, this dependence became all the more obvious.

With films being produced and their theaters being ser-
viced, the majors would turn their salesmanship towards the
remaining thousands of theaters. Since these houses did
not have the strength of a major producing chain, they were
categorized as to their potential. The houses with higher
gross potential were given priority in the matter of playdates.
The distributor would decide how long after the first run
each sub-run theater would play a film. Independent circuits with many theaters were much more valuable to the
majors for playoffs than the single small-town house. Consequently, smaller theaters would be forced to sign contracts
which would set out the date and rental rate for the engagement. To minimize the risk on a year's investment in product,
contracts were signed for all the pictures, one year in advance in a practice known as "block-booking." If a theater
owner did not like these terms, he would not be playing any
of the films from that company. With all these contracts, as
well as the standard bookings with its own theaters, a studio
would merely produce films to fulfill those agreements. Considering that of the nearly 17,000 theaters in the country
only 3,000 were controlled by the majors, distributors soon
found out that they would need the other independent chains
as much as those which were company owned. This did not
mean, however, that the majors would become overly generous.
The independents were mostly "forced" into signing contracts
which they felt were unfair, but if they wanted to book films
from the five major studios--Fox, Metro, Warners, R.K.O.,
and Paramount--and the three smaller ones--Columbia, Universal, and United Artists--they had to comply.

The interdependence of studios and theaters in the motion picture industry was a normal business relationship

but difficulty results from the fact that while selling of entertainment is a commercial process, making films is largely creative and artistic in nature. Moviemakers, like artists in other fields, are generally inclined to experiment with new techniques and are not above wanting to interpret or affect their surroundings. Exhibitors, on the other hand, may not know much about the art of the film, but they know what has been good box office before. Consequently, theirs is the conservative influence; they are the traditionalists of the trade, exerting their influence in the direction of the safe-and-sound in filmmaking. [3]

With almost all of a company's finances emanating from its theaters, the majority of the power remained, at most studios, with those who were in charge of exhibition. They could decide whether a film would attract sufficient audiences to return its cost. At Twentieth Century-Fox, the situation was quite different. Because Fox made more on a per-picture basis from overhead charged by production and distribution than most of the studios, and less from their theater operations, Darryl Zanuck had more clout in production than other creative executives. However, after Sidney Kent's death and the naming of Spyros Skouras to the presidency, there were very often disputes over what product would be commercially successful. A veteran theater executive, Skouras held his own intuition in higher esteem than Zanuck's. The battles would rage for twenty years.

A total of $2 billion was invested in the film industry in 1939, placing $1.88 billion in theaters, $112 million in studios, and $20 million in distribution. As well, the companies listed their various sources of income in the following order: 1) theaters admissions, 2) film rentals, 3) the sale of film accessories, and 4) dividends from affiliated companies. In some cases, a company might show a loss on their production end but make up for it from exhibition. In short, theaters were the tail that wagged the dog.

Although there was no real correlation between the number of theaters a company owned and the amount of income from film rentals, there was good reason to maintain theater chains. Aside from the competition among the majors, theaters 1) provided an insurance policy through first-run exhibition, and 2) they offered a minimum market for films which might not have been well received.

At Fox, the lowest number of playdates for a film in the 1936-1937 season was 1,763, the highest was 12,232. For Paramount, on the other hand, which had the most theaters, the lowest amount was 4,100; for R.K.O. it was 3,155; and for Warner Bros., 3,838. The obvious fact that appears from these figures is that the other companies had "insurance" playdates by owning more theaters. Fox did not. Nevertheless, when it came to successful films, there was no problem in booking. Paramount's most popular film only beat Fox's by 668 exhibitions.

Paramount owned 1,273 houses in 1940. Fox controlled 538 across the country, with California's West Coast chain amounting to 205. Fox was also strong in the states of Wisconsin, Illinois, Missouri, Kansas, Colorado, and Washington. There were other theaters in Michigan, Iowa, Nebraska, Montana, Idaho, New Mexico, Arizona, Utah, and Oregon. With only one house in New York state, Fox left this territory open to the other four companies, each of which had heavy saturation there. In California, Fox held about 90 percent of the houses, and about 70 percent in Colorado, but only one-half of one percent in New York.

The favored position of the majors, however, was their dominance in the first-run situations where the majority of grosses would be earned. Table IV (p. 54) shows the results of a survey of major holdings in 1940.

This dominant profit-making enterprise, however, was a thorn in the side of independent theater owners who wanted better terms and playdates on pictures they played. Banding together, independent exhibitors made their feelings known and voiced their complaints in political and legislative circles. This resulted in the filing of an antitrust suit by the Department of Justice on July 20, 1938. "The eight majors were accused of combining and conspiring to restrain trade in the production, distribution, and exhibition of motion pictures, and with attempting successfully to monopolize such trade in violation of the Sherman Act. The majors were specifically charged with 28 offenses, all of which were alleged to be instrumental in creating the monopoly." [5]

Although there never was a trial, a precedent had been set--the independents, with a concerted effort, could bring the majors to account. Negotiations between the Department

TABLE IV

NUMBER OF FIRST-RUN THEATERS OPERATED IN 35 CITIES

Paramount	63
Warner Bros.	35
20th Century-Fox	30
R.K.O.	29
Loew's	<u>24</u>
Total	181

of Justice and the majors resulted in a consent decree, whereby some of the monopolistic procedures would be limited. On November 20, 1940, the five majors, Fox, Metro, R.K.O., Paramount, and Warners, agreed to:

> (1) Modify, temporarily, the practice of block-booking by restricting sales to blocks of five films at a time;
> (2) Eliminate blind selling by having trade showings before the release of films;
> (3) Refrain from forcing shorts, newsreels, westerns, reissues, etc.;
> (4) Provide a system of arbitration with limited powers for handling the problem of clearance;
> (5) Refrain from entering upon a general program of expansion of theater holdings, and to seek court approval in the question of acquisitions of further theaters. [6]

For all these concessions, the government agreed to postpone any further court action in the anti-trust suit for a period of two years, the length of the decree. The decree could be renewed if agreement was forthcoming from all the parties involved.

The system of arbitration which was set up consisted of 31 tribunals across the country involving some 1,200 arbitrators. These members, who were judges, lawyers, jurors,

and legal advisers, were paid $10 per diem as a token re-
imbursement for their time. The total cost of the arrange-
ment, $300,000 annually, was borne equally by the five
majors. In theory, it cost them $60,000 a year to hold on
to their theaters for a little longer, a sum they were most
willing to pay. Under the terms of the system, only an
exhibitor could initiate a complaint, and the defendant in
the complaint, i.e., a major, would have to provide a de-
fensive argument. In the 342 complaints raised by exhibitors in the two years of the board's existence, a majority
were settled in favor of the exhibitors. The main complaint
was regarding the time a theater had to wait to get a film
after its first run. Others involved the cancellation privileges of an exhibitor, which were usually very minimal.

By the time the first decree had expired, the producers
were more than willing to sign another document for two more
years. Wary theater men noted, though, that the majors
had still been acquiring theaters in the two-year period.
Fox alone had expanded by 30 houses, and other terms of
the decree were going unobserved. For one thing, some of
the majors were booking pictures in blocks larger than five,
and playdates were still unsatisfactory in many cases.

Willing to sign a more liberal decree, the majors were
simply stalling for time, for it was well-known in the industry
that exhibitors were still pushing for anti-trust action. After
eight months of negotiations on a new decree, a settlement
could not be reached and further court action was taken. The
government wanted to separate the production organizations
from the theaters very quickly, and a trial was begun October
8, 1945. Among the accusations were that "(1) the majors
gave their own theaters first crack at the better films and
(2) required independents to book films in blocks." [7]

There was much speculation in the industry as to what
was to happen. If the trial ruled that there was no monopoly, or that owning theaters was not monopolistic, the majors
might be allowed to keep their chains in some limited capacity.
However, they might also be forced to sell off, or separate
one of the two divisions. "Rises in production costs in the
past year or two have caused more than one studio to reap-
praise its multiple functions in the light of the government's
persistence on the anti-trust front. Generally, it is conceded
that any major, given a choice of the two, would hang on to

its theaters (greater, steadier return on investment) and get rid of its studios." [8]

In May of 1948, the Supreme Court ruled, after three years of testimonies, investigations, and retrials in District Courts, that the five majors would have to divest themselves of their theaters. A final date was not yet set for divestment, but price fixing, block-booking, and pooling agreements were immediately labelled monopolistic. This ruling not only affected the five majors which held theaters, but the three smaller companies, in the practices of booking.

Although final action on the ownership of theaters had not been decided upon, the majors agreed to sign another consent decree to avoid years of legal costs disputing the court's rulings. In this decree, the majors each outlined specific actions which would be taken to set up separate theater corporations or to sell the chains to independents.

Previously, many industry analysts and spokesmen had favored the more profitable theater chains, but opinions had changed for one reason--television. Company presidents estimated their backlog of negatives would greatly enhance the profits of the production end, which was thriving in the post-war years.

Although Fox had been less dependent on its theaters than most companies, a sizeable 80% of its $14 million profit in 1947 came from theater revenue. Only one year earlier, its profits of $22.6 million had been split fifty-fifty. Whereas the exhibition end held up within 10 percent, profits in production and distribution had dropped due to sharply rising costs and a drop in foreign grosses.

Business Week reported,

> In one sense, the loss of theaters might have a good effect. In the present setup, producer-owned theaters often get films for first run at a comparatively low rental. Since it's only a bookkeeping transaction anyhow, no effort is made to collect all that the traffic will bear.
> Most of the sales officials are sure that they could get much more for their films if they sell them to the highest bidders. That would boost the production-distribution end of the gross. [9]

Nevertheless, the divorce decree was not good for the majors in the long run. It did not take long to discover that, on a competitive basis, while the majors could get higher rates on the top pictures, no one would bid much for the program pictures. Contracts could no longer guarantee the rate and length of a playdate. A film would play as long as business held up, thus doing away with "insurance playdates." Nor would the theater executives figure as importantly as the production chiefs in filmmaking policy. No longer would the tail wag the dog.

CHAPTER 6

■ BOOM YEARS ■

None of the major film companies operated in a vacuum.
Each was directly affected by the fortunes of the other and
the industry as a whole. There was an absolute interdependence among the majors for a steady supply of each others'
pictures and playdates. Even the three companies which did
not own theaters were dependent on the major chains for key
city first-run theaters. So vital was this interdependence
that when a slump hit, all the companies suffered, and when
boom times came, each one profited. Such a boom occurred
during World War II and resulted in record-breaking earnings for the industry.

Darryl Zanuck was in an ideal position to take maximum
advantage of this boom. Producing an average of 50 pictures yearly, Zanuck and been steadily increasing Fox's
profits since his takeover in 1935. His policy of building
up stars and stories had resulted in enormously popular product, and also left Fox with a roster of talent including
Tyrone Power, Don Ameche, Henry Fonda, Gene Tierney,
Alice Faye, Sonja Henie, and Jane Darwell. Prestige had
also been brought to the studio with pictures like THE GRAPES
OF WRATH, JESSE JAMES, and IN OLD CHICAGO. Zanuck
had changed Fox's record of profitability in films from two-
in-five to one-in-two, and almost equalled the record of
M-G-M. Fox's film rentals for 1939 were second only to
Metro's, which were about 30 percent higher, buoyed by a
bumper crop of titles including GONE WITH THE WIND, GOOD-
BYE MR. CHIPS, and EDISON THE MAN. M-G-M's incomparable
talent roster with Clark Gable, Judy Garland, Mickey Rooney,
Greta Garbo, Robert Taylor, Spencer Tracy, Melvyn Douglas,
Greer Garson added probably 100 percent more drawing power
than any of Fox's stars.

Working from a weaker point in the area of star talent, Zanuck was still able to fashion high-grossing "A" pictures. Of the six top-grossing Fox films of 1940, Zanuck personally produced five. Henry Fonda starred in three, Don Ameche in three, Alice Faye in two, and three were in Technicolor. Two of these films were musicals; two were biographies; one, an action western; and the last, a fine drama. These were Zanuck's stars. In addition, Zanuck introduced others in these six films who were to earn many million for the studio.

Betty Grable had been in films for eight years, but without a starring role in an "A" picture until TIN PAN ALLEY. Fox's top film of 1940, it started Grable on her phenomenally successful career at the studio. THE RETURN OF FRANK JAMES introduced Gene Tierney, who would appear in many more Fox pictures during the next 15 years. Carmen Miranda had been very popular on Broadway and Zanuck brought her to the screen in the hit DOWN ARGENTINE WAY.

There were also more expensive failures in 1940, a problem which plagued Zanuck for the first time. CHAD HANNA with Henry Fonda and THE BLUE BIRD starring Shirley Temple were both high-budget Technicolor vehicles. Neither returned its negative cost. BRIGHAM YOUNG--FRONTIERS-MAN was Tyrone Power's first period picture to flop, much to Zanuck's disappointment, and THE GREAT PROFILE was a sad attempt to revive John Barrymore's past glory. With the exception of CHAD HANNA, all were Zanuck productions.

These failures were symptoms of an uncertain box office. A general slump in the industry had begun in 1939. As the United States was drawn closer to war, the mood of the country was beginning to change, and so were audience patterns. Again, there was a growing selectivity among general audiences catalyzed by further rises in admission. As a result, domestic rentals fell off by about 20 percent from 1938.

Revenue in Europe was evaporating as well as more countries were threatened by invasion. Europe was at war, and a 20 percent decline in foreign grosses hit studios at the bottom line.

With smaller markets to contend with, the losses on certain pictures were taken in stride. Budgets were still very close to $1 million, even on the "A" pictures, and with the protection of guaranteed playdates, a film's losses were never too great to bear. The studio was still turning out many more successful films than unsuccessful ones, and the profits of one hit would pay for the losses on two disasters.

Between 1942 and 1945, Hollywood had to keep operating under the severe limitations imposed by war-time measures. Not only did the studios lose production chiefs to the Armed Forces, they also did without important stars, writers, directors, and producers.

William Goetz was left in charge of Twentieth Century-Fox's production during Zanuck's absence from 1941-1943. Goetz had to contend with the sundry problems resulting from the war-time economy. Measures were imposed by the War Production Board limiting the consumption of basic materials to provide more for the war effort. On May 6, 1942, the W.P.B. issued a limit of $5,000 for the sets on any motion picture. This meant that lumber, nails, paint, and material had to be used and reused as many times as possible. Sets which were built for previous films were redecorated to suit new scripts and stories. The Welsh coal mining town of HOW GREEN WAS MY VALLEY became the small Norwegian town of THE MOON IS DOWN two years later.

At the same time, a limit was set on the amount of film which could be used. Studios were ordered to cut their total film consumption by 50 percent. To comply, no reprints of scenes were permitted, and only one take was ever printed. Distribution had to be trimmed as well, since release prints used up almost 17 times as much footage as production. There were serious consequences involved in these cutbacks, such as the slower return of capital by cutting down on distribution, and alternatives were suggested. Some studio engineers brought up the remote possibility of slowing down the speed of cameras and projectors to 67½ feet per minute from the standard of 90. The reason 90 had been used as a standard was for the clarity of sound reproduction. With technical advances, sound could be improved at the original speed, but there would still be the expensive changeover of gears, motors, and shutters for projectors. The estimated saving of 500 million feet annually was ruled out, however, because the time was not appropriate for changing parts and mechanisms, especially with materials in short supply. Film use was curtailed voluntarily at the studio and all scripts carried the stamped message "Less Shooting Over Here Means More Shooting Over There--Save Film."

There were, however, some advantages, as Business Week reported in its article about cutbacks. "Incidentally, there's one war-time break for picture producers: They have a new set of villains. Up to Pearl Harbor all foreign dastards were out, because film-buying countries threatened boycotts. Now, Japanese and Jerry villains promise to be popular in most countries for a long time to come." [1]

Another advantage was that the war-time boom economy spilled healthily over into the motion picture industry. With little else to do during the war years, everyone went to the movies. Since there were 24-hour schedules at factories, theaters obliged and kept their doors open as well. This produced stratospheric attendance figures at the year's end. The average film gross was rising so fast that there were more successful films than ever before. What might have been a hit only two years earlier reaped smash grosses, and even the average film became a hit. In fact, there was little disputing the notion that it was almost impossible for a film to lose money in these years.

Entertainment was clearly the key to success in 1942 and action films, war stories, or frothy musicals were constant proof of this. THE BLACK SWAN and SON OF FURY both featured Tyrone Power in his final pre-enlistment swashbuckling roles, and both were very successful. Leading the year's hit pictures, though, was a Zanuck production, TO THE SHORES OF TRIPOLI, starring John Payne as a Marine, and MY GAL SAL, a nostalgic Gay Nineties musical with Rita Hayworth and Victor Mature. Other big hits included SPRINGTIME IN THE ROCKIES, another Betty Grable musical, with Carmen Miranda thrown in for good measure; FOOTLIGHT SERENADE which teamed Grable with Victor Mature; and TALES OF MANHATTAN, a multi-starred episodic feature. Each of these features earned domestic rentals either at or very near the $2 million mark, an unprecedented number of smashes for Fox.

Whereas costs had only risen slightly from 1940, profits jumped sharply. However, because England froze Fox's British film revenues in 1940, it produced a European surplus of $2.8 million, which was shown on the corporate records as a loss of $517,000. When the money was released the following year, profits of over $4 million were reported. In the first year of the boom, 1942, profits more than doubled to $10,609,000. Because the average cost of a film at Fox in 1940 was $474,000, and the average cost two years later was $499,000, profits would continue to be very substantial indeed.

The realities of war did eventually intrude on the euphoria. Due to cutbacks of all materials, production in 1943 was cut at Twentieth Century-Fox from the previous annual average of almost 50 films to only 31 features. Even with cuts on the production schedule, negative costs exceeded the previous year, totalling $37,876,000, or an average of $751,000, up by 33 percent.

The rises in cost passed virtually unnoticed because audiences were rushing to theaters in record numbers, and each year seemed to set new all-time figures. Record profits were made possible by increased first-run attendance where the highest percentage of box-office gross was made. These were the flagship houses of the majors, and admissions were set at premium prices. The greater amount of money that was made enabled the studio to produce more expensive films.

Darryl Zanuck had organized the studio so well that the everyday mechanism of getting films into production still operated in his absence. Bill Goetz left no lasting imprint upon the studio after two short years in the top position, but did head a very profitable production unit. When Zanuck returned in 1943, he simply picked up where he left off, but Goetz conspicuously left for a production position at Universal Pictures.

Sidney Kent died March 19, 1942, while Zanuck was away, and was replaced by Spyros P. Skouras, the head of Fox West Coast Theaters. While Kent trusted Zanuck's commercial taste implicity, Skouras constantly tried to assert his judgment in Zanuck's production unit. Acrimony built and the two executives never got along very well. Their strained relationship widened the gap between the studio on the West Coast and Skouras' corporate head office in New York. As a matter of strict policy, Zanuck would never let Skouras see a film until it was completed and shipped to New York for release. Skouras would sometimes "advise" Zanuck on various personal pet projects like THE SONG OF

BERNADETTE, or the value of CinemaScope in the 1950's. However, it was clearly understood that Zanuck had the final say on all projects, and ultimately held himself responsible for their success or failure.

Zanuck had been building up Fox's prestige as an "A" studio, and into the forties, the once-prolific program of "B" films began to dry up. Following the policy he had set at Twentieth Century, Zanuck put all his efforts into the top product, for he could show stockholders that, usually, the higher-budget films made the largest amounts of money. With the number of productions down, and a limited budget for the total program, the films which were ultimately cut back were the "B" films.

As Zanuck took over the reins again in 1943, Fox was enjoying another wildly profitable year. Such high-budget pictures as Betty Grable's SWEET ROSIE O'GRADY and CONEY ISLAND, THE GANG'S ALL HERE, GUADALCANAL DIARY, HEAVEN CAN WAIT, and CLAUDIA were returning very impressive grosses.

For the box-office year of 1944, Darryl Zanuck went on an all-out effort to collect a larger share of the huge filmgoing market. Boosting budgets to record figures, he embarked on some very ambitious projects. Some of these were failures; but again success outranked disaster, and Zanuck continued to live the charmed life of a Hollywood producer. In the process, he boosted film rentals by over $18 million for the year, a rise of nearly 30 percent. This figure even outdistanced a rise in theater grosses of 25 percent.

The average budget continued rising dramatically, from $751,000 in 1943 to $1,253,000 in 1944. Not all films were very expensive, but Zanuck had invested heavily in THE SONG OF BERNADETTE, WILSON, and THE KEYS OF THE KINGDOM. The average budget on these features was approximately $2.5 million. BERNADETTE proved to be an absolute smash hit, the biggest in Fox's history, with a record $4.7 million in domestic rentals. WINGED VICTORY, another Zanuck personal production, was the next highest-grossing film, with $3 million on a $1.5 million negative cost. Zanuck's pet extravaganza, WILSON, was, perhaps, his most bitter failure. He lavished an extraordinary amount of energy on the project, but the 154-minute epic biography could not interest audiences. On a $2.9 million negative cost, Zanuck estimated that the studio lost nearly $2 million. THE KEYS OF THE KINGDOM, another expected blockbuster, could not earn back its $2.65 million cost.

There were many other films on the Fox 1944 program which were successful, even though they were not budgeted as blockbusters. Zanuck's two other pictures, LAURA and THE PURPLE HEART, both performed very well on costs nearing $1 million. Musicals again proved to be surefire box-office successes, especially when they starred Betty Grable. PIN-UP GIRL and DIAMOND HORSESHOE were evidence of her continuing popularity. Carmen Miranda showed up in two moderately successful Technicolor musicals, GREENWICH VILLAGE and SOMETHING FOR THE BOYS.

These returns, coupled with the huge hits, showed that Zanuck was firmly in control once more. Rentals had risen substantially, but company overhead had skyrocketed by more than $11 million. Earnings for the year were slightly lower than in 1943, but it was no fault of Zanuck's. Once the overhead had levelled off in the next year, he was able to show his most profitable record of hits.

Total expenditures for 1945 and 1946 were almost identical, at approximately $34 million for 24 productions. Rentals for 1945 totalled $71,468,000, down slightly from the year before with profits of $12 million. The following year, though, with lower rentals of $63,561,000, profits rose to $22,619,000, with a higher overhead as well. The reason was simple. Theaters had their best year ever, with attendance bringing in approximately $200 million by September, 1946, for a year-end industry total of $1,512,000,000. An estimated 80-90 million people went to the movies weekly.

While business continued to grow, and profits increased, anti-trust feeling was rising among the independent exhibitors, who were not making such large profits.

> Hollywood is uneasy at being considered a monopoly and one that is raking in the coin despite higher taxes, labor costs, and other production expenses. Exhibitors are faintly sensitive to the charge that moviegoers must now pay 44 cents for a single feature

where they paid 22 cents for a double feature before the war, and that a downtown movie under 88 cents is a rarity.

The startling fact which glares out of the financial statements of the big producers is the skyrocketing of net returns to totals that make the public angry. [2]

Within seven years, the profitability of Fox had increased more than fivefold.

Profitable films in Fox's 1946 season were abundant, as nine features grossed over $3 million. It was certainly the best year yet in the motion picture business and every company made huge profits. R.K.O., which had made under $1 million in profits in 1942, showed nearly $14 million in 1946. Paramount jumped from $15 million in 1945 to over $40 million the year later. However, for sheer gross volume, Fox led the industry with $185,673,000 in 1945, almost $25 million ahead of next highest, Paramount.

The returns of 1946 showed the ceiling on rentals had shifted several notches higher with all films on the chart relatively more successful as well. The number one industry-wide spot was held by Fox's LEAVE HER TO HEAVEN, with domestic rentals of $5.5 million and a foreign return of $2.7 million totalling an astounding $8.2 million. Following this adult story on Fox's roster of hits were two family pictures, MARGIE and SMOKY, then ANNA AND THE KING OF SIAM. Other hit films were CENTENNIAL SUMMER, DO YOU LOVE ME?, DRAGONWYCK, SENTIMENTAL JOURNEY, and THREE LITTLE GIRLS IN BLUE.

Grosses were so extraordinary there was concern over whether this was just a temporary phenomenon.

> Returning servicemen and former war workers flush with savings have been the major factors in holding the first-run grosses to the high levels. But a prominent circuit executive says that indications point to a sharp dropoff in the key first runs and more expensive theaters perhaps by this fall, estimating that excess spending money will by that time have diminished to the point where many patrons will get back to normal and economize by attending the lower admission theaters.

This will hit producers where it hurts the worst.
It is estimated in Hollywood that 75 per cent to 80
per cent of the gross on a major picture comes from
the first 100 first-runs in key cities. And the industry executives, foreseeing a decline in the major
income-producing first-run business, have been
seeking innovations in films that might help to re-
verse the trend. [3]

The innovation Darryl Zanuck used was to spend more
money and make more spectacular films. With the proof that
hit movies could earn between $5 million and $10 million,
each studio was preparing its own bigger and better blockbusters to attract audiences. Zanuck bought the rights to
FOREVER AMBER, a controversial and racy novel about a
seventeenth century courtesan, and authorized a $4.5 million
budget. Zanuck was going to allow director Otto Preminger
to give it as much color and scope as possible. AMBER was
Fox's most expensive undertaking ever, and Zanuck was
counting on sexual elements of story to bring people into
the theaters.

On the surface, with world rentals of $8 million, FOR-
EVER AMBER was considered a hit at distribution level.
However, production overages led to a final negative cost of
$6.3 million. With the additional expense of advertising,
publicity, and distribution overhead (chopping off about
30 percent from theater remittances) the movie could never
recoup its costs. On such a high budget, FOREVER AMBER
would have had to earn over $20 million at the box office to
return the $12-$13 million in rentals necessary to cover
ancillary expenses and leave enough to pay for the negative.
Only one movie had done that before—GONE WITH THE WIND.

Runaway production costs would be the bane of Hollywood's existence forever more. Zanuck got a double dose
of it in 1947. Delayed by bad weather in Mexico, CAPTAIN
FROM CASTILE, was originally budgeted at $2 million but
more than doubled its final cost to $4.5 million. Keeping a
massive cast and crew on location for months longer than
anticipated became a nightmare to Fox's budget planners.
Adding salt to the wound were the disappointing rentals on
CAPTAIN FROM CASTILE, which yielded "only" $6 million
worldwide and a loss of $2 million. On the average $1.5
million picture, such returns would be wildly successful, but
new extravagance would take its toll on profits.

However, the situation was not quite as bleak as first blush would indicate. While the studios owned their theaters, the 50 percent to 60 percent which was retained by the chains eventually flowed back into the company's coffers. As well, on each production, an overhead figure of approximately 35 percent was added to the final costs to pay for the studio's executives and general staff. This was in addition to the sometimes exorbitant charges made by individual departments covering music, special effects, sound or costumes. The 28 percent skimmed off the top of a gross also went to the company. The higher the gross, the higher the overhead charges. Additionally, advertising and publicity costs went to the studio's own departments, not outside firms. So, all the money stayed within the same pool. Even when the studio showed losses, there was always some skepticism by industry insiders that the tears shed were only for show. Before talent shared participation points in movies, there was no earthly reason for studios to show massive profits. Such funds were absorbed into the system to keep it well oiled.

The lavishness of some 1947 productions raised Fox's average budget to $2,328,000. For the year, the company turned out only 18 films at a record cost of $41,914,000. Zanuck had succeeded in turning Fox into an "A" company with lush, expensive product. But his timing was bad. Audiences in the domestic market were beginning to drop, as predicted a year earlier. Fox's total domestic rentals were down by $10 million from 1945, and the foreign market had shrunk from $28 million in 1944, to $17.7 million in 1947. Darryl Zanuck took heed from these figures when he claimed in January, 1949, that

> The "easy market" is gone and so Hollywood likewise must do away with the "easy" methods of production. The necessary streamlining has been accomplished in most quarters and I believe the future can be faced with great confidence.
>
> For the several years past, production costs in the film industry mounted, but production did not bring its "money's worth" because the effort wasn't made to insure this. When the bottom dropped out of the war-flushed attendance boom, readjustment toward efficiency became necessary. Costs were cut mainly by eliminating unnecessary footage. [4]

Zanuck did manage to trim budgets considerably for 1948 and 1949 productions, to an average of $1.8 million, and there were many profitable films; but it was evident to producers that attendance was beginning to drop and the profits might never again be as great as during the war years. Spyros Skouras echoed company dissatisfaction with the trends when he pointed out that falling attendance in Britain, Australia, New Zealand, and Argentina might cost Fox 50 percent to 66 percent of foreign revenues. He announced that films would have to be given longer runs to allow them to make back more money. He added that exhibitors should be more "broad-minded" on the subject of "block-buster" films, and be willing to pay premium prices. One exhibitor, though, expressed a common opinion that "every time we announce one of those $1.25 affairs, business is bad for a week before and three or four weeks after." [5]

If it had not been for Darryl Zanuck's taste for controversy, 1948 and 1949 would have indeed been undistinguished in earnings. The top films of the years were GENTLEMAN'S AGREEMENT, PINKY, and THE SNAKE PIT, all black-and-white features made on reasonable budgets. Zanuck's social conscience blended with his taste for showmanship to deliver three entertaining and profitable films. Zanuck was now producing films for more sophisticated and mature audiences than in previous years. A wider spectrum of material was allowed on the screen by the more liberal Motion Picture Code Office and Zanuck took full advantage. He was ready to adapt the studio to new production trends.

There were several other changes in the industry. Studios could no longer get away with placing actors on a sound stage with a rear-projection screen behind them showing exotic locations. Audiences were beginning to tire of such artificiality. Much more costly location shooting was becoming not only common, but a necessity. Stan Hough explains it this way: "The audiences at the end of World War II, maybe because so many people travelled, became very sophisticated. For instance, if you mentioned the word "process" [rear-projection] to a director, you probably got thrown out of the office.... So you went there." [6]

"Going there" meant several things to the studio. For one, it would provide more realistic surroundings for the story. But it also meant being at the mercy of the weather and totally without the control of studio production. It meant higher costs. More importantly, though, it meant less work at the studio. Less work meant less money charged by a department and therefore less to contribute to overhead.

There were greater threats to the film industry than just rising costs, and location shooting. Television was making deep inroads into the film-going audiences. That was a factor which worried every executive. If audiences were declining and costs were rising, there would, eventually, be a crossing point at which more films would be unprofitable.

At this time of upheaval, the studios were in the process of losing their theaters. Another source of steady revenue was drying up. Fox had risen to the top, under Darryl Zanuck's firm guidance and an optimum environment for the industry. The size of the studio had increased from 108 to 284 acres, and from five sound stages to 16. In 1949, Fox was at peak strength, with 4,000 employees, and Zanuck claimed that his per-film return was still the most profitable in Hollywood. It was an auspicious moment for Fox, but, unfortunately, a fleeting one.

CHAPTER 7

■ ENTER THE FIFTIES ■

The immediate post-war euphoria which had gripped the motion picture industry was very quick to evaporate. Ominous signs loomed over the horizon, and many feared the widespread popularity of television and faltering attendance figures. The post-war economy was one of inflation and uncertainty. Costs rose sharply, not only in the film business, but for the average consumer. Rising costs meant curbing such unnecessary luxuries as filmgoing. Theaters felt the pinch, and the immediate reaction was to raise prices to compensate for smaller audiences. However, higher admissions only kept more patrons away.

As always, in times of a box-office slump, Zanuck cut budgetary figures drastically. The cost of an average film at Fox dropped from a high of $2,328,000 in 1947 to $1,229,000 in 1952, the lowest figure since 1944. Because of Fox's expanded number of releases, total negative costs for 1950 and 1951 were in the range of $45 million, and $42.8 million for 1952, among the highest on record.

What happened, though, in production, was a basic change in policy. Whereas in the late thirties or early forties, all the "A" class films would be budgeted between $1 million and $1.5 million and a "B" picture ranged between $100,000-$300,000, there was a lesser distinction in the budgets of the early fifties. Due to skyrocketing costs, any film's budget could easily reach $1 million. So for each production, the studio was taking a greater risk. This became especially pertinent when, in 1948, the government outlawed the practice of "block-booking." Every film would have to stand on its own merit to secure booking. Recoupment was even more risky once Fox gave up its theater chain in 1952.

With the break-even figure considerably higher on almost all productions, Fox had to gross more on every picture
to make up for the difference. This became increasingly
difficult as audiences shrank. Zanuck also sensed that
audiences were changing and that decisions at the studio
would have to reflect these changes. With the country in
the throes of the McCarthy communist witchhunt and the
Korean War, the last in line of what he called "message
pictures" was not faring well at the box office. VIVA
ZAPATA's lukewarm results convinced him that "today, audiences seem to be shopping for anything that sounds like
adventure or escape. They want to get out and away from
the gloomy news of the moment." [1]

In a memo to studio talent, Zanuck pointed out that Fox
would pursue a policy of strictly entertainment films. He
started out by trying to decide exactly what would be the
key to successful films.

> What exactly do they want? It is certain that they
> do not want every excellent picture. It is also
> certain that every excellent picture is not a box-
> office hit. Many excellent pictures have been de-
> feated by unsatisfactory or unpopular subject matter.
> In this regard we have had our own bitter experience
> with pictures like VIVA ZAPATA!, MY COUSIN
> RACHEL, and we are presently disappointed on the
> returns from THE PRESIDENT'S LADY and MAN
> ON A TIGHTROPE, as well as TONIGHT WE SING.
> Other studios have had similar and even more bitter
> experiences with pictures I thought contained won-
> derful entertainment values.
>
> One thing we know for certain--there is not a
> so-called propaganda or "message" picture on the
> successful lists. We have seen some damn good
> pictures in this category fall to the bottom of the
> heap. I wonder what would have happened to PINKY,
> THE SNAKE PIT, and GENTLEMAN'S AGREEMENT in
> this present market. Perhaps the industry made too
> many pictures that tried to lecture, but the records
> and the facts show that there is not one so-called
> "intellectual picture" in the top or secondary category.
> They are all showmanship shows and based either on
> sex or adventure or in the escapist category.
>
> It is well to remember this in considering the

pictures we are now working on and in buying stories for the future. When you think that a picture that says nothing like MISSISSIPPI GAMBLER can double the gross of VIVA ZAPATA! and LILI then you must pause and take heed. I do not say that some great intellectual picture will not come along and violate most of what I have said--but if it does you can be certain it will contain some of the indispensable ingredients I have listed above. [2]

Thus, away from the gloomy news he went, directing production more towards the glossy, flashy entertainment vehicles on which Hollywood had been founded. The years 1950 through 1952 resulted in a disproportionate number of musicals, light comedies, and action films. Technicolor adorned the productions of DANCING IN THE DARK; THE GIRL NEXT DOOR; OH, YOU BEAUTIFUL DOLL; TICKET TO TOMAHAWK; and I'LL GET BY. Although these films were moderately successful productions, they never were as profitable as their M-G-M counterparts. Metro had a separate blue ribbon musical unit made up of talents who understood the genre, boasting stars like Gene Kelly, Fred Astaire, Ginger Rogers, and, until 1950, Judy Garland. Fox never placed as much specialized effort into musicals and offered talent which was not as popular, like Dan Dailey, Mark Stevens, June Haver, Dick Haymes, and Mitzi Gaynor. Fox still had Betty Grable, who encored her way through CALL ME MISTER, MEET ME AFTER THE SHOW, MY BLUE HEAVEN, and WABASH AVENUE, bathed in all the Technicolor glory the studio could afford. Her popularity sustained the box office and these films ranked among Fox's top 20 for the three-year period.

Intended box-office blockbusters figured largely in the production slate. These were the films given all the story and production values enabling them to break records for the company. Although Zanuck had never been solely dependent on stars at Fox, he suddenly found himself, in 1951, with the two top-drawing personalities in the business. Zanuck had starred Gregory Peck in many successful motion pictures, including TWELVE O'CLOCK HIGH, a hit of 1950, and he had cast Susan Hayward in several films. But teamed together in DAVID AND BATHSHEBA, the duo spelled box-office dynamite, and the film reaped a towering $8 million

in worldwide rentals on a cost of $2.1 million. The follow-
ing year, Zanuck starred them together in another of his
personal productions, THE SNOWS OF KILIMANJARO, and
the results were even better, nearing $9 million in world
rentals.

The huge rentals of these films made Zanuck more dependent on stars than at any previous time. Simultaneously,
his star build-up of Marilyn Monroe was beginning to pay
off. Having started in bit parts, she was now on the
verge of superstardom. A modestly budgeted DON'T BOTHER
TO KNOCK (1952) featured Monroe in her first starring
role as a psychopathic killer. Even though the critics did
not react favorably to the film, audiences did. Monroe later
became Fox's most legendary all-time star, and most of her
subsequent films were smash hits.

Fox entered 1950 auspiciously, with many hit productions,
placing the company close to top industry-wide performance.
CHEAPER BY THE DOZEN, a light, homespun comedy, was
Fox's leading hit, with world rentals of $6 million. BROKEN
ARROW earned $5.5 million, TWELVE O'CLOCK HIGH did
$4.3 million, and ALL ABOUT EVE, $4.2 million. Considering
that the total cost of these films was approximately $7 million,
the returns were handsome indeed. This was due to judicious
budgeting. No film cost more than $2 million and Zanuck
cut back the budget of the Tyrone Power epic, PRINCE OF
FOXES, by filming black and white instead of Technicolor.
After the disastrous episode with CAPTAIN FROM CASTILE,
Zanuck would not let any budget get out of hand. Unfortunately, this budget paring also limited the box-office
potential of PRINCE OF FOXES, since audiences were growing accustomed to their period pictures in glorious, vivid,
Technicolor.

By 1951, the motion picture industry was in locked com-
bat with television and the average moviegoer demanded
more color and scope when paying admissions. Once again,
this resulted in higher budgets. With an uncertain domestic
market foreign distribution became more important. Fanatic
nationalism and a divided Europe during World War II had
prevented American movies from being shown. With the Allied
victory and American influence heavily dominant in rebuilding
Europe, grateful allies and one-time enemies throughout the
continent were more receptive to Hollywood entertainment.

Like Americans during the Depression, Europeans flocked
to the cinemas for escapist entertainment. With no competition from television and struggling regional film industries,
American movies won audiences hands down, providing the
most lavish and glamorous entertainment. With the success
of foreign markets, movies which travelled well (westerns,
swashbucklers, war stories, adventures, i.e., action)
could even surpass their domestic grosses.

Zanuck could not emphasize enough the importance of
foreign markets. Since he only sent out financial reports
to producers when business was bad, his following memo
underlined the importance of securing a foothold in Europe,
Central and South America, and the Orient.

> This is another one of my monthly reports on box
> office grosses. This report, like some of the pre-
> vious ones, deals primarily with the foreign market
> as it stands today.
>
> We must realize that no company could exist with-
> out the foreign revenue. We have no television com-
> petition to speak of, outside of England, and new
> markets are opening up around the world.
>
> Of course the most important foreign territory
> remains England. Next comes Italy, Japan, Central
> and South America, West Germany on certain pic-
> tures and a grouping of France, Belgium and Swit-
> zerland. They are treated as a unit.
>
> The loss of the foreign market to an American
> picture can be enormous and can turn a successful
> picture in the domestic market into a failure. By
> the same token, certain pictures that have failed
> in the domestic market have been turned into pro-
> fitable ventures because of an extraordinarily large
> foreign gross.
>
> This was particularly true of BIRD OF PARADISE
> and ANNE OF THE INDIES. It was also true of 5
> FINGERS. As an example, 5 FINGERS grossed
> domestically $1,200,000, and thus considering the
> cost it was a failure. The picture was released in
> the foreign territory and it was a smash hit. It
> has already grossed in the foreign territory $1,361,000
> and will probably reach a total of $1,550,000. Neither
> ANNE OF THE INDIES nor BIRD OF PARADISE gross-
> ed in the domestic market the cost of the negative.

This means that both pictures would have shown
an enormous loss. In the foreign market, however,
BIRD OF PARADISE has already grossed $1,300,000
and will probably gross another $150,000.

ANNE OF THE INDIES has grossed in the foreign
market $1,200,000 and it still has additional revenue
coming in.

Let us examine the typical American subjects and
see what happens to them in Europe. Now some
of these pictures are fine pictures and most of them
did splendid business in the domestic market--but
look at the results in the foreign market. JACKPOT,
which dealt with radio give-away prizes, was typically
American. In spite of the fact that it had Jimmy
Stewart in the cast it grossed in the foreign market
$650,000. The same Jimmy Stewart was in BROKEN
ARROW. BROKEN ARROW was a big, action spectacle with excitement and not too much talk. In
the foreign market it has already grossed $1,850,000
and will probably do more.

I'D CLIMB THE HIGHEST MOUNTAIN was a smash
hit in this country and grossed $2,300,000 domestically.
In the foreign market it will gross less than $400,000
because it deals with a religious sect and problems
arising from it that have no European parallel.

TAKE CARE OF MY LITTLE GIRL was a successful picture in the domestic market. It is the lowest
grossing picture we have in the foreign field, primarily because it dealt with sororities which do not
exist abroad. In the foreign market it will gross
$180,000.

AS YOUNG AS YOU FEEL did fairly well domestically but since it dealt with an American business
problem it does no better than TAKE CARE OF MY
LITTLE GIRL.

BELLES ON THEIR TOES was a smash picture in
the domestic market and grossed approximately
$2,000,000. It was typically American and will do
about $550,000 in the foreign market.

WAIT TILL THE SUN SHINES NELLIE, a typical
small-town film, will do approximately $325,000 in
the foreign market or $1,000,000 less than it did in
the domestic market.

STARS AND STRIPES FOREVER was a big hit
domestically. It will gross about $2,350,000

domestically but at this price it will just manage to squeeze through and get out of the red because it is so typically American that it will not gross more than $700,000 or $750,000 in the foreign territory.

WHAT PRICE GLORY did fairly good business domestically but it will end up deeply in the red because in the foreign market it will be lucky if it reaches $600,000.

Compare the above with LURE OF THE WILDERNESS which will gross approximately $1,250,000 in the foreign market.

Let us examine the musical situation. Certain musicals have had big appeal abroad but our record in this department has been disastrous--the only exceptions being WITH A SONG IN MY HEART, which was more of drama than a musical, and ON THE RIVIERA, which cashed in on the amazing popularity of Danny Kaye in England.

ON THE RIVIERA has already grossed in the foreign market $1,600,000 and it may go to $1,800,000. SONG IN MY HEART has already grossed in the foreign market $1,100,000 and it may go to $1,300,000.

Compare this, however, with some of our other musicals. BLOODHOUNDS OF BROADWAY is estimated to gross approximately $500,000 in the foreign market. I have already mentioned BELLES ON THEIR TOES. GOLDEN GIRL is estimated to gross $500,000 in the foreign market. MEET ME AFTER THE SHOW is estimated to gross $550,000 in the foreign market. CALL ME MISTER is estimated to gross $485,000 in the foreign market. I'LL GET BY is estimated to gross $490,000 in the foreign market. MY BLUE HEAVEN is estimated to gross $550,000 in the foreign market. It is practically played out and so far it has only grossed $473,000. TONIGHT WE SING is a catastrophe in this country. It did very well, however, in Canada and it is hoped that some of the loss can be absorbed in Europe.

It is also felt that CALL ME MADAM will have a very large gross in England and not do too badly in the rest of the foreign field. Because of the sex angle in GENTLEMEN PREFER BLONDES it is anticipated that it will be by far our largest foreign grossing musical. In this case it is a question of the two personalities being big enough to overcome the

foreign objection to most musicals. The objection
is based on the fact that, outside of England, all
pictures are dubbed in most of the important ter-
ritories--but you cannot dub the songs as this would
mean redoing a complete musical job and it would
cost a fortune. Therefore you dub the dialogue
with one voice and when the singing starts you have
to use the songs in English and in the original voice.
Audiences just will not accept it.

Let us now examine the western or outdoor film.
I have already mentioned the enormous success of
BROKEN ARROW in the foreign field. However not
all westerns are successful abroad. In most cases,
however, they give a very good account of themselves as compared to comedies or musicals or typically American stories.

GUNFIGHTER with Gregory Peck will do about
$800,000 abroad. RAWHIDE will do about $1,000,000
abroad. CONVICT LAKE will do about $600,000
abroad. RED SKIES OF MONTANA is disappointing
as it will do only about $500,000 abroad. OUTCASTS
OF POKER FLAT is a real disappointment as it will
only do about $250,000 abroad. PONY SOLDIER,
on the other hand, is estimated to do $1,000,000
abroad. TWO FLAGS WEST will do about $775,000
abroad.

From these figures it appears that big westerns
that have size, like BROKEN ARROW, PONY SOLDIER
and RAWHIDE, have an excellent chance in the foreign field. The others mean nothing.

Now let us look at the war stories or stories that
fit in this general category. Amazing business was
done by AMERICAN GUERILLA IN THE PHILIPPINES
but a great deal of this was due to the business in
the Philippines themselves as well as Central and
South America. In the foreign field it will gross
$1,400,000 or more. Another surprise is HALLS OF
MONTEZUMA. It will do $1,300,000 in the foreign
field or more, in spite of the fact that both pictures
glorified the American forces.

FROGMEN does quite well. In the foreign field it
will gross $950,000.

THE DESERT FOX of course presents something
special because of its enormous popularity in England
and Germany. In the foreign field it will do approximately $2,200,000.

> FIXED BAYONETS, on the other hand, was a complete disappointment in the foreign field. It will do about $375,000. DECISION BEFORE DAWN was also a big disappointment. It will do about $750 or $800,000. We expected big things from it from Germany and yet it is an out and out flop, doing less 10% of THE DESERT FOX. I have already mentioned the disappointment with WHAT PRICE GLORY.
>
> In reviewing this category we again see that pictures with action and size have the best chance. [3]

As Zanuck had mentioned in 1949, the "easy" method of filmmaking had to be abandoned and Hollywood had to meet the challanges of a more difficult market. Action was greatly emphasized, not only for foreign, but domestic rentals as well. Zanuck seized upon another element which he had always tried to emphasize in his films, but was thwarted by censorship—sex! With the more mature handling of adult relationships, Zanuck again struck hard. In analyzing current hits, he came upon the following conclusions:

> We have three pictures that base a great deal of their success on sex. I refer to MOULIN ROUGE; COME BACK, LITTLE SHEBA; and SNOWS OF KILIMANJARO. In addition to sex, KILIMANJARO also combines elements of spectacle and adventure, but the box-office sock of the picture remains the sex scenes between Peck and Ava Gardner....
>
> This is a contrasting list of pictures. We have hits based on sex and hits based on "poetry." The sex story in MOULIN ROUGE is the basic reason for its enormous success. This to a lesser degree is true of COME BACK, LITTLE SHEBA. They all have one thing in common—sex....
>
> Yet we see in both PETER PAN and HANS CHRISTIAN ANDERSEN very little evidence of sex. There are two enormous attractions and they have a special appeal to both young and old. In a way they are adventure stories. They are upbeat, happy and gay. They are at the opposite end of the pole from any of the pictures listed above from the standpoint of content or subject matter....
>
> This report does not necessarily prove that a picture must have sex to survive or become a big hit. It indicates, however, that more pictures with this

content are successful than any other type of picture. It indicates that even a heavy, downbeat, depressing story can be lifted if it contains a really strong, violent sex situation....

Another observation--MOULIN ROUGE is not a success because it deals with Toulouse Lautrec and his paintings. This is all part of a wonderful, colorful background, but the main item is the story of a prostitute and the other women in the life of a little cripple. It had a feeling of almost "dirty sex" in every scene....

In closing I ask you to keep this note confidential as it concerns pictures from other studios as well as our own. There is never any set rule or formula for success but when you analyze big hit attractions you find they always contain one or more of the ingredients I have specified above. If I could find one "exception" that was really a big box-office attraction then I would not be writing this note. [4]

Zanuck had good reason to search for showmanship elements, for although rentals were up for 1950, profits were down to $9,553,000, the lowest they have been since 1941. The expansion of the markets was not keeping up with the quickly rising production costs. Based on average figures, the "A picture had doubled in cost from 1940 to 1950. With the great costs of maintaining studios and distribution offices, there was reason for gloominess in the industry. The most startling fact of all was that admissions had been dropping at an average of $65 million annually since 1946. Total theater revenues were, in 1952, $1,134,000,000, the lowest amount since 1943.

If there was a pessimistic pall over the industry, the trade papers were not revealing it. In the January 3, 1953, issue of Variety, Fox boasted that 50 percent of its upcoming productions would be in Technicolor to offset the competition offered by television.

20th Century-Fox has invested $100,000,000 in your immediate future! Because we look forward to the future with the optimism, faith, and confidence which has made our industry great. Because you must be fortified with the kind of attractions which will meet the challenges of today's market.... And watch for

THE ROBE. It will be the greatest box-office draw of all time. [5]

Their prediction for THE ROBE was not that far off.

CHAPTER 8

■ THE COMING OF CINEMASCOPE ■

As early as March, 1945, Twentieth Century-Fox was becoming involved in television. Through the General Pre-
cision Corporation, which owned 11 percent of Fox stock, the
company had an indirect interest in Scophony Corporation
of America, a theater-television company. As well, National
Theaters president, Charles Skouras, set up a television
department to watch for major developments in the new industry. Fox later offered to buy the American Broadcasting
Corporation, but the deal was never completed. Fox was
obviously interested in the new medium's great potential.

In 1948 Fox's president, Spyros P. Skouras optimistically
forecast that television would be the greatest boon to motion
pictures since the advent of sound. Skouras did not consider the negligible seven-inch screens a threat to the motion picture industry, because Fox was developing a greater
form of transmission. The Eidophor system was based on the
principle of projecting video images onto a large screen in
a theater. It would adapt the elements of television to fit
the needs of theater-owners.

Skouras added that motion pictures or major live events
would be telecast to theaters across the nation. With this
system, he envisioned a hook-up with theater chains which
would increase film grosses four- to five-fold. This was
announced at a time when the major companies still owned
their theaters.

Two main factors disrupted Skouras' optimism and gave
rise to rampant pessimism. After several years of experi-
mentation, development, and a $10 million investment, the

81

Eidophor system still needed much work. More money and time would have to be invested, and both were in short supply in the race against free television.

By 1952, Spyros Skouras, along with the entire industry, worried about the fate of motion pictures.

Television sales had been halted by the war but were now booming. The casualties would be theater and production companies. Broadcasting hours only spanned the late afternoon and early evening, but the lure and novelty of television cut into film audiences drastically. Motion pictures had triumphed over radio but T.V. offered free visual entertainment to homes at the flick of a switch. Millions tuned in to Milton Berle and Ed Sullivan. Neighborhood theaters struggled to compete giving away door prizes, playing bingo, sponsoring amateur nights. Every trick in the showman's manual was hauled out of mothballs to improve film grosses. Nothing helped.

As the sales of television receivers rose steadily, average theater attendance reacted inversely. Major companies were feeling the pinch but were virtually helpless. They knew there was the need for a change that would reestablish moviegoing habits, but no one was sure what that change should be.

Television had a small, round image in fuzzy black-and-white which flickered. Ideas spread through the film industry that a new format which could reproduce reality more faithfully would be an ample rival to television. If motion pictures were bigger in screen size, they would naturally be better.

By late 1952, new screen processes were beginning to come into the marketplace. Three cameras were used to film THIS IS CINERAMA and three projectors produced a deeply-curved, wide-screen image which gave the sensation of depth. Audiences could be roller coastered at frightening speeds, flown through the air, and pulled over water, providing the illusion of participation.

At the same time, Arch Oboler, a writer and producer, was developing a "true" three-dimensional process for his film BWANA DEVIL. Shot with two cameras from different angles, the third dimension was revealed to audiences through the use of polarized glasses. These glasses, which often caused headaches, unscrambled a blurred image, so that audiences were forced to use the bothersome viewing aids.

For a while, Cinerama and 3-D seemed to draw audiences. However, Cinerama films played so long in their roadshow engagements it was only necessary to produce one film yearly. This would not rescue an entire industry. Also, after several early 3-D productions like HOUSE OF WAX showed phenomenal grosses, the novelty began to wear thin. The treatment 3-D was given by the studios was to blame. Initially, the process was used to hurl objects at the audience, rather than utilize depth for dramatic effect. When major films were finally given more serious treatment in 3-D, the golden goose had been killed. Such major releases as KISS ME KATE, DIAL M FOR MURDER, and HONDO, which were photographed in 3-D, were released almost exclusively in standard versions.

Fox had dabbled in 3-D, on lower-case products such as INFERNO and GORILLA AT LARGE, but like other companies, never took it seriously. Darryl Zanuck had mentioned that he considered the success of HOUSE OF WAX "a freak" and nothing more. After all, quality films like FROM HERE TO ETERNITY or THE SNOWS OF KILIMANJARO were smash hits without 3-D.

Spyros Skouras, nevertheless, was looking for a new combatant against the video threat. Flying to Switzerland in late 1952, he met with Dr. Henri Chrétien, who was working on a widescreen process which he called Anamorphoscope. Chrétien began developing his process in 1928, but interest in wider screens had waned during the introduction of sound. The J. Arthur Rank Organisation of London had optioned the exclusive rights to Anamorphoscope but lost their enthusiasm. The day after Rank's option ran out, Skouras made the legal arrangements with Chrétien's optics laboratory to develop the process for practical use. CinemaScope, as it was named, became a trademark of the Twentieth Century-Fox Film Corporation.

Skouras was obviously impressed with CinemaScope, for he remarked to reporters in his broken English, "In bed that night, I don't sleep. Then, I do an' I dream. I am dreaming of Egypt, of lions outside in the street, of Bens-Hur and the Quin of Seba, of Betsy Grabble, in colors, everything on the big screen. Oh, I had wonderful dreams." [1]

Skouras' dreams became everyone's hope in Hollywood as producers anticipated a regeneration of the film industry. American Cinematographer devoted a lengthy article to CinemaScope, a format 2.55 times as wide as high, opposed to the industry standard of 1.33 to 1.

> CinemaScope is not stereoscopic movies--not the same as the 3-D films also causing a flurry in Hollywood. CinemaScope films do not require the use of viewing spectacles, do not require special dual projectors. But the result on the screen, which does present an "illusion" of three-dimension pictures, is said by many to be superior to 3-D films. [2]

> From the optical point of view, (the lenses) consist of two separately achromatized systems: a converging system of two lenses, cemented together, and a diverging system consisting of three lenses, cemented together. [3]

> Although close-ups are reproduced dramatically in CinemaScope films, fewer may be needed because medium shots of actors in groups of three and four show faces so clearly that the most minute emotions and gestures are obvious.
> In the beginning, it is likely that most Cinema-Scope productions will be basically outdoor spectacle dramas. This will undeniably solve the lighting problem--which undeniably will be great when it comes to shooting the large wide angle sets indoors on the stage. Also, it is likely there will be less emphasis on effect lighting, admittedly not so important where films are shot in color.
> Film cutting problems in the new medium ... will not be as great as was at first expected because there won't be as many cuts in CinemaScope films as with standard productions. C-pictures will be like stage plays where the spectator visualizes close-ups and medium shots when he focuses his individual attention on the principal player or some specific bit of action. [4]

Wisely, Darryl Zanuck did not decide to treat this valuable new development as just another novelty. He assigned one of the studio's biggest budget undertakings to initiate CinemaScope, the $4.1 million production of THE ROBE. Although shooting had already begun, Zanuck shut down the production so that it could be realigned to fit the new wide screen.

There were some initial problems. Henry Koster, director of THE ROBE had never shot a CinemaScope movie before. For that matter, no one had. Sets had to be redesigned to accomodate width rather than height and Director of Photography Leon Shamroy had to reassess his style of camerawork. Add to this the availability of only one lens in existence and THE ROBE's production must have been fraught with considerable anxiety. Just to be safe, though, a second camera was used with standard lenses to re-shoot every scene and provide a regular release version of THE ROBE in case CinemaScope did not catch on. This was sound thinking because when THE ROBE finished production, there still were no theaters yet equipped to run CinemaScope anywhere in the world.

Having shot some test footage to demonstrate the vast potential of CinemaScope, Darryl Zanuck touted the new process to his stable of writers, directors, and cameramen. Not all of them were overwhelmed. Delmer Daves, who had directed BROKEN ARROW and BIRD OF PARADISE for Zanuck remembered the birth of CinemaScope with distaste.

> That was a dramatic time. Little Caesar (Zanuck) had made his decision--and he loved drama. He ordered all his directors and writers to come to Fox Sunset and not to tell anyone. We didn't know what it was all about.
> We were herded into a big, abandoned stage there, with the first CinemaScope screen stretched across the end. Zanuck ran samplings of what the thing could do and later the lights came on and he said, "Isn't this the greatest thing you ever saw? This is the future of films." Most of the people found it wise to keep their mouths shut with Zanuck because if you disagreed with him, he would stride around with his little cane and give edicts.
> I was terrified by CinemaScope and made a quick

review of the films I'd made. It would have been
disastrous for them. Nevertheless, he finally got
around to asking for a few comments. A lot of
directors just said, "Great, Darryl. Can't wait to
do one." I had several questions to which I didn't
see any answers. One was from the standpoint of
composition. Was this the end of the close shot or
the two shot? What could you do about all of that
out-of-focus space when you're on someone two feet
away from the camera? Was all the intimacy of
filmmaking going to be lost? Darryl didn't have
any answers. [5]

With all the tremendous enthusiasm from the studio and
the industry for the new ultrawide screen, Skouras and
Zanuck made the bold decision to completely switch over to
CinemaScope for all major films. And bold it was, for at the
time there were only a handful theaters in America equipped
to run CinemaScope. Fox was counting on theater owners
to install $20,000 worth of lenses, screens, and sound
systems in every house, for the privilege of running THE
ROBE and future productions.

On March 12, 1953, even before THE ROBE had begun
shooting, Zanuck sent a memo around the lot with instructions regarding CinemaScope.

Upon completion of the production of several
standard 35mm films now in production and two other
pictures scheduled for production in the very near
future (namely BE PREPARED and WATERFRONT),
Twentieth Century-Fox will concentrate exclusively
on subjects suitable for CinemaScope.
Effective now we will abandon further work on
any treatment or screenplay that does not take full
advantage of the new dimension of CinemaScope. It
is our conviction that almost any story can be told
more effectively in CinemaScope than any other
medium but it is also our conviction that every picture that goes into production in CinemaScope should
contain subject matter which utilizes to the fullest
extent the full possibilities of this medium.
This does not mean that every picture should
have so-called epic proportions but it does mean
that at least for the first 18 months of CinemaScope

production that we select subjects that contain elements which enable us to take full advantage of scope, size, and physical action.

This certainly does not mean that every picture has to contain a roller coaster or an underwater sequence or be an outdoor film or contain sets the proportion of the sets in THE ROBE. As a matter of fact, CinemaScope unquestionably adds a new dimension to the production of musical pictures. As an example, the opera sequence in TONIGHT WE SING would have been enhanced by CinemaScope at least 500 per cent.

For the time being intimate comedies or small-scale, domestic stories should be put aside and no further monies expanded on their development. The day will undoubtedly come when all pictures in this category will probably be made in CinemaScope. But in the present market we want to show the things on CinemaScope that we cannot nearly as effectively on standard 35mm film. We have a new entertainment medium and we want to exploit it for all it's worth.

At the present time I am investigating each of your individual assignments with a view toward stopping further work on any subject that does not fit in the above format. I wish that you, too, would give this your immediate attention and give me any recommendations that you have in connection with this matter. I know that you will be prone to say, "CinemaScope will help this certain picture." This is true but at this point in our development of CinemaScope we must be guided by selecting only those subjects which have obvious ingredients which will not only be helpful to the story but helpful to the exploitation of CinemaScope. The so-called "intimate stories" must be put aside for the time being.

If CinemaScope does nothing else it will force us back into the moving picture business--I mean moving pictures that move. 6

To maintain the quality of each CinemaScope production in exhibition, Fox only released their films with four-track magnetic stereophonic sound. No concessions were made to theaters which would not install new screens or sound systems. Proud of their achievement and buttressed by Academy

Awards for technical advancement, Fox felt that every exhibitor should do his best to enhance the presentation of CinemaScope films. There was, of course, some skepticism on the part of exhibitors, who felt that this might just be another passing novelty. Nevertheless, the rules were made clear. Fox would supply CinemaScope product only to those with proper equipment.

When drive-in theaters refused to install sterophonic sound, claiming that it was an unnecessary extravagance, Fox promptly let it be known that no drive-in would play their new films. Finally, in late 1954, concessions were made when both parties agreed that stereo was not needed in a car. Fox's move was not altogether altruistic, for other companies were making CinemaScope films, and the drive-ins would soon have all the films they needed. The only one to lose out would be Fox in not getting extra play-dates.

It was estimated that by 1954 almost 15,000 theaters across the nation had been equipped with CinemaScope. Fox had made an investment which paid off royally for all aspects of the industry and elation spread. Variety reported, "CinemaScope not only is boosting theater grosses, it's also helping exhibs to stay in business and in some instances had actually been instrumental in reopening houses that had been shuttered. Records of 20th-Fox bear witness to the extent to which showmen have been impressed by Cinema-Scope as a [box-office] tonic." [7]

Any other studio or independent producer who wanted to use CinemaScope had to apply to Fox and pay a fee of $25,000, or a blanket charge for any number of films of $100,000. In addition, Fox had the right to approve every screenplay for films shot in that process, and demanded nothing less than top-rate material. This was all done in an effort to protect the exclusivity of the process.

Perhaps the Fox advertising department was prophetic in claiming THE ROBE would be the biggest draw of all time. By the end of 1954, it became the company's highest-grossing film with $17.5 million in domestic rentals and a worldwide total of $25 million, second only to GONE WITH THE WIND, with over $30 million. Until it was surpassed by THE LONG-EST DAY a decade later, it remained Fox's all-time champion.

Fox rode the crest of the wave of CinemaScope, which had ostensibly "rescued" the industry from impending doom. Wide-screen films pleased audiences and a CinemaScope production doubled the rentals of a standard screen film. For the 1953 release schedule following the record set by THE ROBE were the smash figures of HOW TO MARRY A MILLIONAIRE, the second CinemaScope release, starring Marilyn Monroe, Betty Grable, and Lauren Bacall. World rentals totalled $8 million, and this was followed by another Monroe vehicle, GENTLEMEN PREFER BLONDES, which in standard screen took in $5.3 million. Even BENEATH THE 12-MILE REEF, an average adventure with underwater scenes in CinemaScope, brought world rentals of $5.7 million. The wide screen certainly enhanced the box-office power of motion pictures. In 1953, Fox's two greatest assets were CinemaScope and Marilyn Monroe, in that order.

Finances had been needed to develop CinemaScope and Fox had staked $16 million in contracts to supply equipment, and the equipment itself. When theater owners rejected the suggestion to install stereophonic equipment, Fox was stuck with an $8.5 million guarantee with manufacturers for the production of magnetic-striped prints. What the company finally settled on was a single compatible print, usable in magnetic stereo situations or those with standardized optical sound. This development in 1956 also resulted in an annual saving for Fox of $3 million.

Due to its enormous gamble Fox's revenues soared 13 percent in 1953 with only three CinemaScope productions in release. By 1954, profits had risen 400 percent in the first 39-week period to $5,732,063, from $1,443,037 the previous year. The box-office power of CinemaScope was dramatically emphasized by the continuing program of successful films released by Fox that year. All films grossed uniformly well, and if budgets could be held down, the program would show great profits.

Zanuck and Twentieth Century-Fox succeeded in exploiting the new process to the fullest. Scope and action were in abundance in RIVER OF NO RETURN, GARDEN OF EVIL, HELL AND HIGH WATER, and KING OF THE KHYBER RIFLES. Lush settings created atmosphere for THREE COINS IN THE FOUNTAIN, and THE EGYPTIAN. Spectacle played a great part in PRINCE VALIANT and DEMETRIUS AND THE GLADIATORS.

In short, the motion picture industry and Fox had been granted a brief respite in their continuing struggle for survival. For this shining moment, Fox was again leading the entertainment industry.

CHAPTER 9

■ TROUBLE IN PARADISE ■

The fifties began as troubled years, and very soon after the initial impact of CinemaScope had passed, they continued true to form. Production costs had risen greatly, and the studio more than ever needed audience support for all of its films. With production shrinking as individual budgets rose each project became more critical in the year-end profit position.

Fewer films, as well, had alarming effects on Hollywood because there was less need for studio personnel. Stables of writers were no longer necessary at Fox to script only two dozen features. Suddenly there were more producers, directors, and performers than projects to assign them to. As a result, the studio staff was trimmed considerably by not renewing contracts.

Those directors who did remain with Fox were the ones who worked well with Zanuck. Among them Henry King, Jean Negulesco, Henry Koster, Walter Lang, Henry Hathaway, and there were others who stayed from picture to picture like Richard Fleischer, Samuel Fuller, Edward Dmytryk, Delmer Daves. There were graduates from other departments as well. Robert D. Webb, Henry King's assistant director for 15 years, worked his way up to direct several lower cost features. Nunnally Johnson and Philip Dunne both directed from their own screenplays. Among those to leave the company were dynamic and creative younger directors including Elia Kazan, Joseph L. Mankiewicz, and Robert Wise.

Talent was to be the greatest single cause for chagrin

in the following years. "Independent" became an important buzzword in the industry, as actors, directors, and writers were more aware of the lack of control they had in a studio production. Scripts were edited and revised on the advice of the production chief. Producers interfered with directors on how to shoot sequences, and the studio head would recut all films.

This situation was less appealing than ever to certain actors and directors and the climate was such as to allow for change. "Independent" production left all creative control in the hands of the owner of the producing company whether it be a director, writer, or performer. Financing for such independent productions was available dependent upon the box-office importance of the talents involved. In 1950, the United Artists Corporation was reorganized by Arthur Krim, Robert Benjamin, and Max Youngstein, to become a financing organization and distributor for independent producers. Such deals became extremely tempting and sometimes lucrative for those who were more interested in making pictures their way than assembly-line studio procedures.

At Twentieth Century-Fox, there was little question among directors and writers as to who was the boss. Zanuck had little problem in that respect. However, Fox had become dependent on star names to draw audiences. The importance of Marilyn Monroe, for example, was acknowledged by everyone at the studio. It did not take long for Monroe to discover that she could demand more from her contract than Fox had originally given.

Almost every film after GENTLEMEN PREFER BLONDES, which established her fame, became an ordeal for the studio. Under the terms of her contract, Monroe was to start production on PINK TIGHTS in December 1953. The screenplay had been written by I.A.L. Diamond, and was to be produced by Buddy Adler, who had just come to the studio, and Henry Koster was to direct. Everything was set to roll but the production was forced to shut down when Monroe failed to report to the set. The studio tried to locate her, but she could not be found. Finally, it was discovered she was honeymooning with Joe DiMaggio. She was immediately placed on suspension by the studio, however, everyone knew that Monroe was worth more to Fox on film than on suspension. Producer Adler optimistically announced that the film would finally roll in May 1954, with co-stars Frank Sinatra and Bob Hope.

To keep Monroe's temperament in check, the studio brought in Sheree North to provide competition for M.M. Almost immediately, North was assigned to PINK TIGHTS and a costume test was shot with North singing the title song. But before PINK TIGHTS rolled, the studio assigned North to HOW TO BE VERY, VERY POPULAR, another project which Monroe had rejected. When Monroe returned she was assigned to THERE'S NO BUSINESS LIKE SHOW BUSINESS and once again PINK TIGHTS was delayed.

On January 10, 1955, a daily trade paper humorously reported that

> PINK TIGHTS drew another replacement, a not altogether unusual occurrence for the film. This time it was Tommy Noonan who replaced Johnnie Ray-- who had previously replaced Frank Sinatra.
> Sheree North previously replaced Marilyn Monroe in femme lead, Samuel G. Engel has replaced Sol C. Siegel as producer and Henry Levin has replaced Henry Koster as director. Actually, 1955 has replaced 1953 as starting year for the 20th-Fox production. [1]

The new rebellious nature of actors also irreparably harmed particular films in this period. Darryl Zanuck had cast Marlon Brando as the idealistic young doctor in Mika Waltari's THE EGYPTIAN. Brando had more than proven his acting ability in A STREETCAR NAMED DESIRE, JULIUS CAESAR, and THE WILD ONE, and there was no doubt that his presence would bring prestige to THE EGYPTIAN.

Brando, however, was a very single-minded person, and had decided that he did not like Philip Dunne's screenplay. After a first read-through of the script he left Los Angeles and refused to return to the studio. Shooting was subsequently postponed until a suitable lead could be found. Zanuck tried to cast Dirk Bogarde, but the actor was under contract to the Rank Organization and could not get a release. Zanuck groped around wherever he could to find new talent. John Cassavetes, who was then an aspiring New York actor, was flown to the Coast for a test. He was joined by John

Derek and Edmund Purdom. From these final contenders, Purdom was chosen in what proved to be a disastrous blunder.

Variety reported,

> Darryl Zanuck launches THE EGYPTIAN today, (March 3, 1954) at 20th-Fox, two months and one-half after its original scheduled Dec. 19 shooting date as a $4,000,000 Technicolor production.
> Studio reported that a total of 21,000 feet of tests had been shot during casting of picture, an unusually high figure even for such a high-budget film. Usual casting footage is between 8,000--9,000 feet. When finally edited, EGYPTIAN is expected to total 10-11,000 feet for its release print, approximately half of that of casting footage. [2]

This was just the beginning of a myriad of problems. In 1955, during Fox's location shooting of CAROUSEL in Maine, Frank Sinatra walked off the set after two days of production, complaining about the camera system the crew was using. Fox had been experimenting with a new process called Cinema-Scope 55, which was shot on a larger 55mm width negative and then printed down to a sharper 35mm release print. As in the early CinemaScope production of THE ROBE, Fox was also shooting a 35mm version, so that each take was photographed twice. Sinatra refused to go along with this situation and the production was shut down. Again, there were costly delays.

In each of these events, the studio lost precious production time and more precious budget funds. But it was not the only drain on studio money. Popular stars demanded and were paid higher salaries for fewer pictures. Many, in fact, would only sign one-picture contracts, since this would keep them out of long-term studio control. In a supply and demand environment, if their films were successful, they could command even higher fees, but if they were in flops, their salary plummeted. However, with the star system at its peak in the fifties, demand usually outpaced supply, pushing salaries generally higher.

With Marilyn Monroe and Susan Hayward, Zanuck had become star-conscious in his production slate. Soon, he brought many of the biggest names in Hollywood to his studio including Clark Gable, Fred Astaire, Errol Flynn, Humphrey Bogart, Bette Davis, Spencer Tracy, and Gary Cooper, stars who at one time were tied exclusively to other studios. These star names once meant surefire box-office hits, but times had changed, and their glitter had tarnished with age. Many of these well-known talents had lost fans to the likes of James Dean, Marlon Brando, Burt Lancaster, Kirk Douglas, Kim Novak, Rock Hudson, and Elizabeth Taylor. Fox found that the results of star-casting did not perform as well as expected, even with the help of CinemaScope.

Unfortunately, the problems did not end with talent. Good properties, best-selling books and hit stage plays, were difficult to come by, because every production head knew that popular stories very often made hit films and bidding wars ensued for a good piece of literary material. Best-selling novels, with their built-in title recognition, were sought by the studios and every company proudly announced its important acquisitions. The original screenplay was more problematic because the studio had to promote the title and subject matter in an advertising campaign to create public awareness.

Prices continued to skyrocket for properties, but in some cases, the six-figure sums were well worth the cost. Fox paid $175,000 to film George Axelrod's THE SEVEN YEAR ITCH. Rights to ANASTASIA cost Fox $500,000, but the movie version brought enormous prestige and a Best Actress Oscar for Ingrid Bergman. A bargain was occasionally to be had, as Darryl Zanuck found with Alec Waugh's novel, ISLAND IN THE SUN, which was purchased for a mere $100,000. Ernest K. Gann signed a deal with the studio by which he could earn up to $400,000 from SOLDIER OF FORTUNE. This sum was based on Gann's participation in the profits of the film, a demand which would have chilled negotiations before studios became desperate for properties. Even without participation, Fox paid the regal sum of $1 million for screen rights to Rodgers and Hammerstein's THE KING AND I.

The rising cost of literary works could not continue an upward spiral indefinitely, and by 1957 successful novels or plays did not always mean hit movies. Françoise Sagan's A CERTAIN SMILE was purchased for $150,000, but the film was a box-office dud. A HATFUL OF RAIN did not perform well despite its $250,000 outlay for a hit play. John O'Hara's TEN NORTH FREDERICK brought a $500,000 fee which ended up being a gross overpayment.

Not only were these deals expensive, but they involved many months and perhaps another $100,000 to translate into a script. Many properties were bought and developed, but only after a script was written did it become obvious that the property would not suit a motion picture. Great expenses were run up on stories which would never be filmed. THE PAINTED DAYS, a novel which was bought at Philip Dunne's suggestion cost $41,800.51 to script but was never shot. KATHERINE, a period film set in France, ran into heavy censorship problems from the Breen office of the Motion Picture Producers Association and, after an expenditure of $158,514.08, was put back in the files. A remake of RAMONA was also suggested and scripted by Dunne to the tune of $71,938.55, but was subsequently abandoned.

The way such costs escalated can be seen from a project entitled SABER TOOTH which originated in a memo from Philip Dunne to Darryl Zanuck on October 2, 1952. Dunne suggested that Fox do a science-fiction adventure story, but both he and Zanuck wanted to steer clear of the shoddy exploitation epics and produce a high-quality motion picture. Dunne proceeded to write several drafts of the script.

A first draft screenplay was finished in August 1953, and Zanuck noted "I have always liked the story as I think it has enormous potentialities as well as being the first semi-science-fiction story in CinemaScope." [3] With the intervening advent of the wide screen, the project had now become a prospective "A" picture. Zanuck added, "All science-fiction pictures are basically 'B' pictures--it depends on how well they are written, directed and produced." [4]

By late August the iconoclastic Samuel Fuller, who had directed PICKUP ON SOUTH STREET at Fox, was brought in as a co-writer with Dunne. The script was to go through various changes at Zanuck's suggestion. When Dunne wanted to begin planning the production, Zanuck advised him, "This is not necessary now because there is no possible way, confidentially, that we can start the picture before the first of the year. We made THE ROBE and we haven't got any more money left." [5]

Other projects occupied the various creative persons involved in SABER TOOTH until December 17, 1953, when Dunne received a memo from Zanuck which stated, "I vaguely remember an idea we once had titled SABER TOOTH. It was assigned to a producer and writer--and I can't remember the names--but apparently the script, like the story, disappeared in the crater of an extinct volcano. Perhaps you can bring me up to date? In talking with Hedda Hopper on the phone today she told me more about the story than I know." 6

A new script was prepared by Sam Fuller in January, 1954, and then more rewrites were suggested for a revision. However, Fuller's contract expired before the completion of the script, so Zanuck waited for a completed revision before any further plans were made. In April, 1954, it was agreed to continue work on the script, since it was nearing Zanuck's approval. A final script was agreed upon by late October, and the project was to be budgeted.

A little more than two years after Dunne sent Zanuck his first inklings about the project, SABER TOOTH was pegged by the estimating department to be a $2.5 to $3 million film. Although Zanuck and Dunne had agreed the film would not be done cheaply, $3 million was too much of a gamble. Sid Rogell, a production executive, pointed out to Zanuck that

> there is so much cheap science fiction being produced in "B" pictures and on television that this (budget) should be considered very carefully from an investment standpoint.
> I called Jack Karp at Paramount yesterday to inquire about their picture, WAR OF THE WORLDS. He told me the picture cost $1,600,000, and while it opened big, it soon fell off. It did fairly well abroad and they will make a slight profit. He asked me why I wanted the figures and I told him we were considering a big science fiction picture which might cost as much as $2,000,000. He said he thought we must be nuts to even consider such a thing. 7

After $97,540.04 of story costs, SABER TOOTH came to an end. It was not the first project to be terminated, and

it was not the last. There had been notable changes,
though, in studio operations because of rising costs which
altered the studio position on "chancy" material. In the
thirties or early forties, with so many pictures being made,
the studio was not afraid of taking some chances. However,
with costs in the fifties beginning at $1 million, there was
need for caution, especially since the importance of each
film had risen. It was estimated that for similar reasons
two-and-one-quarter projects were shelved for each one
that was produced in the mid-1950's.

For Fox to maintain its dominance in the theatrical main-
stream, strong literary material had to be corralled. This
was a matter Darryl Zanuck pondered over constantly, revealed in a memo dated October 26, 1955.

> In analyzing the motion picture production situa-
> tion today, we are all aware that it is practically
> impossible to obtain the services of top people in all
> of our pictures. The same situation exists at every
> studio. Occasionally you can grab a top name if it
> is something that they desperately want to do but
> this does not happen frequently.
>
> The independent deals have come to the point
> where they are practically "untouchable." We have
> gambled with new personalities and we will continue
> to gamble but we cannot sit around and wait for
> top names.
>
> We have got to meet this problem by once again
> emphasizing our determination to acquire as many
> pre-sold properties as we can. With a famous stage-
> play or a best-selling book we at least start out with
> something of value. The best example last year was
> BATTLE CRY. They had no one in the cast and yet
> they have an enormous hit.
>
> We have made the mistake of trusting our own
> judgment entirely too much. We should turn over a
> new leaf and begin to trust the judgment of the
> public. By this I mean that if a book becomes a
> genuine best-seller, we should buy it even though
> we may not be completely "sold" on it. The same
> thing applies to stageplays.
>
> When the public flocks to see a show or eagerly
> buys a book then there must be something of value
> in it. Sometimes we, from a professional standpoint,

cannot properly evaluate or put our finger on this
<u>something</u>.

Of course certain plays and books that are successful can never be turned into pictures because
they may deal with subject matter that is just not
suitable for the screen.

None of us liked MARJORIE MORNINGSTAR but
we should have bought it. This is a genuine best-
seller. It will be difficult to lick but at least you
start with something of value. We have passed up
too many things that the public has accepted and I
want to re-emphasize that if the public goes for it
in a big way then we should be smart enough to
trust the public more than we trust ourselves.

We have paid entirely too much attention to the
problems of censorship. I now wish we owned CAT
ON A HOT TIN ROOF. I wish we owned THE BAD
SEED.

We have repeatedly listened to censorship warn-
ings and we have cost ourselves important properties.
We backed away from I'LL CRY TOMORROW because
we thought it was too downbeat and too difficult.

Starting with a best-seller or a hit screenplay
does not guarantee a box-office success but at least
you begin with something of importance and something
that is pre-sold. You have a chance of attracting
top actors and top directors.

We almost passed up THE MAN IN THE GRAY
FLANNEL SUIT, ANASTASIA, and BUS STOP. These
would have been fatal errors.

I am willing to wager that Metro finally gets a seal
on TEA AND SYMPATHY in the same way that Warners
will get a seal on THE BAD SEED. We have got to
take more gambles than we have taken in the past
in the purchase of material. There is always a way
to "solve" what appears to be forbidden material.
We turned down STREETCAR NAMED DESIRE because
we thought it couldn't be licked. Usually when you
finally manage to lick one of these difficult problems
you turn out to have a very successful picture. The
fact that the story is censorable or difficult or un-
orthodox usually means that it is something off the
beaten track and not in the usual formula groove--
this means that it is something "different" and when
you have something different, in most cases, it
happens that you end up with a hit.

> I do not want to bore you with repetition but I
> want to again emphasize that we should begin to rely
> more on the judgment of the public than our own
> judgment. [8]

Although the motion picture code had relaxed somewhat
in the post-war forties, and again in the mid-fifties, the
threat of an audience boycott over sensitive subject matter
continued to dog every serious producer. Without the code's
seal of approval, theater chains would not to play a film and
audiences would be encouraged to stay away by their local
community leaders. No major studio could afford to gamble
at such stakes. Losing a large segment of the film-going
audience could spell disaster for the studio. Even by 1955
the studios were still cowering in the shadows of the Code,
and would be forced to follow suggestions relating to the
handling of material.

When a script was completed, it was sent to the Code
office, where it would be scrutinized for offensive dialogue,
situations, or scenes. If the film were clear of objections,
there would be no problem. Often, though, with the constant push for more mature stories in the fifties, suggestions for revisions were legion. What the Code office demanded for KATHERINE, obviously undermined the integrity
and power of the story. A letter addressed to producer
Frank McCarthy, sent by Geoffrey Shurlock of the Motion
Picture Association of America outlined these objections.

> ... It will be necessary, of course, to secure
> proper technical advice with reference to the char-
> acterization of the Prioress, as well as with reference
> to the various other religious personalities and reli-
> gious angles to this story.
> Parenthetically, we might mention that we feel
> that in the choice given to Katherine in the opening
> scenes of this story, the sympathy seems to be
> directed against religion in a rather unfair way, and
> there seems to be some danger that the character of
> the Prioress might be played in such a way as to
> make religion seem something from which it would be
> good to escape.
> Furthermore, Nirac's line, "I was a child with many
> fathers," seems offensively blunt and should be
> changed.

We also note that Nirac frequently uses the expression, "Mon dieu." We have always discouraged this particular expression as not containing the consistent reverence as required by the Code.

The acceptability of Hugh's assault on Katherine will depend entirely on the taste and discretion with which it is presented on the screen. It seems to us entirely unnecessary that the shoulder of her gown should have to rip.

... We seriously question the taste involved in John's provoking Katherine's passion with a deliberate kiss, particularly considering that this girl has only just a moment before pronounced the marital vows. This scene, in order to be acceptable in the finished picture, will have to be handled with extremely great care.

... The agonies of childbirth, as described in this script would not be acceptable on the screen. The pains which are wracking Katherine would have to be gotten over merely by suggestion rather than shown in detail, as presently indicated.

... The use of the word "damn" is unacceptable.

... The kiss between Katherine and John should not be "brutal."

... Nirac's line, "If his grace is busy tonight, I can show you a trick, ma belle," is unacceptable. We have always tried to keep the vulgarity of a belch off the screen.

Katherine's dialogue, "Does not care in whose arms you lie?" seems unacceptable. It is necessary to remove those lines of dialogue from the story in which persons of importance might seem to be acquiescing in this adulterous relationship.

In her further dialogue, towards the middle of this page, it would be better were the reference to "mistress" be simply omitted.

Throughout this story there has been no actual acknowledgement by John of the sinful relationship in which he has been engaged. We think that this added element of a voice for morality would be essential for the proper telling of this story under the Code. We ask that some thought be given to introducing this acknowledgement on this page. His plea with Katherine is currently simply on the basis that he still loves her. The added element of

> acknowledging his wrong would produce a proper
> balance of moral considerations in the telling of this
> story of adultery in which the two sinners are
> eventually happily united. [9]

These objections were made to a script which overall
was deemed "acceptable under the provisions of the Production Code." The studio had more serious problems when
the subject matter itself was offensive to the Code office.
Nevertheless, these were problems which the producers had
faced since 1933. What made them so frustrating to producers
in the mid-fifties was that European films were dealing
with sophisticated adult material, and ending up in the
American marketplace, offering new opportunities for critics
and movie fans alike. But because major studios were sig-
natories to the powerful M.P.A.A., which had established
the Code, all a producer could do was to comply.

There was money to be earned nevertheless in controversy,
a fact proven by two films released without Code approval.
THE MOON IS BLUE and BABY DOLL both gained infamy and
sensational publicity by not having a Code seal. The
majority of studios, however, were not willing to risk the
wrath of the Association and countless civic groups by producing unapproved material. This lack of sophistication
eventually promoted a flood of racy foreign films, and opened
up a new market for independent distributors to handle them.
The major studios lost part of their audiences to this avant-
garde competing product. Although not a large market
share, it was the beginning of audience fragmentation which
would perplex studio publicity people into the 1960's.

What American films lacked in adult sophistication was
made up in lavish spending. One thing foreign producers
could not afford was big-star names, glamorous costumes,
luxurious sets, and Hollywood-style action. As always, the
bigger films were, the more expensive they became, and not
necessarily better. CinemaScope, itself, contributed to rising
budgets, for the wider, larger screens only showed up the
deficiencies in studio-based films. There was a greater need
for reality in sets which prompted more location shooting.
Entire films were taken to distant locations for production.
GARDEN OF EVIL was shot almost entirely in Mexico, and
HOUSE OF BAMBOO went on location in Tokyo. THREE
COINS IN THE FOUNTAIN had a good portion of location

TABLE V

SET COSTS OF FOX PICTURES

TITLE	EXPENDITURE	PERCENTAGE OF TOTAL COST
Wilson (1944)	$232,881	7.7
Keys of the Kingdom (1944)	337,307	12.6
The Dolly Sisters (1945)	171,326	6.8
Carnival in Costa Rica (1946)	219,769	6.8
Forever Amber (1947)	462,604	7.3
The Razor's Edge (1947)	342,215	10.2
The Big Lift (1950)	12,980	0.8
Broken Arrow (1950)	65,330	3.2
I'd Climb the Highest Mountain (1951)	12,683	1.0
American Guerilla in the Philippines (1951)	12,795	0.7
Way of a Gaucho (1952)	68,103	3.0
Stars and Stripes Forever (1953)	87,925	4.9
Prince of Players (1955)	92,503	5.8
The View From Pompey's Head (1955)	55,574	4.5
Hilda Crane (1956)	45,000	3.9

work in Rome, and Otto Preminger photographed the pictorial Rocky Mountains of British Columbia as his setting for RIVER OF NO RETURN.

The one obvious drawback of a great amount of location work was that it further cut the need for huge, expensive sound stages. It also reduced the need for contracted set designers, carpenters, art directors, and it meant that the studio's great backlog of standing sets were no longer as useful. The decline in entirely studio-made pictures resulted in a drastic drop in the set costs for movies after the post-war boom, as seen in Table V's comparison of expenditures (p. 103).

With the exception of studio-bound films like THE KING AND I, THE SEVEN YEAR ITCH, outdoor adventures like THE TALL MEN, SOLDIER OF FORTUNE, WHITE FEATHER, THE RACERS, THE LAST WAGON, and BETWEEN HEAVEN AND HELL had little need for sound stages. Fox was fortunate for taking the plunge into television production with a ½ hour series, MY FRIEND FLICKA, in 1956. At the same time the entire original Fox Sunset studio became the hub of Twentieth Century-Fox Television.

Also produced on the Sunset lot was the 20th Century-Fox Hour, sponsored by General Electric, recycling already released movies as the basis for new teleplays. Thus, what had previously been unusable "old" films were revitalized for the television format. At a cost of $69,000 per episode, Fox's total cash outlay for the series was $2 million, and the network sale was double that amount, providing a 100 percent profit. Television was suddenly beginning to pay off.

Taking the cue from United Artists and Republic Pictures, Spyros Skouras began looking enviously towards revenues from the possible sale of motion pictures to television. Fox had a backlog of 600 features in their pre-1948 (which was a cut-off date established to protect theater operators) library. There was little theatrical value left in these films. Aside from the perennial reissues of perhaps STATE FAIR or JESSE JAMES, the less-known productions were on the shelf forever. Reissues had never provided much revenue, except for a brief period during and after the war, when there was a shortage of product. Skouras also felt that the future lay in new CinemaScope productions, not in the old formats, again cutting down reissue value.

With profits dropping in the main market of theatrical releases, it was inevitable that some move would be made to cash in on the library of older films. Even though there was discussion within the company that a hold-off would result in higher prices later, Skouras in May, 1956, went ahead on an experimental deal with National Telefilm Associates. Fox leased, not sold, the rights to 52 of their old films to N.T.A. for 20 years, netting between $2 million and $3 million. Skouras announced at the time of the sale, "Never in the history of commerce has an industry been subjected to such competition, competition which supplies the same thing for free which we are trying to sell." Skouras, unfortunately, was underestimating the precedent he had set by the sale. Not only would television be competitive, but it would now have the product with which to compete even more fiercely.

With audiences now watching movies on television, it became painfully clear that while a film like THE ROBE could earn $16.5 million in rentals domestically, expensive Cinema-Scope ventures such as PRINCE OF PLAYERS or THE VIRGIN QUEEN, each costing around $1.5 million, could still be box-office disasters. With higher budgets, a failed film was more likely to be injurious to the company's profits.

Each of these individual problems fell, ultimately, on Darryl Zanuck's shoulders. After 21 years with the studio, Zanuck was making fewer pictures than ever, and coping with more problems than ever. In mid-1956, Spyros Skouras tried to quell rumors that Zanuck was about to leave Fox, but the production chief publicly announced that he was re-negotiating his position with the studio. Very shortly after, he made the decision to leave Fox and enter into independent production. This decision was a culmination of the problems which were wracking Fox and the industry, as well as Zanuck's personal dissatisfaction with the job.

"Zanuck told me he got on a plane to New York," said Nunnally Johnson,

> and on the plane was Pat Boone, who at that time was quite big. Zanuck felt that one of the scripts he had in his briefcase would suit him. He talked to Boone and gave him the script. Boone told him that he had nine people who had to say yes before he could say yes himself. So (Zanuck) would have to deal with nine sons-of-bitches to get this one singer. He said, "I can't go on in this business any longer. Everybody's got a corporation." [10]

Although money was not a major factor in Zanuck's decision, Philip Dunne claimed that it did play some part.

> [Zanuck] started telling me how much money Frank
> Ross had made and kept on THE ROBE. He'd kept
> it because he got a capital gain on the whole thing
> because he'd developed the project and sold it.
> Zanuck figured out that on this one picture Frank
> had made and kept as much money as Zanuck had
> made and kept in 10 years. Made and kept is the
> thing. He said, "I'm in the wrong business." I
> always had the feeling that he resented this very
> much, and was beginning to feel trapped. I also
> think he was tired. He would never admit it and he
> never looked it, but I think he was just plain tired.
> I think that at the rate he had gone, he had to burn
> himself out sometime. Creatively, he had to burn
> out. [11]

Dunne elaborated on his notion that Zanuck no longer had the same energy and enthusiasm towards making pictures.

> You would notice it in the meetings. He'd begin to
> lose a little of that enthusiasm.... There were
> moments ... that you would go in and sit there in
> silence for long periods. He wasn't sparking. I
> think he was just bored with the whole thing and
> getting a little tired and not able to drive himself as
> he had in the beginning. He was very young when
> he started. He was older now and middle age was
> creeping up. The genius of the studio, and I'm
> using the word in its old sense, was dim now. [12]

By mid-1956, Darryl Francis Zanuck, the man who had built up Twentieth Century-Fox as a film corporation of standing, was about to break his 10-year contract as vice-president in charge of production. Fox's single most valuable resource since 1935 was leaving the studio when its employment was at an all-time peak of 4,186 and its product included some of the most popular titles in the industry--THE KING AND I, ANASTASIA, LOVE ME TENDER, and BUS STOP. Under the Zanuck administration, Fox had become world renowned by "the best fanfare in town." What was to follow was a gross case of mismanagement which would very shortly claim Zanuck's studio as a disaster area.

CHAPTER 10

■ THE BUDGET MYSTIQUE ■

Aside from budget breakdowns locked away in production files, there is precious little public information about what money went where within the studio system. Major studios were always reluctant to disclose accurate figures to talent or their competitors. The exception to that rule was in the case of publicity. Even there, figures were distorted to make a film sound like the greatest ever produced. The catchline "millions in the making" tried to convince the public that cost equalled quality. More often, though, nothing was mentioned about the average release. An approximate budget of a film was based on innuendo, hearsay, and bits of inter-studio shop-talk.

Stan Hough summed it up, "It's always been close-mouthed. Other studios didn't want their competitors to know what they were making pictures for. I know when the heads of studios got together, they lied to one another. They would say, 'Hey, Sam, how much did you make A TREE GROWS IN BROOKLYN for?' 'Well, we made it for two [million] six [hundred thousand].' And it was usually about a million low. Probably cost three, six." [1]

Only the producing studio really knew what a film cost, and others were seldom informed. Studio executives saw copies of overall budgets, as well as producers and directors, but department heads only saw what related to them. The studio was tight-lipped on budgets for privacy, prestige, and a desire to keep figures flexible for accounting purposes. That way, if one picture went over budget, losses could be transferred to another which was more modest in cost. It is no coincidence that studios have been accused of keeping

three sets of accounts: one for themselves, one for producers, and one for the Internal Revenue Service.

Nevertheless, while talent was kept on contracted salaries, there was no way to find out the actual cost and profit
figures. This attitude accounts for the current lack of information on what films actually cost. Even budgets themselves were not thoroughly reliable. As Sam Engel suggests,
"We went in with the results of the last production meeting.
Then we'd get the budget. But that and 10 cents would
get you a cup of coffee. You never knew how many sets of
books they kept anyway, or how they bookkeeped it. This
overhead was always a matter, I think, of flipping a coin.
They'd charge you departmental costs, and on top of the
whole thing, they'd charge you 30 percent. Then, of course,
you never knew what the hell distribution was charging." [2]

There was a general procedure which was followed in the
early stages of every project. When a script was approved
as being in final form, a copy would be sent to each department which would be playing a large role in that production.
If the film were to be a musical, the estimations of the music
department would be very important, as well as for costumes,
sets, and numbers. A film with much special effects work,
either through process or matte work, was dependent on the
estimates of Ray Kellogg, who was in charge of special photography. In the 1950's, the phrase, "Kellogg shot," became
commonly used when a script called for superimposure or
trick effects.

When each department filed its report, the head of the
estimating department would put together a tentative budget
which would then be sent to Zanuck and the New York office.
All budgets had to be approved by the studio and the distribution group. The script would then be formally approved
or rejected depending on the cost and projected returns.
Zanuck would also analyze cost from an overall production
point of view,

> Invariably, he'd tell the production manager, "You're
> our of your head. I want you to cut $250,000 out
> of this budget," [recalls Nunnally Johnson.] The
> fellow said, "I can't possibly do it, Darryl." And
> he'd say, "Don't come back until you've done it."
> And he did it. I suppose the production manager

had the sense to add $250,000, so it didn't bother him too much.

[Johnson continues], I paid little attention to costs. I didn't think anybody in the whole studio that had anything to do with figures was honest. I remember once, as producer, they always sent me an invoice to sign, and this set cost $18,000. How the hell could I tell what it cost? So I signed automatically.

Now, one day, I wanted a sign for "Keep off the Grass." Two days later, I got this invoice for $175. I kept that somewhere just as an example of the kind of nonsense that went into the cost of a picture.

When I did THE MUDLARK at Shepperton Studio (England), they [Fox] were paying $250,000 a picture. They had failed to take the studio option on the picture before, so it was $500,000 on THE MUD-LARK. They just put the cost they had to pay anyway on the next picture--mine! It was very foolish of me to be so careless about this thing because it meant that the studio could say my pictures cost too much, or weren't profitmaking.

I just couldn't believe that any of their figures meant anything. I could have sat down and written figures that would have been just as sensible. One time I did a picture with Eddie Goulding, who had just been sitting around. So when I went to Zanuck, I told him I wanted Goulding, but only for one picture. I didn't want them to put on the picture he should have done but didn't and they had to pay him for anyway. I think later they did it, and it was slipped in some other way. Under "miscellaneous." I didn't pay much attention to the cost, because as I say, I didn't believe in it. [3]

Not only were methods occasionally suspect, but so were motives. Very often films were made because some contract talent was not being used, as in the example of Sam Engel's Gracie Fields picture, WE'RE GOING TO BE RICH. There were other examples Engel was involved with as well.

People we had under contract had to be used. They were miscast many times in order to use them. Which is a mistake. I had this experience with Ty Power. We had one more picture he had to give us under his

> contract. Now, I'd written a story called PONY
> SOLDIER and I was going to put young Jeffrey
> Hunter in it. It cried aloud for a young kid of
> 19 or 20 years old. But because Ty Power had
> one more picture left, Zanuck said, "We're going to
> use Ty Power," who was miscast.
>
> Not only that, but we went the wrong season of
> the year on location. We went up to Arizona and
> sure enough we got snowed in. All because of the
> greed to use Ty Power because he cost us "x" amount
> of dollars. [4]

There were, as well, reasons to produce films other than
the sheer idea of profit. During the war many countries
froze their currencies, and large funds were built up for
the major studios within these countries. One way of freeing
this money was by using it for local production. Therefore,
the studio would send a crew out to make a film like WAY OF
A GAUCHO, which Philip Dunne produced in Argentina.

> The whole thing was supposed to be shot there. In
> the meantime, the company made $2 million on the
> picture before it was even released, or so I was told,
> because they wrote off all the costs of the picture on
> the official rate of exchange, and we were spending
> pesos at the black market rate of exchange, which
> is the only way anybody could spend any pesos. They
> showed a tremendous write-off on the picture. That
> was the reason for making it. It was not successful. [5]

WAY OF A GAUCHO went over budget by $413,000, with
$154,000 in retakes, and the total budget stood at $2,239,000.
Although the film did not make a profit at the box office,
according to Dunne, the profits showed up elsewhere.

There were more practical reasons for production as well.
Fox had run up such a high budget on THE ROBE that
Zanuck decided to make a sequel and charge much of the
original's overage to DEMETRIUS. As a result, it recycled
many of THE ROBE's sets and defrayed some enormous costs.

Various elements contributed to a budget, and if these
elements were controlled judiciously, a film could be made
within its estimated range. The genre of film obviously had
a great deal to do with its final cost. However, one of the

TABLE VI

NUMBER OF SHOOTING DAYS OF "A" PRODUCT

TITLE	ESTIMATED	ACTUAL	COST (MILLIONS)
Anna and the King of Siam (1946)	67	78	2.20
The Homestretch (1946)	87	102	2.65
Razor's Edge (1946)	83	95	3.35
Smoky (1946)	87	76	1.38
Three Little Girls in Blue (1946)	78	100	2.33
Captain From Castile (1947)	89	112	4.50
Forever Amber (1947)	99	129	6.37
My Darling Clementine (1946)	48	59	2.23
Boomerang (1947)	56	48	1.14
Gentleman's Agreement (1947)	55	62	1.98
Kiss of Death (1947)	63	68	1.53
Sitting Pretty (1948)	47	49	1.33
The Snake Pit (1949)	66	68	2.64

most expensive factors was time. The amount of shooting days could make the difference whether a film came in on budget or not. Extra production days meant keeping an entire cast and crew for a longer period, and sometimes including penalty salaries for non-term contract actors. Studio overhead would be increased and department charges would be higher. Thus, in scheduling a film, one of the first

TABLE VII

NUMBER OF SHOOTING DAYS OF "B" PRODUCT

TITLE	ESTIMATED	ACTUAL	COST (MILLIONS)
Shock (1946)	24	29	.363
Strange Triangle (1946)	24	27	.398
Johnny Comes Flying Home (1946)	24	24	.341
It Shouldn't Happen to a Dog (1946)	24	30	.455

considerations in estimating a budget was the number of production days. From Table VI (p. 111), and Table VII (above), a rule of thumb can be drawn between the number of days and the total cost. Obviously, the more expensive period productions with large casts and spectacular sets cost more to shoot on a per-day basis. In the budget-conscious late 1940's, producers trimmed expenses on their "A" pictures by shooting fewer days with more contemporary stories to cut down on sets and costumes.

The differences in schedule vary proportionately with the importance of the film. Blockbuster productions like FOREVER AMBER and THE RAZOR'S EDGE were assigned lengthy schedules and large budgets, whereas "B" product was shot in approximately 24 to 30 days, utilizing less expensive talent. Stan Hough added that the CHARLIE CHAN and MR. MOTO series were shot in even less time.

> I know we made them in 16 to 18 days. Rigid discipline. We had to have a shot at 8 o'clock in the morning or the studio fell on our head.... There were some rigid rules in the "B" pictures. First of all, we had to get six to seven pages a day.... But that was mandatory. Unless you came in with your day's work, you probably wouldn't be around the next day. The directors knew it, the producers knew it, and the actors knew it. Whatever had to be done to get that amount of work was done. [6]

On the other hand, Hough was also familiar with CAPTAIN FROM CASTILE, having been assistant director, and noted, "Now CASTILE was shot virtually entirely in Mexico. Lots of weather problems. Again, it was a costume picture, and a gigantic operation, and we were way behind." [7] So, time did mean money in these cases.

Musical numbers meant considerable amounts in some budgets, for cast, costume, and choreography. The actual amount of shooting time was usually lengthened for these highly-complex and heavily-populated sequences.

Various other departments contributed heavy charges to certain films. Special camera effects, which contributed largely to science-fiction films, ran up costs on THE DAY THE EARTH STOOD STILL of $152,000. This figure was at least 15 percent of the film's budget. Sets for the same film totalled $64,750; art direction cost $8,060; set design, $6,368; sketch artists, $2,260; and model builders, $1,167. However, each of these factors played an important role in the success of the film.

Music scoring was also a major factor in budgets and was considered a vital element of every film. On THE DAY THE EARTH STOOD STILL, Bernard Herrmann's score was budgeted for $41,000. The same composer, on a higher-budget film, THE EGYPTIAN, charged $111,000 for a musical score. Another high-budget film, THE RAZOR'S EDGE, had a musical score costing $89,000, and a considerably lower-budget film, LAURA, was scored for $22,000.

Generally, an entire budget of a film was lowered in every area if it were a "B" picture; a top "A" film would, on the other hand, run up greater expenses. When Cinema-Scope was introduced, it added an average cost of $250,000 to every budget for more elaborate sets, costumes, and locations. The budgets on Tables VIII, IX, and X (pp. 114, 115, and 116) point out how monies were allotted to various productions over the years.

Approved for $1,296,000, STANLEY AND LIVINGSTONE went $42,302.23 over budget. Note the enormous amount assigned to overhead (Table VIII).

I'D CLIMB THE HIGHEST MOUNTAIN was produced at a

TABLE VIII

Budget for STANLEY AND LIVINGSTONE (1939)

DESCRIPTION	COST
Story Rights and Expenses	12,000.00
Scenario	123,743.83
Music Department	33,531.94
Direction and supervision	115,703.22
Staff cost	81,773.21
Cast	159,322.60
Extras	26,860.67
Singers and Chorus Salaries	1,888.45
Art Cost	14,507.17
Set Cost	57,892.56
Strike Labor	6,680,51
Transportation	3,937.17
Operating Labor and Material	23,047.54
Miniature Cost	980.86
Camera Department	21,343.13
Sound Department	7,129.27
Electrical Department	18,430.51
Special Effects	6,764.32
Snow Dressing	77.85
Set Dressing Cost	16,354.91
Animal and Action Devices	3,510.80
Wardrobe Department	17,328.60
Make-up Department	10,166.64
Scenic Art Department	6,302.09
Process Department	22,930.07
Re-recording Department	12,755.25
Editorial Department	6,597.99
Production Film Cost	21,263.33
Still Department	4,068.32
Title Department	788.07
Insert Department	1,106.30
Optical Printing Department	909.22
Fades and Dissolves	1,979.28
Insurance and Tax	30,887.59
Location expenses	114,657.84
Stock Film Library Cost	4,246.03
Miscellaneous	9,690.34
Overhead	336,769.21
Total	$1,337,926.69

TABLE IX

Budget for I'D CLIMB THE HIGHEST MOUNTAIN (1950)

DESCRIPTION	COST
Story Rights and Expenses	40,000.00
Scenario	25,899.06
Music Department	46,344.25
Direction	77,083.34
Cast	187,993.01
Production Department Service	196,033.73
Administrative Overhead	98,016.87
Art	10,242.64
Set Cost	12,683.05
Strike Labor	1,768.53
Re-recording	15,023.38
Titles, Inserts, and Fades	9,965.89
Projectionists	2,539.10
Talent Tests	6,043.28
Editorial	11,808.94
Insurance and Tax	15,271.40
Prod. and Dir. Secys.	1,712.86
Staff	22,850.37
Extras	17,730.85
Operating L and M	40,654.71
Camera	33,896.72
Sound	12,087.35
Electrical	26,848.19
Mech. Eff. and Show Dressing	147.50
Set Dressing Cost	14,591.30
Animals and Action Devices	18,493.00
Women's Wardrobe	17,523.41
Men's Wardrobe	9,587.31
Make-up and Hair Dressing	9,981.97
Spec. Effects and Scenic Art	6.84
Process Department	879.94
Production Film	48,065.21
Stills	8,493.57
Transportation	54,524.64
Location expenses	77,445.21
Miscellaneous	18,696.52
Total	$1,190,933.94

TABLE X

Budget for PRINCE OF PLAYERS (1955)

DESCRIPTION	COST
Story Rights and Expenses	22,500.00
Scenario	102,000.00
Music Department	36,111.82
Director	53,750.00
Producer and Assistants	2,500.00
Cast	266,452.22
Direct Production Service	116,675.15
Art	19,384.82
Set Cost	92,503.48
Strike Labor	21,890.53
Light Platforms	7,431.58
Re-recording	23,614.13
Titles, Inserts, and Fades	18,075.91
Projectionists	4,106.90
Talent Tests	1,603.44
Editorial	6,882.96
Insurance and Tax	23,584.76
Dance Director and Staff	40.15
Prod. and Dir. Secys.	2,068.24
Staff	20,225.53
Extras	46,821.26
Operating L and M	27,695.38
Camera	11,731.20
Sound	15,053.70
Electrical	45,358.98
Mech. Eff. and Snow Dressing	6,274.69
Set Dressing Cost	29,896.28
Animals and Action Devices	5,282.24
Women's Wardrobe	29,871.94
Men's Wardrobe	42,086.61
Make-up and Hair Dressing	17,715.26
Spec. Effects and Scenic Art	2,823.52
Process Department	311.18
Production Film	35,922.45
Stills	5,217.15
Transportation	47,988.00
Location Expenses	2,580.04
Miscellaneous	50,326.69
General Overhead	262,496.56
Total	$1,526,855.08

cost of $126,140.95 over its approved budget (Table IX).
Note the added Production Film figure of $48,065 for Techni-
color shooting compared to STANLEY AND LIVINGSTONE's
$21,263 figure. Also note the inconsequential amount spent
on Process Photography compared to the previous title. This
reflected the trend to shoot on location. Nevertheless,
set dressing costs were almost the same on both pictures,
showing the rise in labor expenses between 1939 and 1950.

PRINCE OF PLAYERS ended up $45,944.92 under budget
(Table X). The low amount for location expenses indicates
much of the movie was shot within reasonable proximity of
the studio. The high costs for Wardrobe is attributed to
the number of costumed stars and extras needed to fill the
CinemaScope screen.

Interesting to note is the fact that in 1939, the budget
for STANLEY AND LIVINGSTONE was the absolute high-end
of the spectrum. By 1950, I'D CLIMB THE HIGHEST MOUN-
TAIN was the lowest cost Technicolor Fox film of the year,
running less than half of some black and white features.
The highest "A" budget that year was for DAVID AND
BATHSHEBA at $2.17 million. When PRINCE OF PLAYERS
was made in the throes of CinemaScope budgeting, the highest budget of 1955 was $3.568 million for a Tyrone Power-
Susan Hayward epic, UNTAMED. PRINCE OF PLAYERS
ranged among the least expensive wide-screen product for
the year.

If the studio was secretive about budgets, the executives were downright adamant about not letting anyone know
what the pictures grossed. Virtually no one on the lot knew
what their films made at the box office, other than a few
reports in the trade papers.

> One of the things is [says Sam Engel], that they
> didn't want talent, that goes for actors particularly,
> and directors, writers and producers, to know how
> well we did, for fear they'd want raises. That was
> basic. There was no question about that. And why
> should they tell you that they're making money?
> That's all an agent has to hear, and he's in there
> the next morning on the doorstep. [8]

There was some regret among producers that Zanuck

had not kept them informed until he began sending his memos of the early fifties.

> The high command never let us in on anything [Engel continues]. The only time we'd hear from them was if things turned sour. But we were never told anything. If we had a hit, we never got figures except what we picked up in Variety or the Reporter. So you were never told. And a big mistake that was, of course, because it would have been good to know even though they were almost insured grosses. But there was still a difference if a certain picture did more or did less. And you could learn something from the subject matter or the casting. But you never knew. 9

CHAPTER 11

■ THE ADLER YEARS ■

In 1956, total figures showed that since 1950 the motion picture industry had slumped by $207 million. From a post-
war peak of approximately 90 million, audiences had dropped
to an estimated 65 million. More pessimistic figures came
from business analyst Sindlinger and Company which placed
weekly attendance at 38,482,000.

Many exhibitors felt that television was the main reason
for the drop and great animosity developed between producers
and theater owners when more features were sold for broad-
cast. At Twentieth Century-Fox, television sales undoubtedly
produced needed revenue. N.T.A. reportedly paid $29.5
million to cover the leases on 390 films which would be released in a staggered order at the rate of 50 to 68 annually.
This yielded approximately $75,000 for each film and, unlike
a reissue, there were few expenses. There was little doubt
that the major companies would benefit from the sales in the
short haul but the longterm damage would be inestimable.

Figures did not lie, and a Sindlinger survey showed that
when THE WIZARD OF OZ (1939), was aired on television for
the first time on November 3, 1956, national box-office receipts
dropped by $2 million. Such a precipitous decline was only
a sampling of what was to follow for theater owners across
the country.

Back at the Fox studio, the day-to-day chores of
churning out theatrical motion pictures was to continue without the dynamic presence of Darryl Zanuck. Zanuck, through
his D.F.Z. Productions would turn out between one and five
features annually with an aggregate cost of no more than
$9 million. No single film could cost more than $4 million;

if it did, it would be the only Fox-financed project for the year. To make the deal even sweeter, Zanuck would keep 50 percent of the profits. With Fox putting up all the money, he had nothing to lose but time.

Problems arose at the studio with the man who was now making decisions, Buddy Adler. An executive producer who had been named as successor by Zanuck himself, Adler had gained success at Columbia Pictures. Beginning his activity at the studio known as "Poverty Row," Adler rocketed into the big league with his 1953 production of FROM HERE TO ETERNITY. Not only did the film bring $12 million in domestic rentals to the studio, it also won many Academy Awards, including Best Picture. It was not long before Adler began looking to the more important major companies for employment.

Adler signed a deal with Fox on May 13, 1954, and by September 13 was assigned to several major productions. For his Fox debut, Adler produced the screen version of Ernest K. Gann's SOLDIER OF FORTUNE, starring an aging Clark Gable, and in the same year, THE LEFT HAND OF GOD, with Humphrey Bogart. Both films were directed by Edward Dmytryk and proved to be moderate successes. After this initiation, Adler was given six more of the studio's top properties. Included in this package were BUS STOP and THE REVOLT OF MAMIE STOVER, both for Marilyn Monore; ANASTASIA, the stage hit; THE WAY TO THE GOLD, a suspense story; THE DAY THE CENTURY ENDED; and SOLO, a Frank Sinatra-June Allyson vehicle.

By April 25, 1955, Buddy Adler was named a member of Darryl Zanuck's executive staff. A pair of projects boosted his prestige at the studio. ANASTASIA and BUS STOP were both smash hits in 1956. Because Monroe turned down MAMIE STOVER, the project was produced with Jane Russell in the leading role and was a failure due to a Breen office-emasculated script. CENTURY was retitled BETWEEN HEAVEN AND HELL and turned over to contract producer, David Weisbart. SOLO was cancelled and GOLD was postponed indefinitely.

When Buddy Adler took over Darryl Zanuck's office, the studio was floating on a string of moneymakers. THE KING AND I, ANASTASIA, LOVE ME TENDER and Zanuck's personal production of THE MAN IN THE GRAY FLANNEL SUIT were showing excellent returns and left Fox with a high dollar volume at year-end. Talks which Zanuck had initiated with Pat Boone resulted in two more very popular films, BERNARDINE and APRIL LOVE. When the Zanuck properties were exhausted, Fox's troubles began. Adler was simply not a good judge of film projects.

Buddy Adler was most certainly not able to fan the flames lit by Darryl Zanuck. Most producers, in retrospect, remember the successor with little affection. Nunnally Johnson was probably representative of the Fox team when he stated,

> To tell you the truth, that's a very delicate subject. I was never very impressed with Adler. He produced one picture, FROM HERE TO ETERNITY, and they made him head of the studio. I had very little to do with him. What I had to do didn't impress me greatly. I don't know that operations changed at all. The man who was the focus of the thing just wasn't as good as the man who occupied the position previously. [1]

Samuel Engel concurred, but for different reasons.

> They bring over a man who'd only had a smattering of experience. His screen credit for FROM HERE TO ETERNITY was in dispute.... He was a very, very nice, warm guy. Very pleasant. Sort of a semi-playboy.... I never knew what he was doing there, but it never dawned on me that they ever thought of him as a successor to Zanuck. [2]

Being as efficient and aggressive as his predecessor would have been difficult for Adler, since Zanuck was a "boy wonder" when he started in the business. Adler was solidly into middle age and his health was not to last for long. Zanuck had also established career-long relationships with men like Johnson, Engel, Dunne, John Ford, Henry King, and numerous others since the very beginning of Twentieth's history.

Zanuck knew how to bring out the best in talent, but Buddy Adler let the studio go on its own. Zanuck's great strength was his ability to suggest or assign projects and follow them through. This was Adler's weakness. Story conferences were virtually abandoned. When they were held, notes with suggestions were late in preparation, if they were prepared at all. Suggestions were very often for legal or censorship problems rather than creative additions to the story.

Thomas Stempel, Nunnally Johnson's biographer, noted:

> One of the interesting things I noticed in going through Johnson's memos in the collection at Boston University was the change in the tone of the memos after Zanuck left. The Johnson/Zanuck memos have an ease and a sense of professional competence and mutual respect about them; a feeling that these men know what they're doing and that they know that the other one knows what he's doing too. This changes in Johnson's memos to Adler. In the first few months after Zanuck left, Johnson wrote to Adler in a memo dated March 20, 1956: "It is an odd fact that the projects assigned to me by Darryl almost invariably turn out better than those I pick for myself, which leads me to believe that I leave something to be desired as a picker of stories. Accordingly, I would like to look to you for suggestions for my next one.... All I ask of it is that it provide something that I will make some money out of.... Please answer this. I have no file for Adler, Buddy--Inter-office Memos, and I would like very much to have one." After this, everything seems to go downhill, and the tone changes to a rather cool one and there is even some exasperation on Johnson's part. [3]

It was not only Adler's personal relationship with studio talent which was lacking, it was professional associations as well. Johnson's description of Adler portrayed him as a man who "liked to walk out and take a bow at the openings. Adler was a smart-looking fellow and always appeared to be carrying some kind of secret. He was just wondering what time dinner was, really." [4]

Films which were produced under Adler's regime pretty much confirmed the problems at the studio. Many of them, without any doubt, would never have gone into production had Zanuck been in charge. Producer-director Johnson

even admitted that Zanuck would not have permitted him to
do THE MAN WHO UNDERSTOOD WOMEN, which was based
on Romain Gary's THE COLORS OF THE DAY. "I think
Zanuck would have stopped me from doing that," he recalls.
"He might have called me in and said, 'Look, I don't think
this story is good enough. It's too precious.' Generally,
he'd make suggestions of other ways to work out the story." 5

Another film which was lacking in story to Johnson was
John Huston's THE BARBARIAN AND THE GEISHA.

> At any rate, I think their whole trouble was Huston.
> I remember Adler said to me one day at lunch, in
> quiet excitement, that John had arrived with a print
> of the film. They were going to look at it right after
> lunch.
> I happened to see (Adler) around six, when I
> was leaving the studio. He was white and said, in
> effect, "I don't know what the hell this guy's done,
> and he's leaving tonight." I think there was some-
> thing like 15 days of shooting to get the bridges be-
> tween scenes Huston had shot. And it just didn't
> come together.
> Zanuck would have flown the footage back from
> wherever they were shooting and would have long
> before told John what he thought was happening or
> what was wrong. Huston would never have come up
> with such rubbish as was brought in. And if he had,
> Zanuck would have kept him there until he shot the
> stuff to make it a picture. Not that it was specifically
> rubbish, but there was evidently complete indifference
> to the coherence of a story. 6

"It was aimless with Buddy," Sam Engel summed up.
"And whatever good things happened, happened by chance
and not by design. The best word to describe it is that
it drifted ... like a ship without a rudder." 7

Philip Dunne compared the Zanuck and Adler regimes
more succinctly:

> The big asset that Zanuck had that really made the
> thing go was his unquenchable enthusiasm for what
> he was doing. He loved it and he was in love with
> the story. Good or bad, he made himself love it.

> You went out from there thinking, "We're going to
> have the greatest (film) the world has ever seen."
> Everytime. Good or bad. This was invaluable. You
> run into the other kind, the frightened producer like
> Adler, who had no love for it, who was mistrustful,
> suspicious, and frightened all the time. You walked
> out and you said, "My God, what am I doing? Why
> are we doing this picture?" Right there is perhaps
> the short story of what happened to 20th Century-
> Fox. [8]

Aside from Philip Dunne's personal opinion of Adler,
there were certain aspects of studio policy which he felt were
drastically wrong. Rather than trying to make better inexpensive films, Dunne complained that Fox's policy was simply
to make inexpensive films. One of the first problems he discovered was that location shooting was forbidden and that his
production of THREE BRAVE MEN would have to be filmed on
the back lot.

> On THE VIEW FROM POMPEY'S HEAD, they had said
> the same thing. The art directors always want to
> keep it on the lot. They come up with the idea of
> doing the whole thing there. I said, "No." I went
> to Zanuck and I said, "Look, I want to go to Georgia.
> I want to go to Pompey's Head, which is in Brunswick,
> Georgia." He said, "Absolutely," and he dictated a
> note to all the people in the production department
> ... and said, "This picture will be made in Brunswick,
> Georgia, or wherever Phil Dunne says it will be made."
> Now this is the difference between the two men right
> there. The result was you were always "Not quite-
> ing." This was not a time, as in pre-World War II
> Hollywood where you took pride in creating the world
> on your back lot and spent the money on it and had
> the resources to do it. This was a time when people
> were venturing out into real backgrounds. This was
> a picture that needed to be done as ON THE WATER-
> FRONT was done. I think that if I'd been able to
> go back there I would have been able to elevate the
> picture 50 percent at least in authenticity and feeling,
> but we were stuck with the back lot. [9]

These problems which directors and producers encountered
were not to disappear. Dunne discovered on his next picture,
TEN NORTH FREDERICK, based on the John O'Hara novel,

that the studio was trying even harder to cut costs.

> Again, this could have been a slightly better picture. I thought it was good. Adler hated it all the way. He said, "I don't like tragedies." Everything had to have a happy ending. He stifled it in every way he could. It was supposed to be in color. It came out in black and white. I hate black and white CinemaScope. We had a very limited budget. I had no new sets. I had to use warmed-over sets and re-dress them. The house itself was the star. It was in the title TEN NORTH FREDERICK, but it was never right. I did what I could with the props. The locations were not quite good enough. I wanted to go East. Generally, the whole thing was done reluctantly by the studio, and released the same way. [10]
>
> This is another Adlerism. This comes into it, but peripherally. I did (Gary Cooper's) close-ups first after getting a master (shot) in bits and pieces. I said "I'll bridge it with a close-up." Coop's close-up, one take, perfection. Then I came around to (Suzy Parker's). There were 18 lines and we had 18 takes. I got two lines out of one take, two out of another, one here, and one there. I couldn't get the whole scene in one take, or in four or five takes. They had a studio rule, promulgated by Adler. Adler could be dominated by the production department. Sid Rogell, who was the production manager, said, "We're going to save on film. We'll only print one take." So Adler made it a rule: only one print. In this case, I said, "Print all 18." I had to or I had no scene. The next thing I knew there was a whole delegation down on the set. "What? Printing 18 takes? What is this?" I said, "Well, if you'd rather take 18 days to get the scene, that's the alternative." Adler said, "It's a rule from now on, you don't print more than one take." So I took two days to get the next scene. They took that rule off in a hurry. [11]

There were, of course, other points of view. Stan Hough represented the production department at the time.

> I think that panic had set in by that time and all kinds of so-called excesses were to be eliminated.

The one-take thing, however, goes way back. This is not something new. Again, that stems from excess directors who used to print three and four and five takes.

There was one fellow, I remember, who went for 48 takes and printed 2, 13, and 27. So, the story goes, Zanuck the next day said, "Bring him into the projection room," and they ran the takes and he asked him to separate the three he'd picked. And he couldn't do it. He had it all mixed up.

If you say two takes to directors, they'll want three. Here again, I represent the other side of the desk. Directors ask for a lot of these kinds of things in a sense. I've also worked with directors as an assistant and we didn't work with one take. We simply added an "A" or a "B" and went right ahead with the second take. That's been going on a long time.

I think that regime reflected an attitude of panic in the business and probably went too far. It's true that sets were used two, three, four, five, six times. Phil (Dunne) says "warmed over" sets. Well, I come from the "B" school where you shot every nook and cranny. I never heard of people saying, "Hey, I saw that set last week in another movie." I think that maybe they went too far. But I would doubt that Phil was shorted that much. No question though, the panic was on, and they cut back on construction crews unrealistically. 12

Buddy Adler was not the only one who affected production adversely after Zanuck left. Spyros Skouras had always wanted more control of the production end of the business, but Zanuck had the strength and good sense to keep him as far away as possible. Philip Dunne attests:

We were sitting in the projection room one night and Zanuck said "Lock the door." He had the projectionist lock his door, too. He said "Spyros is on the lot." Later we heard this knocking on the door and this voice, "Let me in. Darryl, let me in." He wouldn't let him in. He was absolutely right that he would just not permit any interference with the studio operation. That's why he was successful. 13

He [Skouras] didn't realize that Zanuck was his meal
ticket. He thought he could run the studio. He was
anxious to get rid of Zanuck, obviously, and get his own
man in there. When Buddy came in, that meant Skouras,
and it meant right away that everything was done for
the wrong reasons. 14

Sam Engel experienced a particularly bitter episode in
his career during the filming of BOY ON A DOLPHIN.

When I got BOY ON A DOLPHIN it was a book which
was nothing like the final story. It wasn't intended
to be and only suggested a Cook's Tour idea of
Greece and I liked it as an adventure romance story.
I made the story up and we went and made it. But,
because it was Greece, and because of Mr. Skouras,
you can imagine what happened. He and his brother
and everybody were writing the script and rewriting
it, until finally I said, "If you want to take it over
Spyros, you can take it."

Engel then imitated a gruff Greek voice saying,

"What you talking about? What you talking about?
You the greatest producer." You know, all that stuff.
Anyway, it wound up that we had to write it as we
shot it. A deadly idea. There's nothing worse than
to start a picture with an unprepared script. It's
just deadly. I was in Greece for about half of it and
then I came home because I had to shoot the second
unit back here. While they were shooting there, I
did the underwater stuff, matching it to what they
were still shooting. I think my cablegrams to Negulesco, directing it by cable, must have cost something
like $50,000." 15

Due to the fact that Buddy Adler did not watch over pro-
duction as closely as Darryl Zanuck, the Fox lot became
mainly a conglomeration of individual producers, each working
on one specific project. Aside from Buddy Adler's personal
productions of INN OF THE 6th HAPPINESS or SOUTH PACIFIC,
Eugene Frenke produced HEAVEN KNOWS, MR. ALLISON and
THE BARBARIAN AND THE GEISHA; Nunnally Johnson, THE
THREE FACES OF EVE; Herbert B. Swope, Jr., THE
BRAVADOS and THREE BRAVE MAN; Samuel G. Engel,
BERNARDINE and BOY ON A DOLPHIN; and Charles Brackett,

TEN NORTH FREDERICK. There were also independent producers who received Fox financing but made their own films. David O. Selznick produced A FAREWELL TO ARMS under such a deal, and Darryl Zanuck turned out THE SUN ALSO RISES, ISLAND IN THE SUN, and the ROOTS OF HEAVEN between 1957 and 1958.

One name, however, stood out among all the others working through Twentieth Century-Fox. Amidst the troubles at the studio and in the industry, he was one of the few to flourish at the studio in the Adler years. Jerry Wald, in his own words, described his position at Fox as a "dependent independent." Fox supplied the financing, facilities, and the offices, and Wald chose and developed his own properties. He had been doing so successfully since 1956.

Jerry Wald had first been a successful and prolific writer at Warners in the early thirties. His versatility in scripting allowed him to proceed from Dick Powell musicals (20 MILLION SWEETHEARTS) to higher-budget films by the end of the decade (THE ROARING TWENTIES). When the producer of THE MAN WHO CAME TO DINNER walked off the 1941 production, Wald, who had written the script, was assigned to replace him. Some of Warner Bros. most commercially successful films of the forties were produced under Wald's aegis, including DESTINATION TOKYO, OBJECTIVE BURMA, ACROSS THE PACIFIC, and JOHNNY BELINDA. After the Warners years came partnership with Norman Krasna at R.K.O. Although some good films resulted, Wald's record did not match the one he had set at Warners.

Several years at Columbia Pictures brought forth more profitable films, including THE EDDY DUCHIN STORY, an executive producership at that studio, and a camaraderie with Buddy Adler. Wald then came to Fox for an eighteen-picture, five-year deal. He very shortly established an impressive "track record" and by 1957 had produced four films which grossed a total of $36 million. Included in this group was one of Fox's most successful films ever, PEYTON PLACE. Nunnally Johnson noted that because Wald operated his own organization, Jerry Wald Productions, and had a share in the profits of PEYTON PLACE, the studio resented him. As Johnson said, "they never forgave him for that." 16

There is also evidence that Wald did not get along well

with the studio administration and the head office in New
York. There were many disputes involving a subject very
dear to the company--money. Wald constantly complained
that Fox was not spending enough advertising dollars on
his films. He advanced funds but then found out that Fox
would not repay him an amount of $80,000. It was a trifling
amount, considering the grosses coming in on his pictures.
Bitter arguments ensued, with charges and countercharges,
but Wald was finally repaid only after threatening to break
his five-year contract. Fox, at that time, needed all the
profitable producers it could get. Wald stayed and produced
four pictures annually.

Jerry Wald had established himself as a daring producer
willing to take a risk on difficult material like PEYTON PLACE.
He very often noted that Hollywood writers lacked the courage
and incentive to come up with anything new in story matter.
Of 62 submissions in 1957, 30 stories were westerns, 20 were
melodramas. Only one possessed any sort of topicality and
this was not very original. Noted Wald, "It seems to me that
too many writers lack the courage to go out and develop
original material on their own; they are nearly all looking
for an idea to be thrown in their laps and the guarantee of
a weekly salary." 17

If Wald's description could be applied to producers,
Buddy Adler would probably fit the mold. Looking for virtual
"sure-sell" material, Adler announced month after month the
heavy purchases of novels and plays. Zanuck had always
advised the same procedure, but had also spent great efforts
in developing original material at the same time.

Even though Jerry Wald himself bought novel after novel,
the properties he developed were much more daring than anything Adler attempted. Among Wald's acquisitions following
PEYTON PLACE were THE LONG HOT SUMMER, THE SOUND
AND THE FURY, IN LOVE AND WAR, and THE BEST OF
EVERYTHING. All were fairly sophisticated adult stories
dealing with romance, marriage, and sex. An emphasis on
the latter element made THE LONG, HOT SUMMER, and THE
BEST OF EVERYTHING box-office successes.

The latter Adler years were characterized by blandness
and a general staleness in subject matter. Fox was virtually
remaking films which had been done better before. With a

lack of dynamism behind the production arm of the company, there was no doubt why the films suffered. With his health failing Buddy Adler spent less energy on the studio and eventually died of cancer, July 11, 1960.

What Twentieth Century-Fox needed at this very moment was someone aggressive and knowledgeable in production; someone who could judge screen material and assign talent to various properties; someone who could guide productions through each stage and end up with a commercial and entertaining product. This type of person was exactly what Fox did not get. With Adler's death, Spyros Skouras assigned Bob Goldstein, the head of Fox's European operation, to take over as studio boss. The position was short-lived and Skouras made a more permanent choice with Peter Levathes.

Levathes had been the head of Fox television and was not nearly equipped to run a studio. His weaknesses in production caused despair among many producers and directors on the lot. Sam Engel was particularly bitter about the appointment.

> Skouras came out and told me he was going to pick a successor to Zanuck and he spent a whole day with me.... He informed me of a board meeting Tuesday morning and he was going to let them know, then he'd call me. I took him to the airport Sunday night. Lap dissolve. Now Mr. Adler dies ... and [he] puts Levathes in. The mistake I made was I stayed there. [18]

Many agreed that to stay at Fox under the Skouras-Levathes administration was a disaster area. Philip Dunne expressed his feelings in a letter to Darryl Zanuck, then residing in Paris.

> I have so much to say now that I don't really know how to begin. So perhaps I won't begin at all, but merely tell you that you are sorely missed by all the people with any pretensions to integrity and professionalism who are still to be found at 20th Century-Fox. That includes Dick (Zanuck) himself, Charlie Brackett, Jerry Wald, Mark Robson, Walter Lang and all the rest of us who shared the stimulus of your leadership in the great days of what was once a great studio.

It also includes the old-timers among the back-lot workers. I managed to corral the cream of them for a picture I have just finished ... and I heard your name come up 20 times a day in terms of "I wish" and "if only" and "those were the days." I can no longer bear to enter the mortuary that used to be the commissary, so I bring my lunch every day and eat with the grips and electricians on the set. You have many friends you may never have heard of among these skilled and devoted people.

But the spirit is going out of them fast. We managed to rekindle a little of it on our set, to fan an ember into a brief glow, but it was tough going.... There is much more to say than I can hope to put in this letter. But there is one thing that should be said, and that is if the studio is to be saved, someone has to move--and move fast. I was never much of a company man, as you know, but now I see the studio dying before my eyes, I have conceived a great affection for the old place. After all, I have spent most of my professional life here. I almost wish the liquidators would take over and give it a quick and painless death, rather than see it eaten out from the inside by the rats, termites, lice and nameless creeping things that now infest the place. If I sound like some Cato mourning the great days of the Roman Republic, that is exactly how I feel. [19]

CHAPTER 12

■ DECLINE AND FALL ■

"I am taking a tremendous chance. I'm really sticking my neck out. But television is here, and we can co-exist profitably only by making better entertainment. We must produce more and important pictures to get people away from their home sets." [1] This proclamation was made by Spyros P. Skouras, along with the announcement that Twentieth Century-Fox would release 55 productions in 1957 and 65 in 1958. Skouras even hoped to see the year of 100 releases. He predicted a boon to the studio since it would mean expansion, full employment, and lower overhead per picture.

This type of thinking was positive to the point of unreality. In fact, the studio was just barely surviving because almost every important production went on location for most of its shooting schedule. To keep the sound stages in use, a deal was made with Robert Lippert, a theater owner and independent producer, for a series of low-budget, black-and-white CinemaScope films budgeted between $100,000 and $150,000 per feature. Lippert had produced many low-budget films and was familiar with the tight schedules and the problems involved. Lippert's company became known as Regal Films, and the process they were filmed in, Regalscope.

Regal's first feature STAGECOACH TO FURY had been released in 1956 and made a tidy profit over its minimal negative cost. This prompted Fox to expand the series. From a slate of three features that year Fox increased its investment to $4,362,000 for 23 films. World-wide grosses on this total negative cost reached $10,357,000 and soon prompted Regal to increase budgets to $250,000.

At the same time Skouras had allotted $55 million for Fox's

"A" pictures in a "frontal attack" against television. In his attack there was a notable effort to invest in projects which involved exotic or foreign settings. Much of Darryl Zanuck's ISLAND IN THE SUN was shot in the Caribbean, which boosted costs by 15 percent. With many pictures being filmed on location, there were the problems of going over budget. THE YOUNG LIONS had the misfortune to hit torrential rains in almost every location and was even struck by a locust plague, causing delays which amounted to $1.3 million, almost 50 percent of the original budget. Among the other productions which were being given the "values" of location shooting were A FAREWELL TO ARMS, THE BARBARIAN AND THE GEISHA, and THE SUN ALSO RISES.

These multimillion dollar productions soon forced producers to outdo one another. Such battles produced the "blockbuster" era and for a while these epic extravaganzas seemed to hold guaranteed audience appeal in their size, scope, and grandeur. The $10 million budget became almost a syndrome with producers, as films like AROUND THE WORLD IN 80 DAYS, THE TEN COMMANDMENTS, GIANT, and WAR AND PEACE all grabbed huge audiences and became long-running hits.

Fox, too, had its blockbusters but nothing quite in the category of the "roadshows." THE KING AND I proved that a $4.5 million production could still yield good world rentals of $11 million. SOUTH PACIFIC, which was a co-production with the Magna Theater Corporation, returned $17.5 million domestically on a $5.5 million budget. Producers assumed that the more a film cost, the more it would make. Thus, the catchline "millions in the making" became commonplace. Whether it was millions of dollars, francs, yen, or lire often was overlooked as the studios tried to equate prestige with seven-digit figures.

Blockbusters, however, soon proved to make competition difficult for the major studios. If a roadshow picture were successful it might occupy one theater in a limited two-performance-a-day engagement for a year or more. It would siphon audiences away from the less-important product, and sometimes make it impossible for another film to get that prestige engagement. Many "A" films ended up in saturation playdates in many theaters, the type of playoff generally relegated to exploitation features.

Suddenly every studio was thinking "roadshow." However, many resulting features cost so much that they could never earn back their negative cost after the deductions for advertising and promotional costs. Fred Zinnemann had begun shooting THE OLD MAN AND THE SEA at Warner Bros., but his footage was deemed unusable and John Sturges was brought in to reshoot the film. When finally completed, the production cost $4 million so the studio planned to release it as a roadshow. Problems arose, though, from its scant 86-minute running time. An overture was added and the roadshow engagement policy was tested, but failed along with the film. Since the epic proportions audiences were accustomed to were lacking in this personal story, the film was a quick disaster.

Bigness failed as well in Warners' MOBY DICK, a $4.5 million Technicolor adventure adaptation of the Melville classic. Ventures such as this proved that lavish entertainment on the wide screen did not always mean a guaranteed return on the investment.

No studio learned this lesson more painfully than Fox. Since blockbusters also brought extensive financial risks, Spyros Skouras decided to stay with the "middle picture." These films were bigger than the average "A" film, but not as expensive as the blockbuster.

Skouras pursued this policy of what he called "double A" pictures, which included such films as INN OF THE 6TH HAPPINESS, A CERTAIN SMILE, THE ROOTS OF HEAVEN, THE YOUNG LIONS, THE HUNTERS, and THE BRAVADOS. In early 1958, though, there was a disappointing audience shift away from the "middle picture." Since Fox had directed its entire program towards this type of vehicle, returns were disappointing. The "middle picture" was found to be the most risky of all film ventures, since audience support was not quite strong enough to guarantee returns on a film budgeted between $1 million and $4 million.

Suddenly, Spyros Skouras became very concerned about the remainder of his 1958 program of pictures. Even at the head offices in New York, concern was expressed over the wisdom of such an enormous program costing so many millions. Very simply, the slate of Adler-Skouras productions was not capturing a proportionate share of film-going audiences.

Since roadshows were tying up theaters for very lengthy periods, new Fox product was not getting the same treatment from exhibitors as with the introduction of CinemaScope. Certain theaters became prestige houses and ran only road-shows, and it was in these houses that Skouras wanted his films to play. The problem became so acute at Fox that Skouras had to appeal to theater-owners across the country, saying that he had once "bailed out" exhibitors and now needed to have the favor returned.

Skouras, a theater man himself, should have understood the breed he was dealing with. Survival in the theater bus-iness was based on making money and because Fox's pictures did not attract large audiences, little help was forthcoming. In an attempt to cash in on the roadshow policy for survival, Skouras decided that his more important releases would initially go out in key cities on a reserved-seat basis. The Fox organization also felt that this would give the films the added publicity boost needed in subsequent runs. A roadshow was usually better known by the public due to its initial publicity hype and a long run.

THE BARBARIAN AND THE GEISHA, THE ROOTS OF HEAVEN, and THE DIARY OF ANNE FRANK were the first films to be tested under this new policy. Fox was immediately thwarted, though, when the ABC-Paramount Theaters refused to play the films as roadshows and claimed that a general mass release would yield greater revenue. This was a nice way of saying that the films just were not worth the inflated "roadshow" admissions. These films were ultimately released on a general playoff to universally poor results. THE ROOTS OF HEAVEN had gone $1 million over its $2.4 million budget, but returned only $3 million domestically. THE BARBARIAN AND THE GEISHA did not even bring in $1.5 worldwide and THE DIARY OF ANNE FRANK fared only a little better. These were the pictures which were going to save Twentieth Century-Fox.

Surveying the returns for 1958, one striking fact appears. Aside from SOUTH PACIFIC (which was a co-production) and PEYTON PLACE, produced by Jerry Wald Productions, the most profitable film of the year turned out to be a low-budget exploitation horror film called THE FLY. On its budget of approximately $500,000, this film showed a 300 percent return of $1.5 million, by far better than any other

Fox-produced film of 1958. The success of THE FLY, which was given a heavy advertising campaign and saturation bookings, pointed out a severe deficiency in Fox's planning. Whereas the company had geared itself for big profits from multimillion dollar budgets, the best showing came from a low-budget film. It would have seemed obvious that more of these low-risk gambles should be taken. The Regal program had proven to be profitable when budgets remained low. Why not take a chance on ten $300,000 features rather than one $3 million project?

This attitude had been uncultivated at Twentieth Century-Fox and could be traced back to the introduction of Cinema-Scope. With the studio geared towards the high-cost "values" of wide-screen pictures, the smaller dramatic films were completely ignored. When Darryl Zanuck sent around his "CinemaScope memo," all other projects were abandoned. Among these was ON THE WATERFRONT, which Elia Kazan and Budd Schulberg had been developing at Fox. Unfortunately, Zanuck decided that the film simply did not fit CinemaScope proportions and the project went to Columbia where Harry Cohn had one of his most profitable films of the decade.

Throughout the fifites, every company made some dramatic, lower-budget features and some were astoundingly successful. United Artists, which never had the same strength as the larger majors, released a group of black-and-white films which had no pretensions to blockbusterdom. Some of them turned out to earn more than many of Fox's supposed "double A" pictures. THE MOON IS BLUE, MARTY, TWELVE ANGRY MEN, PATHS OF GLORY, and ATTACK were all distinguished films at the time of their release. For United Artists, they were also more profitable than the expensive ventures like THE PRIDE AND THE PASSION or SOLOMON AND SHEBA.

Fox never picked up on the growing market for "small pictures" and made a mistake in doing so. The industry was constantly changing and audiences in the major cities were making films like MARTY or THE SWEET SMELL OF SUCCESS very profitable indeed. It was in small towns that these films were considered to be "poison" at the box office, and small towns had always been the "bread and butter" of the industry. At this time small town theaters were closing in droves due to the adverse effects of television. The "bread and butter" market virtually disappeared and it was not long before the major cities could make or break the success of a film entirely on their own. This meant that films would be made primarily for the key runs. Regardless of these changes, Fox's policies stayed the same.

Fox soon experienced another milestone in its history. In 1958, with foreign markets growing and domestic ones shrinking, foreign rentals surpassed the U.S.-Canada take by $500,000. It was the first time Fox recorded such an event, but it was a somewhat ominous sign of the future.

Although certain films were earning rentals upwards of $25 million, the average costs made many unprofitable. With overall profits dropping steadily, new sources of income had to be found. Television had already used up a total of 9,000 titles from various studios and a sale of post-1948 films became inevitable.

Another drain on funds was the extremely large Fox organization. The many distribution offices around the world needed large staffs to control bookings, film shipment, and storage warehouses for thousands of prints had to be available. Nothing, though, was quite as expensive as the cost of operating the studio. With many unused sound stages, and an extensive backlot of standing sets, there was not enough revenue to make it profitable.

It became obvious that location shooting was a phenomenon which would not pass and that sound stages would never be used again as much as in the past. Declining production also made studio space more expensive per feature. With these burgeoning problems, Spyros Skouras decided, in November 1958, to sell 176 acres of its Westwood studio for the development of Century City. Webb and Knapp of New York paid $40 million for the acreage. Fox also leased the Sunset studio to Four Star Television and moved T.C.F. Television to the Westwood lot.

By 1959, it was estimated that Fox films had to gross $100 million annually just to meet the costs of the company. This meant that almost $2 million was spent weekly on the production and distribution of its films. When grosses dropped, it became obvious that overhead would have to be cut. Smaller profits meant the program for 1959 would be sharply curtailed to a total of 35 releases, of which only 16 were major productions. The remaining 19 features were filler product.

On January 29, 1959, Spyros P. Skouras, president of Twentieth Century-Fox, announced a 25 percent cost slash throughout the entire operation. Almost immediately, nearly 1,000 workers were cut from the payroll. Executives were forced to take a 50 percent cut in salary if they earned over $1,000 weekly. This was the first time in six years that such measures had been taken. Similar cuts had been made in 1952, just before the coming of CinemaScope. Skouras also added that the cuts would remain in effect until there was an improvement of conditions at the studio and within the company.

If conditions were to improve, it was not to be in 1959 with a release schedule filled with productions doomed to failure. Such major films as THE MAN WHO UNDERSTOOD WOMEN, THESE THOUSAND HILLS, and BELOVED INFIDEL grossed less than $1 million domestically, putting them deeply in the red.

The top-grossing film of the year was JOURNEY TO THE CENTER OF THE EARTH, with $8 million in world rentals on a cost of $3.4 million. Following in descending order were SAY ONE FOR ME, RALLY ROUND THE FLAG, BOYS, and BLUE DENIM. Darryl Zanuck's production of COMPULSION was a minor success in the world market, but its moderate budget made it profitable.

Then came the losers including THE DIARY OF ANNE FRANK ($3.5 million budget), WARLOCK ($2.4 million), HOUND DOG MAN ($1 million), THE REMARKABLE MR. PENNYPACKER ($1.5 million), WOMAN OBSESSED ($1.7 million), and HOLIDAY FOR LOVERS ($2 million). On a slate of twenty major releases, only two could be considered bonafide profit makers, JOURNEY TO THE CENTER OF THE EARTH and BLUE DENIM.

To gain additional funds, Fox made a deal with William Zeckendorf, a land-developing giant, to sell the remaining 208 acres of studio land in Westwood for $60 million. Fox leased some of the land back and Zeckendorf kept all the mineral and oil rights.

More financial disasters followed in 1960 with a package of properties Buddy Adler had purchased. Out of five projects, only one, THE BILLIONAIRE, written by Norman Krasna, came to fruition. It became a Marilyn Monroe vehicle which cost $3.6 million and the year's biggest disappointment. Even though LET'S MAKE LOVE was directed by George Cukor, reviews were unencouraging and audiences scarce enough to make it Monroe's first Fox movie ever to lose money. The big "roadshow" production of CAN-CAN, which Fox had been scheduling for six years, finally completed production and went into release on a "hardticket" two-a-day performance basis. With Frank Sinatra, Shirley MacLaine, Maurice Chevalier, and a Cole Porter score, the film did not return its $5 million cost.

Fox seemed beyond rescue and no release could help the ailing company. Only two films showed any real returns in 1960: SINK THE BISMARK, and THE LOST WORLD. FROM THE TERRACE and NORTH TO ALASKA performed well but on high negative costs which cut profits to a minimum. Samuel G. Engel's THE STORY OF RUTH was a supposed blockbuster which fizzled, largely due to casting problems. Fox had certain "stars" under contract and producers were encouraged to utilize available talent. Among these contractees were such non-boxoffice names as Stuart Whitman, Stephen Boyd, Fabian, Ray Stricklyn, David Hedison, Suzy Parker, Bradford Dillman, and Dolores Michaels. Potential hits were ruined by the "casting imperative" of the studio administration. Fox only had three films with any of the top 20 most popular actors and actresses of the year, and only one of these films lured audiences, NORTH TO ALASKA starring John Wayne.

With the bottom already reached in 1960, Fox proceeded, incredibly, to sink lower in 1961. If the previous year's product was undistinguished, 1961 brought forth a new low in picture-making at the studio. Audiences obviously sensed the change. Based on Variety's top grossing films, Fox had a total of eight films which yielded domestic rentals over $1 million, for a sum of $17.7 million, compared to a total of $57.1 million in 1956. This was the lowest amount since 1945 without considering inflation in admission prices. The coup de grace was yet to come, in the form of the most expensive motion picture made by a major American studio--CLEOPATRA.

CHAPTER 13

■ THE CLEOPATRA YEARS ■

I think that good films are not made by a massive
display of a thousand horses galloping across the
screen ... but more on content and intent and
character, and how those characters relate to the
audience [declared Jerry Wald]. Intent and content
are far more important than all the massive sets and
all the gimmick pictures that you can think of with
the eyeglasses and wide screen, small screen; that
doesn't mean a thing. A big screen only shows up
a small idea much larger.
    There's no such thing as a star that's going to
carry a film for me. My star's the subject matter
... I've seen too many stars be fooled into thinking
that they're so important that they can take a bad
story and pull it over the top of the box-office hill.
It cannot be done. And conversely, I know of many
a good story that's made a bad actor into a good
actor. [1]

Jerry Wald was probably a better choice for studio head
than anyone since Darryl Zanuck. His tastes were similar,
and he had Zanuck's flair for commercial product. As Wald
was saying these very words to Arthur Knight on a TV
Odyssey show, Twentieth Century-Fox was engaged in exactly
the type of film Jerry Wald disliked. A film that took almost
four years to make, two directors, two producers, three production heads, two company presidents, and countless writers--
CLEOPATRA survived it all. But Fox almost did not survive
CLEOPATRA.

With so many people approving and disapproving budgets

140

and making decisions, CLEOPATRA could never be anything but a fiasco. There was one very obvious fact which emerged during the production of the $40 million film. The Twentieth Century-Fox film organization had broken down into a completely inefficient producer of motion pictures.

Originally budgeted at $4 million, the period love story was to have been a CinemaScope vehicle for contract star Joan Collins. When director Rouben Mamoulian was brought into the project by producer Walter Wanger, Collins was dropped and Elizabeth Taylor was signed.

On Spyros Skouras' orders, sets were built in London to duplicate ancient Egypt. CLEOPATRA was under control and in the usual stages of preparation. Until mid-1960 there was nothing untoward about the production. Fox had made more expensive films before, and other companies were slating biblical epics like BEN-HUR at $15 million. However, when the June 17, 1960, start date rolled around, the sets, casting, crew, and script were not yet ready. Shooting was postponed until August and that date, as well, was missed. Soon studio executives were taking an unrealistic approach to the film's budget. Although nearly $2 million had been spent in London, the total amount assigned to the film was slightly over $4 million.

Mamoulian finally started shooting some camera tests in late September, but two problems quickly intervened. One was the weather, which turned notoriously bad in the fall; the other was Elizabeth Taylor, who became ill. Shooting was postponed again indefinitely, and other writers were signed to finish the script. Nunnally Johnson had been hired by Skouras and Bob Goldstein (who had been at Fox since Buddy Adler's death in July), but Mamoulian wanted to work with his own writer. So Nunnally Johnson was paid $140,000 for writing two words--his name on a contract.

By mid-January, there were plans to resume shooting in London. Skouras was trying to settle insurance claims for lost production of between $2 million and $3 million. Finally, when all problems were being resolved, new obstacles arose. Taylor and Peter Finch, her co-star, claimed that the final script was unacceptable.

By this time, Skouras, Goldstein, and production executive

Sid Rogell were issuing charges due to the delay, and
Mamoulian was issuing countercharges. There was talk about
replacing the director, but Mamoulian quit before this could
be done. One week after he left, Joseph L. Mankiewicz was
hired as director, and would also supervise the screenwriting.
At an overhead rate of $45,000 daily, CLEOPATRA was sche-
duled once again for an April 4, 1961, start.

Illness once again took hold of Elizabeth Taylor who was
rushed to a hospital for an emergency tracheotomy. This
left Taylor unable to continue as CLEOPATRA for a least
three months. Production would begin in Hollywood in the
summer months to accommodate Taylor's recuperation and then
move to Rome and Egypt for location work. The $600,000
sets in London would be torn down, and the total cost to
the production by now was nearly $5 million.

With Fox in dire financial trouble with other films, everyone at the studio agreed that CLEOPATRA was the needed
big hit of the coming season. More money was allotted first
by Bob Goldstein, and then by Peter Levathes. Rather than
give up, Fox was going to pour more money into what appeared at the time to be a potential blockbuster. A $14
million estimated budget, however, frightened Skouras, and
he continued to present his stockholders with the unreal
$8 million figure.

November 11, 1961, brought a new budget without the
35 percent overhead charge, which totalled $15,214,348.21.
Producer Wanger did not think the company would stay within
that budget for long. Time proved him to be absolutely
correct. Delays by May 1962 brought the estimated cost of
CLEOPATRA up to $30 million--the most expensive film ever
made! Due to this one film, Fox was on the verge of bankruptcy.

The mistake which Skouras made so often during the
shooting of CLEOPATRA was that when problems arose, he
threw more money in. Skouras had taken on a production which
had gotten out of control. There was no way to shut it
down and declare it a loss, since that would mean a total
write-off of between $10 million and $15 million. Fox was also
committed to many contracts which had to be paid in any
event. There was no way to know that the film would eventually cost $40 million at the outset, so Skouras was not alone

to blame. However, with his lack of control and experience in production, he had no way to solve the film's problems.

There was probably more wasteful spending on CLEO-PATRA than any other film in history. In 1979 dollars, CLEOPATRA's cost stacks up against even HEAVEN'S GATE profligacy. Not only were writers, actors, and set costs unbelievably inflated, but Skouras also bought the rights to a negligible Italian version of CLEOPATRA for $500,000 just to keep it off American screens. The constant travels of Fox executives to the many locations helped to run up steep charges.

If there was ever a worse time to get involved in such a disaster, it was 1961. There were only two partially successful films, one produced by Jerry Wald, RETURN TO PEYTON PLACE, and Irwin Allen's VOYAGE TO THE BOTTOM OF THE SEA. Skouras had assigned such low-return titles as THE SECOND TIME AROUND, SNOW WHITE AND THE THREE STOOGES, ALL HANDS ON DECK, THE FIERCEST HEART, and FRANCIS OF ASSISI. Although each of these was designed for family audiences, neither adults nor children attended any of them in great numbers. Out of 24 releases, at least half did not earn back their negative costs. As a result, Fox showed a loss of $22,532,084, for 1961, the most red ink in the history of the company.

With all of the company's resources being poured into CLEOPATRA, there was little left over for other productions, and the number of slated projects dropped sharply in 1962. If most of 1961's films were geared towards family audiences, the following year was just the opposite. The slate for 1962 included predominantly adult material such as BACHELOR FLAT, THE STRIPPER, LISA, MADISON AVENUE, SATAN NEVER SLEEPS, TENDER IS THE NIGHT, THE INNOCENTS, HEMINGWAY'S ADVENTURES OF A YOUNG MAN, and SOMETHING'S GOT TO GIVE. There were four titles for family audiences including a third remake of STATE FAIR starring Pat Boone, THE LION, GIGOT, and Irwin Allen's FIVE WEEKS IN A BALLOON.

Fox had reached the very bottom with not one of these films returning its cost. Some were inexpensive failures, but others, which were expected to be hits, turned out to be the biggest disasters.

Among them were the catastrophic TENDER IS THE NIGHT, HEMINGWAY'S ADVENTURES OF A YOUNG MAN, SATAN NEVER SLEEPS and STATE FAIR. On an aggregate total cost of these four films of $15.5 million, Fox made only $10 million in world rentals.

SOMETHING'S GOT TO GIVE proved to be a further embarrassment to Skouras and Levathes, adding to the frustration of stockholders. Marilyn Monroe had started shooting with co-star Dean Martin and director George Cukor. Monroe began showing up late, missing days, and disagreeing with Cukor. When the budget began skyrocketing in the same way as CLEOPATRA, Skouras and Levathes decided to shut down production and suffer a "mere" $2 million loss. Shortly thereafter, Monroe committed suicide, and the project was put aside, even though several days' footage had been shot.

Spyros Skouras could not go on indefinitely announcing CLEOPATRA costs along with disastrous revenues on other pictures before stockholders would become enraged. Skouras was as aware of the problems as anyone else and soon decided it might be more appropriate for a new administration to tackle the problems plaguing Fox. But who was to take over the presidency?

Darryl Zanuck had been in Paris for several years, making films through his D.F.Z. Productions. When he left Fox in 1956, he had scheduled three films, including ISLAND IN THE SUN, I MARRIED JOSEPH STALIN, and PARRIS ISLAND. Due to various problems, only ISLAND was filmed, and became a substantial success. Zanuck's next venture, THE SUN ALSO RISES, did fairly well at the box office, but had a large budget nut to crack.

Zanuck had also become romantically involved with Juliette Greco while producing THE SUN ALSO RISES, and spent the next few years trying to make her a star as he did with Bella Darvi. Greco was cast in subsequent Zanuck films, THE ROOTS OF HEAVEN and CRACK IN THE MIRROR. Both were artistically ambitious but neither was very successful financially or critically. Between these two films, Zanuck placed his son Richard in charge of the production of COMPULSION. Fortunately, the courtroom drama scored well with critics, thus revitalizing the Zanuck reputation.

Soon after, Darryl F. Zanuck reached his lowest point as a producer of commercial product. CRACK IN THE MIRROR and THE BIG GAMBLE were both monumental box-office failures and a blow to Zanuck's credibility as an independent producer. Both featured Juliette Greco in vanity showcases. But finally, the Greco romance ended and soon after Darryl Zanuck turned his energies towards the stupendous production of THE LONGEST DAY.

When Zanuck had finished cutting THE LONGEST DAY, he became concerned about the misfortunes back at the Fox studio. Being the largest shareholder in the company, Zanuck and his family had the most to lose if Fox went into bankruptcy due to mismanagement by the Skouras administration.

After much negotiation and discussion, Darryl Zanuck returned to New York and was appointed president of Twentieth Century-Fox. Spyros P. Skouras became a nominal chairman of the board. When Zanuck arrived back at his desk, there was more chaos than when Twentieth Century had merged with Fox. Budgets were out of control, the studio was in deep financial trouble, there was no consistent policy for making pictures, and overhead was much too high. In the six short years Zanuck had been away from the studio, Fox had been transformed from a profitable picture producer and distributor into a sheer disaster area, both financially and artistically. The burden now rested on Darryl Zanuck to once again put the studio back in the big league.

CHAPTER 14

■ DARRYL ZANUCK RIDES AGAIN ■

The industry had changed greatly in Hollywood during Darryl Zanuck's absence. The major studios, once the bastions of commercial film production, were giving way to the new independence of producers, directors, writers, and actors. With production down drastically from the golden post-war years, many former studio contractees were forced to work independently. Those who managed to turn out profitable films were the ones in constant demand, while other careers were on the wane.

By 1962, most major actors and directors had formed their own corporations, so that deals were no longer put together simply by gathering together various people under contract. Now, each element of a project had to be individually assembled. If an actor did not like a director, the one who had more strength in a project would decide the outcome. Producers now were forced more than ever to cater to the whims of actors and directors who could also be their bosses. Writers in demand could pick and choose projects as they had never done before, while lesser talents would slave away for independent producers or for television at lower wages.

Salaries had also skyrocketed with a new breed of superstars and super-productions like BEN-HUR, SPARTACUS, WEST SIDE STORY, LAWRENCE OF ARABIA, MUTINY ON THE BOUNTY, and of course, CLEOPATRA. Stars of renown could command between $500,000 and $1 million for roles in such high-budget films to which they were vitally important. No studio wanted to risk $15 million without a stellar cast. Participation also became a very popular element in deals, not only for actors but for producers and

directors as well. In some cases, a percentage was imperative for the deal as Elizabeth Taylor made clear. CLEOPA-
TRA brought her a precedent-setting 10 percent of the film's
box-office gross. In others, participation was offered to
make the deal more enticing, as when Skouras convinced
Samuel Engel to form his own production company to make
THE STORY OF RUTH and THE LION. Marlon Brando had
signed a deal at Paramount which would give him 100 percent
of profits from ONE EYED JACKS (1961) while Paramount
completely financed the project but settled for only a distribution fee of 27 percent of returns.

When participation became so predominant, participants
became aware of terminology. Gross had always been loosely
understood as the amount given the distributor by the theater.
Now, gross became the term for the amount taken in at the
theater box office. Theater gross, therefore, gave an un-
diluted chunk of money to whomever held a share. This
method of participation came about in self defense--to protect
one's share from the nebulous accounting of major studios
between the time receipts left the theater and funnelled down
to the producer. The majors were notorious for conjuring
up charges against the net remittances, which would cut
down the value of a percentage. The only way a participation of net profits could be protected was if the film were
such an outright smash the studio could not possibly hide
all the money.

Along with the spiralling costs went labor, as unions
tried to protect their members' livelihoods. With work scarcer
those few who worked demanded higher rates. Studios
could no longer afford to keep fully staffed departments,
so crews were assembled for individual films. This raised
the cost of a skilled crew.

Aside from the problems in production, distribution had
changed as well. Audiences were still dropping as movies
continued to be sold to television and admission prices steadily
rose. With fewer films to see and a higher price to pay,
families stayed home to watch free television. With a constantly spreading affluence in America, there were many
other forms of entertainment available to the public. Outdoor
sports were beginning to attract more leisure dollars every
year. Bowling, amusement parks, country clubs, and resorts
were on the increase as roads and superhighways linked the

country from one end to another. There was a lot more competition for the entertainment dollar.

To lure audiences to the theaters, films had to have some special quality--either great performances, spectacle, a terrific script, or sex. In short, movies could not get along on past glories. The family audience, always staple for motion pictures, was dropping off rapidly. This resulted in more sophisticated adult stories and situations. Such films as THE APARTMENT, THE CHILDREN'S HOUR, LOLITA, ADVISE AND CONSENT, ALL FALL DOWN, SUMMER AND SMOKE, ROOM AT THE TOP, DAYS OF WINE AND ROSES, SWEET BIRD OF YOUTH, WALK ON THE WILD SIDE, DAVID AND LISA, THE WORLD OF SUZIE WONG, and SPLENDOR IN THE GRASS were much franker in their treatment of adult relationships.

In addition to satisfying a narrower, more sophisticated, and more particular audience, the studios had the problem, with lower production, of depending more on each individual film. In the case of CLEOPATRA, the entire Fox organization was riding on one picture. It was a situation which was not particular to Fox over the next few years.

Darryl Zanuck was aware of all the pitfalls when he returned victoriously to the studio in mid-1962. His first decision was to shut down the studio and to cease all production--including Fox's unfinished $30 million epic. Zanuck cancelled all shooting on CLEOPATRA until he could screen all the footage and decide what to do with it.

Zanuck did supervise the production of subsequent sequences shot in Spain to complete the film and after spending an additional $2 million CLEOPATRA finally saw the last day of shooting. The next problem to contend with was the reorganization of the studio. Stan Hough, vice-president in charge of studio operations at the time, remembers the changeover vividly:

> We cut back in all departments of the studio. We fired as we went and laid off as we went. In the old days they even carried a symphony orchestra under contract, with 40 or 50 men. Obviously that had to go. At one point, I think we had 200 policemen on this lot. The last time I looked at the figures, we

had trimmed that back to 35. Janitorial services
were curtailed to a reasonable degree. Not every
office had private phones. There were all sorts
of luxuries which existed which we really trimmed
back. We took a hard look at every department.
The department heads had assistants, and assistants
to assistants, and we cut them back. It was very
hard and difficult, heartbreaking in many cases,
because these fellows had been here many years. [1]

Producers and writers still at the studio were given
their leave as well, so that the cost-cutting was done across
the board. Top and bottom were affected equally, and in
this sometimes ruthless way, Darryl Zanuck hoped to considerably trim studio overhead. While he tended to company
matters in New York, Darryl Zanuck left Richard Zanuck
as his representative at the studio, and those who kept
their jobs were elated.

Stan Hough continued,

I think the core of Fox employees, who had been at
the studio for many years, welcomed Darryl back,
and his son Dick, because they were picture-makers.
Most of them, people like myself, felt that we had
been in the hands of everything but picture-makers
in the past ten years. So we welcomed Zanuck back
because, most of all, we thought he could make successful pictures. [2]

There was no doubt about the revitalization of Darryl
Zanuck's career in the fall of 1962. With the release of his
personal production of THE LONGEST DAY, any doubts
about his abilities were put back into storage. Zanuck's
epic portrayal of the Allied landing at Normandy exceeded
anything he had yet attempted. Working from Cornelius
Ryan's best-selling novel, Zanuck cast as many international
stars as he could sign. Shooting schedules were revised to
accommodate such well-known stars as John Wayne, Richard
Burton, Henry Fonda, Robert Mitchum, Robert Ryan, Rod
Steiger, Peter Lawford, and Eddie Albert.

Production on THE LONGEST DAY was an enormous
undertaking and Zanuck engaged three directors, who shared
credit equally. Ken Annakin handled the English-language

scenes, while Bernhard Wicki directed the German-language sequences. To add to the realistic atmosphere, all of the German sequences carried subtitles, an element seldom used in American films. For the many lengthy and complex action sequences, Zanuck entrusted Andrew Marton, a veteran second-unit director of large scale scenes, with the planning and execution. Marton undertook the assignment as commanding general and performed equally well. The results were by far the largest grosses in Fox's history. THE LONGEST DAY helped put Fox back into business. Darryl Zanuck was again free to do as he pleased, without Skouras' interference. Richard Zanuck, who had grown up at the studio, was being groomed for the executive vice-presidency and the responsibilities of production.

As he had done in 1935, Darryl Zanuck reevaluated all productions from the standpoint of budget and potential. There was one major difference between the period after the merger and Zanuck's recent return. The studio now turned out far fewer films and there was no large staff of writers and producers to assign projects to. Now a picture would be packaged step by step, depending on its own special needs, requiring more time and individual attention.

Fox suffered another loss with the death of Jerry Wald in July, 1962. His immediate projects were discontinued and a favorite of his, based on Robert Kennedy's THE ENEMY WITHIN, was shelved by Zanuck. This was the type of project which Zanuck would have relished in the golden late 1940's, when 40 other commercial productions would pay for a controversial subject. The 1960's had brought new and expensive trends in filmmaking permitting only a few films yearly. Each had to be as commercial as possible.

Examining the production chart, Zanuck pored over remnants of the Skouras regime. From many scripts Zanuck selected TAKE HER, SHE'S MINE, written by Nunnally Johnson, based on a play by Henry and Phoebe Ephron. Johnson had completed the script to Peter Levathes' approval in early 1962, but Zanuck felt that the story of young American girl at an American college would have no foreign appeal. Zanuck demanded that under contractual agreement Johnson would have to rewrite the script. Johnson was reluctant since he had been paid for the job and his work had been approved but Zanuck persisted, straining their long-time friendship.

Finally, Johnson agreed to rework the story, using a Parisian setting for the college.

TAKE HER, SHE'S MINE was the first production of the new Zanuck administration and it starred James Stewart, Sandra Dee, and Audrey Meadows. A relatively safe, commercial project, it was directed by a long-time Fox alumnus, Henry Koster, who had guided THE ROBE, A MAN CALLED PETER, and many others. Other "sure-fire" projects were developed as well. Doris Day, the industry's top drawing female star, was teamed with James Garner in a light, domestic comedy, MOVE OVER, DARLING. The screenplay had been salvaged from the ill-fated SOMETHING'S GOT TO GIVE. Stars by the carload were brought to the studio for former agent Arthur P. Jacobs' production of WHAT A WAY TO GO, showcasing the talents of Shirley MacLaine, Paul Newman, Robert Mitchum, Dean Martin, Gene Kelly, Bob Cummings, and Dick Van Dyke.

While Zanuck could cancel those projects he felt would be duds, he could do nothing about productions already rolling. Among them, THE CONDEMNED OF ALTONA, SODOM AND GOMORRAH, and THE LEOPARD which had been made as co-productions with Titanus Films in Rome. Co-productions meant that costs were shared in producing the film, yet Fox had to pay for advertising and print costs to get these subjects into release. None created any excitement at the box office. Other minor films were produced under a continuing agreement with Robert Lippert's Associated Producers: THE DAY MARS INVADED EARTH, HOUSE OF THE DAMNED, POLICE NURSE, THE YOUNG GUNS OF TEXAS, and THE YOUNG SWINGERS.

There were also "pick-up" deals, which meant that Fox bought the American rights to foreign films, either because it was cheaper than producing a second feature for a double bill, as in the case of THE LOVES OF SALAMMBO, or to take advantage of the growing market for foreign "art" films such as LA BONNE SOUPE or DIARY OF A CHAMBERMAID.

No matter where Fox managed to get its product, the top films of 1963 were those which Darryl Zanuck had initiated. Aggregate rentals for two successful films, MOVE OVER, DARLING, and TAKE HER, SHE'S MINE reached $9.4 million domestically, or almost twice their negative cost. With foreign

rentals, these films performed very well, indeed. With THE
LONGEST DAY generating most of its $30 million in world
rentals in 1963, the future looked bright. These were the
"miracle" pictures which kept Fox alive yet another year in
its tenuous existence.

For all the money spent on CLEOPATRA, Fox could have
made ten fairly high-budget films and have a tenfold chance
of coming up with hits. By the law of averages, one film
out of the ten would have been a big hit, two probably substantial successes, two more moderate successes, two break-
evens, and three failures. Even if CLEOPATRA made $100
million, three times the highest domestic figure ever, it would
have only been moderately successful. Breakeven, alone, was
set around $68 million at the box office and that was based
on roadshow runs where the remittance to distributors was
very high. Even though admission was set at an all-time
record of $3, audiences would have to number approximately
25 million in the first-run alone to make the film profitable.
There were not many films that demanded so much audience
support just to break even. Then there was the havoc the
production had wreaked at the studio. How many productions
suffered from cutbacks because of CLEOPATRA? How much
land was sold off which could have been worth more as studio
backlot or as development under Fox ownership? How many
projects could not be attempted because there were not sufficient funds? The questions are endless when it comes to
the many aspects of Fox that CLEOPATRA impacted on.

When CLEOPATRA was released in June 1963, audience
response was initially strong due to interest sparked by a
publicized Elizabeth Taylor-Richard Burton romance, but
tapered off alarmingly. Audiences made the final decision.
CLEOPATRA would not break even from its initial release
and the decision was final. European audiences reacted similarly, and grosses did not meet Fox's optimistic expectations.
Total domestic rentals set a record for Twentieth Century-
Fox, but it was not a record held high with pride. The
$26 million in U.S. and Canada rentals was higher than THE
LONGEST DAY, but that film only cost $7.75 million. Fox
did not even set any historical records with the top gross
still held by M-G-M's GONE WITH THE WIND. Taking all
factors into consideration, the only way CLEOPATRA could
have been a true hit would be to make up for all the disaster left in its wake. This would never be. Nevertheless,

the film did finally show a minor profit after it was sold to television in 1965, for a 1972 airing, for a reported $5 million.

With CLEOPATRA out of the way, Darryl Zanuck could now attempt to move his company forward. Since motion pictures were now virtually all shot on location, Zanuck felt no burning need to be at the studio watching over every production. Richard Zanuck read the scripts, put together the package of stars, director, and writer, and prepared the deals. Darryl Zanuck was consulted for final approval. For the most part, this system worked well. Both Zanucks would follow the production from a financial standpoint, checking that it was on budget, then would view the final product. Darryl Zanuck, after CLEOPATRA, was not as interested in recutting films as he had been in earlier years.

Competition played a great factor in Darryl Zanuck's slate of pictures for the next two years. Roadshows had been doing excellent business since 1960 with smash returns from the likes of WEST SIDE STORY, HOW THE WEST WAS WON, IT'S A MAD, MAD, MAD, MAD WORLD, EL CID, SPARTACUS, and LAWRENCE OF ARABIA. There had also been some very costly failures including MUTINY ON THE BOUNTY, but experiences with roadshows had generally been positive. Other studios continued to invest heavily in roadshows. Warner Bros. would release the $15 million MY FAIR LADY in 1964, and had scheduled CAMELOT for production. United Artists has $30 million tied up in THE GREATEST STORY EVER TOLD and THE HALLELUJAH TRAIL both in preparation. Paramount announced CIRCUS WORLD, THE FALL OF THE ROMAN EMPIRE and BECKET. The road seemed to point to roadshows, characterized by their large budgets, all-star casts, and 70mm stereophonic presentations.

Twentieth Century-Fox was not going to be left behind, and embarked on the most ambitious, let alone most expensive, of all studio programs. Darryl Zanuck proudly announced that his company's 1964-1965 schedule would include such 70mm, Todd-AO pictures as THE AGONY AND THE ECSTASY, THE DAY CUSTER FELL, JUSTINE, THE SAND PEBBLES, THE SOUND OF MUSIC, and THOSE MAGNIFICENT MEN IN THEIR FLYING MACHINES.

Being roadshow productions, many of these films would

take much longer in preproduction, actual shooting, and
then editing and scoring than the normal film. To be sure,
there was much more at stake and no producer would be
foolish enough to rush a roadshow into production. Thus,
there was a production gap in the 1964 release season. Fox's
"major" product that year was fairly undistinguished but
its top-grossing film, WHAT A WAY TO GO, headed the year
at $6.1 million. GOODBYE, CHARLIE headed the list of
remaining films, none of which produced results of any mag-
nitude.

Twentieth Century-Fox was completely overshadowed by
its competitors in 1964 and was oblivious to a changing market. For one thing, British films which had struggled for
years to attract American audiences finally came into their
own. This was, in large part, aided by the great amount
of cultural attention paid to Britain in the early to mid-1960's.
Music, dress, theater, and even fads spread from Britain to
North America with startling speed and influence. Since
young adults and teenagers made up a large part of the
movie-going population in the domestic market, British-made
films suddenly became top box-office attractions.

United Artists virtually monopolized this newly-found
market with shrewd production planning and found itself
with a number of hit films. Such 1964-65 titles as TOM
JONES, A SHOT IN THE DARK, A HARD DAY'S NIGHT, the
James Bond series of DR. NO, FROM RUSSIA WITH LOVE,
all low-cost negatives, and the medium-range GOLDFINGER
met with astounding success. Suddenly, new actors burst
upon the scene and within months became international stars.
Sean Connery, Peter Sellers, Julie Christie, Albert Finney,
and the Beatles joined directors like Tony Richardson, Richard
Lester, Clive Donner, Guy Hamilton, and Terence Young
among the most commercially successful talents in the business.

Other companies were quick to become involved in British-
made films with young talent and many were very profitable.
Universal's low budget spy thriller, THE IPCRESS FILE and
Paramount's ALFIE established Michael Caine as a new star,
and Terence Stamp and Samantha Eggar, who had appeared
in several previous films, rose to stardom with THE COLLEC-
TOR.

Regardless of trends, changes, or fads, the year 1965

was one of solid, old-fashioned success for Twentieth Century-Fox. It was the year of THE SOUND OF MUSIC, informally referred to as THE SOUND OF MONEY. Costing $8 million, the Julie Andrews-Rodgers and Hammerstein vehicle brought rentals of $110 million worldwide through 1966--the highest figure ever for any motion picture. In the domestic market it more than doubled the all-time record of GONE WITH THE WIND. Fox struck it rich with THE SOUND OF MUSIC and stockholders were convinced the Zanucks obviously knew what they were doing. With the release of THE SOUND OF MUSIC, there was no longer any fear of closing the doors on Twentieth Century-Fox. Although land had been sold on the studio lot, contract talent was no longer employed, distribution forces had been cut drastically, especially in Europe, and the studio was of little use for features, there were still monumental profits to be made by a motion picture company. Fox had proven it with THE SOUND OF MUSIC.

It seemed that luck was with the Zanucks in 1965, for there were other substantial hits as well. Due to the international flavor of THOSE MAGNIFICENT MEN IN THEIR FLYING MACHINES, with a cast including American, German, French, and Italian actors, the film performed well in all markets and on a $6.5 million negative cost, proved to be very profitable. Other fairly high-budget productions, like Mark Robson's VON RYAN'S EXPRESS, performed very well in domestic and foreign markets. ZORBA THE GREEK, a low-cost pickup, pulled in a solid $4.4 million domestically. There were losses though, on one major roadshow, THE AGONY AND THE ECSTASY, a $7 million adaptation of the Irving Stone novel which failed to capture the bestseller's potential. Also, the raucous comedy, JOHN GOLDFARB, PLEASE COME HOME, which ran up costs of close to $4 million was a loser, and MORITURI, a $6.2 million Marlon Brando-Yul Brynner war film, showed almost no revenues. That film was probably Fox's worst venture of any year.

Domestic rentals of 1965 neared the $115 million level, a new record for the company, and a welcome relief from the years of red ink. Riding another wave, there was no doubt that it was Fox's year. The question in everyone's mind was whether it would continue, and if so, what would be the follow-up to THE SOUND OF MUSIC?

CHAPTER 15

▪ UPHEAVAL ▪

If a seer had seen the specter of bankruptcy hanging over
the studio system, hardly anyone would have listened in 1966.
Fox, for one, was left in a very healthy financial position
due to the miracle of THE SOUND OF MUSIC. M-G-M also
had roadshow smashes in DOCTOR ZHIVAGO and a 70mm
reissue of GONE WITH THE WIND. While Columbia had not
done well with their epic production of LORD JIM, other
titles such as BORN FREE, CAT BALLOU, and THE PRO-
FESSIONALS attracted very large audiences. The other
majors all had their ups and downs, but, for the time being,
success continued to outweigh failure.

Riding high on its blockbusters of 1965, Fox now had
the funds necessary for a production expansion. However,
it was expanded in the direction of the blockbuster. Stan
Hough summed up the period by saying,

> Someone once said that the worst thing that ever
> happened to this particular studio was that they
> made THE SOUND OF MUSIC, which cost $8 million
> and has done $110 million. Obviously, if there's
> something better than one SOUND OF MUSIC, it's
> two SOUNDS OF MUSIC. Or three. Or four. Which
> brings us to STAR and [DOCTOR] DOLITTLE. That
> was what we called the "roadshow era." It seemed to
> us suddenly that the pulse of the public reflected
> that roadshows were the thing to do. THOSE MAG-
> NIFICENT MEN IN THEIR FLYING MACHINES was
> very successful. CLEOPATRA, even with its costs,
> did very well. [1]

Darryl and Richard Zanuck chose to embark on a policy
of "blockbuster" pictures designed to keep the studio in

profits for many years to come. That great big $100 million market was too hard to resist in the same way pioneer producers in the 1920's went after the golden million, Fox slated big musical productions, each costing more than double THE SOUND OF MUSIC, to draw back the same large audience. Both appeared to be potential blockbusters on the surface. STAR reunited Julie Andrews and Robert Wise from MUSIC to create the bittersweet story of Gertrude Lawrence. Arthur P. Jacobs, an ex-publicist/agent who had a true instinct for "packages," assembled a cast of Rex Harrison, Richard Attenborough, Samantha Eggar, and Anthony Newley for an adaptation of the Hugh Lofting story, DOCTOR DOLITTLE. Before they were finished, the pair had run up costs totalling $30 million, and were a very high risk to the studio.

Before Robert Wise agreed to direct STAR, he had Fox guarantee him another roadshow epic, THE SAND PEBBLES. A first estimating budget on THE SAND PEBBLES set production costs at $8,513,000. First estimating costs on DOLITTLE had been $9 million. What was developing would soon be known as the "runaway budget," a symptom of weak production which had started on a monumental scale with CLEOPATRA. Every major studio was to experience the "runaway," some more injuriously than others.

Nevertheless, 1966 seemed to be rather blissful, like the calm before the storm. Because roadshows were so long in planning, the effects of a major blockbuster might not be felt for two or three years. The year 1966 was also one of fairly profitable films at Fox with only 19 releases and only a fraction of these studio-made. FANTASTIC VOYAGE, a science-fiction adventure, was made at a cost of $5 million and virtually studio-filmed, due to the complex sets and special effects needed. One of the reasons for the high production costs was soundstage-sized sets and elaborate props. Location shooting had become even more popular now that independent producers found it less expensive to go to a foreign setting than recreating it inside a studio.

Television did not carry the enormous financial burden or risk of a large-scale feature. To produce a pilot for a series, the studio might spend $250,000 for a half-hour or up to $700,000 for an hour. When a sale was made the cost of the pilot was amortized over the various episodes.

Returns from series in the 1950's and 1960's were not wildly profitable unless a show ran endlessly like I LOVE LUCY, GUNSMOKE, or BONANZA and could then be syndicated. With orders of 39 episodes though, a series could keep the studio alive. Several series were even better. After dabbling in TV with two and three-season series like HOW TO MARRY A MILLIONAIRE, DOBIE GILLIS, and ADVENTURES IN PARADISE, T.C.F. Television finally became a power to reckon with when William B. Self became vice-president in charge of production. In 1966, Fox Television was in its best shape ever with hit series on all three networks. Long-running series, most of which continued to earn large amounts in syndication included PEYTON PLACE, BATMAN, and VOYAGE TO THE BOTTOM OF THE SEA on ABC, LOST IN SPACE on CBS, and DANIEL BOONE on NBC. Fox carried an average of five network hours weekly, 30 weeks yearly-- the production equivalent of 100 features. Clearly, television had taken over as the "B" unit.

Amidst a spate of successful films, including THE BLUE MAX, TONY ROME, OUR MAN FLINT, A GUIDE FOR THE MARRIED MAN, and ONE MILLION YEARS, B.C., Twentieth Century-Fox was able to survive its 1966 and 1967 roadshows of THE BIBLE and THE SAND PEBBLES. With foreign grosses, both just barely made back their negative costs. VALLEY OF THE DOLLS turned into a blockbuster with its $20 million domestic rentals and helped to keep Fox's stock high. However, distressing and ominous signs dotted the horizon. Costs were again rising uncontrollably on non-roadshow pictures. The $6 million production of HOMBRE, starring Paul Newman, was a high-grosser, but because of its cost it never became a profitable picture.

Even Roger Corman, the king of low-budget movies, was affected when he came to Fox to produce THE ST. VALENTINE'S DAY MASSACRE in 1966. Following the $2.2 million production, Corman promptly went back to making his own type of picture. MASSACRE was one of a handful of Corman's 43 productions through 1967 not to return its negative cost. With inflated department costs and studio overhead there was little reason for producers to bring their projects to major studios like Fox.

Changes in the industry now favored the independent producer by the late sixties. In the golden age of the studio

system, the major companies produced enough films to supply
the theater circuits of the nation, and the "indies" were
the poor relatives hovering around the fringes of the industry.
As well, top talent was always under contract to or allied
with one studio or another, so it would be difficult for an
independent to secure top talent.

Declining output at the major studios led to the rise of
independent producers. Agents packaged their own clients
and made themselves producers, like Arthur P. Jacobs with
his prestigious Apjac company. Actors and directors formed
their own companies for creative control and a grip on profits, like Jack Lemmon's Jalem Productions, which produced
THE GREAT RACE and COOL HAND LUKE; or Blake Edwards'
Geoffrey Productions, which became a co-producer of THE
PINK PANTHER and A SHOT IN THE DARK for United
Artists.

For the first time since the early days of distribution,
an independent producer could make his film, with or without
studio money, and then sell it to a major distributor. If the
quality was not high enough for a major, there were many
new independent distributors who might pick up the film.
At this point in time, the major companies needed product
as badly as the independent distributors. Any film which
looked like it might make some money was likely to be taken
on by one of the majors. Paramount chose ALFIE, produced
independently in England. Fox bought U.S. distribution
rights to ONE MILLION YEARS, B.C. from the same country.
United Artists purchased the rights to a trio of Italian
westerns which became very popular films in the United
States. A FISTFUL OF DOLLARS (1966), FOR A FEW DOLLARS
MORE (1967), and THE GOOD, THE BAD, AND THE UGLY
(1968), made more money than any English-dubbed films ever
released and established Clint Eastwood as a box-office name.
Very often it was cheaper to purchase a film from a producer
than to make it at the studio. For that reason, there were
many features made during the 1960's, using the advantages
freewheeling and innovative independent producers had over
the majors. The subject matter with which the studios dealt
was still limited by membership in The Motion Picture Association of America. Although the perusal of scripts was not
quite as rigid as in the past, the majors were honor-bound
to keep sex, nudity, and racy language off the screens. Independents did not suffer such restraints, and many films
depicted sex in increasingly graphic ways.

THE PAWNBROKER, released without a Code Seal in 1965, was a landmark film in the history of censorship. It was considered the first "important" film to contain nudity. Director Sidney Lumet defended the inclusion of a bare-breasted woman on artistic grounds, but many other films followed with no such integrity. Nudity became a sensationalistic and accepted aspect of motion pictures in the next several years. The impact of nudity would not be lost on the studios. Those motion pictures considered to be "controversial" were released under a subsidiary of a major company, freeing the studio from Code responsibility. United Artists had been the first to overcome a censorship problem with NEVER ON SUNDAY, which was distributed by its European subsidiary, Lopert Films. Then came TOM JONES and KISS ME, STUPID, originally set as a U.A. release, but stigmatized by a "condemned" rating by the National Legion of Decency, an influential opinion-maker.

At Twentieth Century-Fox, International Classics was set up to handle LA BONNE SOUPE (1964) and ZORBA THE GREEK (1965). Universal had Regional Films; Warners, Claridge Films; and M-G-M, Premier Productions, which released the very successful BLOW-UP (1967). Very soon, the studios were forced to keep up with the independent product, and sex scenes with nudity were included in many major films. The reason was simple: audiences wanted them. Films like BLOW-UP, I AM CURIOUS (YELLOW), and BARBARELLA attracted audiences with their sensationalism and produced substantial amounts of money.

Meanwhile, back at the Fox studio, Richard Zanuck was awaiting the release of DOCTOR DOLITTLE and STAR, the cost of which equalled that of ten other films, making their importance tenfold. Both films were unmitigated disasters. The Zanucks had assumed that family-oriented entertainment would attract audiences who did not wish to see the newly exploited violence and sex of the American cinema, and would flock to these two roadshows. It was a miscalculation made worse by the fact that individual films like I AM CURIOUS (YELLOW) or CANDY both carrying an "X" from the new MPAA rating system, made almost as much money as both films combined. A drastic upheaval was about to take place in the motion picture industry which would continue through the next few years.

If there was ever a time when all rhyme and reason
(if there ever was any in films) was missing from the movie
business, it was from 1968 to 1970. It was as though studio
executives had lost all touch with the reality of the industry.
With a proliferation of sex and violence on the screen, the
family trade was lost. Many adults who had been brought
up on the studio movies of the 1940's and 1950's were alienated
and offended by the sometimes shocking trends of the cinema.
The majority of the film-going audience by 1968 consisted of
those between the ages of 16 and 28.

A natural shift occured in the development of subject
matter. If audiences were mainly made up of young adults,
appropriate material would have to be provided. And who
was more likely to provide it than other young people?
Youth became an obsession with the majors, as young writers,
directors, and actors were plucked from film schools around
the country. Names like Francis Ford Coppola, Brian de
Palma, and William Friedkin began to appear on credits. Experience was of little value and seasoned directors and writers soon were forced to do youth material which they neither
understood nor had any feeling for.

The experiment might have been a bold one, but it was
too fast and uncontrolled to succeed. Not only were the
studios unaccustomed to working with the younger talents,
their distribution organization were baffled by the product
turned out. Films like Fox's PRETTY POISON, JOANNA,
THE TOUCHABLES, and THE GURU were not typical of
product the company had been designed to market. As a
result, many "youth films" had difficulty finding their audiences.

The problem was not limited to Fox alone. M-G-M released an entire series of "youth" features to cover all the
topical items of the day: campus unrest, anti-war protests,
sex, drugs, youthful self-discovery, etc. Unfortunately
for M-G-M, such films as THE MAGIC GARDEN OF STANLEY
SWEETHEART and THE STRAWBERRY STATEMENT were dated
before any of the half-dozen titles were even released. All
were failures and nearly drove the great Metro-Goldwyn-
Mayer into bankruptcy.

Fox had its own problems with finding audiences for its
films in the 1968 to 1970 period. Some films would be

TABLE XI

RUNAWAY BUDGET PICTURES

TITLE, COMPANY, YEAR	COST (millions)	DOMESTIC RENTALS (millions)
Doctor Dolittle (Fox, 1967)	17.0	6.2
Camelot (W.B., 1967)	17.0	14.0
Chitty Chitty Bang Bang (U.A., 1968)	16.0	7.0
The Battle of Britain (U.A., 1968)	12.0	2.5
Star (Fox, 1968)	14.5	4.2
Charge of the Light Brigade (U.A., 1968)	12.0	1.0
Gaily Gaily (U.A., 1969)	9.0	1.0
Paint Your Wagon (Para., 1969)	18.0	14.5
The Party (U.A., 1969)	6.0	1.0
The Great White Hope (Fox, 1970)	9.9	2.8
Ryan's Daughter (Fox, 1970)	15.0	14.6
Little Big Man (Cinema Center, 1970)	15.0	15.0
The Adventurers (Para., 1970)	17.0	7.7
Catch-22 (Para., 1970)	18.0	12.2
Darling Lili (Para., 1970)	22.0	3.5
The Only Game in Town (Fox, 1970)	10.0	1.5
The Last Valley (Cinerama, 1970)	6.0	1.0
The Molly Maguires (Para., 1970)	11.0	1.0
On A Clear Day You Can See Forever (Para., 1970)	10.0	5.3

TABLE XII

HIT MOVIES of 1968-1969 SEASON

TITLE, COMPANY, YEAR	COST (millions)	DOMESTIC RENTALS (millions)
The Graduate (Avco, 1967)	3.0	49.0*
Bonnie and Clyde (W.B., 1967)	3.0	24.1*
Planet of the Apes (Fox, 1968)	5.8	15.0
Bullitt (W.B., 1968)	5.5	19.0
2001: A Space Odyssey (M-G-M, 1968)	11.0	24.1
Funny Girl (Col., 1968)	14.0	26.3
Bob and Carol and Ted and Alice (Col., 1968)	2.0	14.6
Oliver (Col., 1969)	10.0	16.8
Easy Rider (Col., 1969)	0.6	19.1
Goodbye, Columbus (Para., 1969)	1.5	10.5
Midnight Cowboy (U.A., 1969)	3.2	20.3
The Love Bug (Disney, 1969)	5.0 **	23.1

*denotes most revenue from 1968
**denotes approximation--Disney never released cost figures

tremendously successful like PLANET OF THE APES, BUTCH
CASSIDY AND THE SUNDANCE KID or M*A*S*H others like
DOCTOR DOLITTLE and STAR would be pitiful disasters.
There was no longer any middle ground as there had been
for so many years. Because a $20 million dollar roadshow
could return as little as a $1 million picture, there would be
severe casualties. Again, this was not a problem peculiar to
Fox alone. Table XI (p. 162) indicates films which suffered
cost overruns and returned much lower rentals than anticipated. If Fox was having a bad time, Paramount was disaster city, causing the abrupt resignation of production head,
Robert Evans. One conclusion drawn from Table XII (above)
is that the studios were never certain whether a blockbuster
would come from a low-budget feature like EASY RIDER or a
large-scale musical like FUNNY GIRL. It was a dicey situation, much resembling the casinos in Las Vegas.

With the disastrous results on so many of these roadshow productions, Fox anxiously awaited the release of its three big-budget attractions, HELLO DOLLY, TORA! TORA! TORA! and PATTON at a total negative cost of $65 million. There was dismay at the studio as well due to the "runaway" nature of the business in the late sixties. Almost every major production was running into budgetary problems. Stan Hough explained the high costs this way.

> I felt during those years that our schedules were too long. Again, because we didn't have complete autonomy, directors and actors who were partners saw fit to extend the shooting time on some of these pictures unbearably.... It was brutal. Pictures that had 60 days scheduled should have been made in 40. And <u>could</u> have been made in 40. I recall some directors, without naming names, for some reason, because they <u>could</u> do better, shot generally three pages of script a day. We should have had that by lunch. I'm of the school where you had to shoot six, seven, and eight a day. Of course, in television they do 10 to 15. But to get three pages, and sometimes two, was incredible. The only thing we could do would be to fire the director, and then the star would go with him. You had to grin and bear it. [2]

There was little grinning and less bearing it when it was announced that Fox's losses for 1969 were set at $36.8 million. The losses from THE UNDEFEATED, CHE, THE CHAIRMAN, HARD CONTRACT, STAIRCASE, THE MAGUS, JUSTINE all added to the DOCTOR DOLITTLE and STAR drain. There was hesitation on the part of Richard Zanuck to continue on the roadshow policy at the time DOLLY and TORA were being prepared, as Stan Hough reveals:

> There's no question that by the time we got to TORA TORA and HELLO DOLLY we had reached an impossible situation. Personally, I didn't want to make TORA TORA. I don't think Dick Zanuck did either, but we thought with DOLLY we could probably make some money. But on TORA TORA there was great doubt. And there was a difference of opinion, as I recall, between Dick and Darryl on TORA TORA. Dick did not want to make the picture

and Darryl did. Darryl thought it was another
LONGEST DAY. But people differ on these things
and it's pretty hard to say if they're wrong. 3

While Darryl and Richard Zanuck would have figured
HELLO DOLLY to be the top-grossing picture of Fox's 1970
slate, it was not. In its place was a moderately-budgeted
film without Barbra Streisand or Walter Matthau, not a roadshow, released without much ballyhoo. M*A*S*H was a wacky,
raucous Korean war comedy which dealt out as much blood
as it did laughs, but the film caught on. Over its long
run, which included a 1973 reissue, M*A*S*H took in more
money than HELLO DOLLY, TORA! TORA! TORA!, STAR,
and DOCTOR DOLITTLE combined. This amazing feat was
accomplished for only $3 million. A lesson was to be learned
from this episode, and suddenly, Hollywood did a quick
about-face on the roadshow. Luckily for Fox, PATTON,
(buoyed by a top script and George C. Scott's star performance), did turn out to be a big success and brought in
world rentals of $45 million on a $12.5 million negative.

Hollywood suddenly became budget-conscious after three
years of lavish spending and overruns. Films like M*A*S*H,
BONNIE AND CLYDE, BOB AND CAROL AND TED AND ALICE,
MIDNIGHT COWBOY, LOVE STORY, and, of course, EASY
RIDER pointed out very clearly that a film did not have to
cost $15 million-plus to reap extraordinary grosses. Nor did
films have to be political or youth-oriented, as Walt Disney's
THE LOVE BUG and Universal's AIRPORT proved. All the
rules that Hollywood had been following were based on the
assumption that audiences had changed greatly in a matter
of three years. They had not really changed and were still
searching out films which provided unique entertainment.
When this point was finally received by producers, the content
of films changed once more.

Darryl Zanuck would no longer be at the studio to see
this turnaround. With losses for 1970 set at $77.4 million,
he had to answer to the ire of stockholders who had watched
their shares plummet in value. With the dismal bottom line
figures impossible to ignore, the Zanucks could not defend
themselves. Losses were not limited to Fox; they were heavy
at United Artists and Paramount as well. The industry was
in upheaval and the Zanucks fell prey to the times.

Bitter proxy fights erupted within the company and

various factions tried to gain control. In the midst of these disputes, a rift developed between Darryl and Richard Zanuck. Darryl stayed on through the battle, but Richard's contract was terminated four years short in December 1970. Zanuck, senior, however, was soon removed from active production and given the honorary title of Chairman Emeritus. The effective rule of Darryl Zanuck at the Twentieth Century-Fox Film Corporation had come to an end.

CHAPTER 16

■ NEW POLICIES AND NEW FORCES ■

At 36 years of age, Richard D. Zanuck left the Twentieth Century-Fox Film Corporation. He had not been so much an infusion of young blood as a continuation of Zanuck blood. His instincts were similar to his father's and his taste in commercial filmmaking ranged from the absurdities of M*A*S*H to the slam-bang action of THE FRENCH CONNECTION, with an occasional lapse into MYRA BRECKINRIDGE or BEYOND THE VALLEY OF THE DOLLS. He had largely supported the production of PATTON, but not TORA! TORA! TORA!, and had brought THE FRENCH CONNECTION to the studio as well as BUTCH CASSIDY AND THE SUNDANCE KID.

Richard Zanuck had run the studio for his father, making deals as well as pictures. With the film industry in turmoil in 1969, however, his record was starting to pale in the eyes of stockholders. Had the studio not made TORA! TORA! TORA! as he suggested, losses would not have been so great. Richard Zanuck might have had a chance to reestablish himself as a credible production chief. The PLANET OF THE APES motion pictures were all moneymakers and Zanuck's record would have immediately improved had he stayed through the release of THE FRENCH CONNECTION, which took in rentals of approximately $75 million worldwide. The reissues of BUTCH CASSIDY, M*A*S*H, and THE SOUND OF MUSIC generated nearly $30 million domestically in the next few years. Like his father, Richard Zanuck had good pictures and bad pictures, but because in 1970 only one picture in eight returned its cost, the odds were against any producer.

Richard Zanuck left Fox and his $350,000 annual salary

along with David Brown, who had been head of the story department since 1956. Both were immediately named as executives at Warner Bros., a part of the giant shoe-selling Kinney Corporation. Zanuck became a senior vice-president, and Brown became vice president for creative operations. The team's first project was PORTNOY'S COMPLAINT, which attracted very poor reception. The tenure at Warners was very short and just over a year later both became partners in Zanuck/Brown Productions with an exclusive contract with Universal Pictures. Among their first releases at Universal was THE STING (1974) which took in $68 million in domestic rentals for the company and won several Academy Awards. The following year they produced JAWS (1975), which promptly became the highest-grossing movie ever at $130 million domestic rentals and over $200 million worldwide.

All was not well at Twentieth Century-Fox in early 1971 after Richard Zanuck's departure. Dennis C. Stanfill, an Annapolis graduate and Rhodes scholar who had been brought to Fox from the financial vice-presidency of the Times Mirror Co. publishing empire in 1969 to establish fiscal responsibility was made president and was temporarily running the creative end of the company. There were immediate hurdles for him to overcome. A group of stockholders encouraged by producer David Merrick, was about to wage a proxy battle to wrest control from current management. William T. Gossett, chairman of Fox's executive committee said that the company needed "a man to lead it in the creative field," but that no one would be appointed until the proxy contest had been determined.

The ensuing stockholders' battle was made public through full-page ads in The Wall Street Journal, with Fox's board of directors trying to gain sympathy and support for their cause. An ad on April 22, 1971, said:

> Two "protectors" of stockholders' interests, a
> stockbroker and a lawyer, calling themselves "The
> Protective Committee for the Benefit of Twentieth
> Century-Fox" announced on March 9 that they were
> launching a proxy contest to gain control of the
> management of your Company.
> About the Powell-Lewis Committee. We submit that
> these two men are opportunists. Neither of them
> personally owned a single share of Fox stock at the

time; neither indicates that he has had any experience as an executive or as a director of any publicly-
owned company, let alone a major motion picture
company like ours. [1]

Charles Lewis, the stockbroker, and Louis Powell, the
lawyer, each bought shares in the company and formed a
group of 18 persons, of which four did not own any shares.
According to the Company advertisement, of the total of
8,561,815 shares of common stock outstanding, one member
of the committee owned 32,400 shares, while the other members owned a total of 21,901, the majority of which were
purchased after Powell and Lewis made their plans to gain
control.

The company added in its favor that it "is now operating
profitably," comparing the first two months of 1971 to the same
period of 1970. As well, "the choice of Dennis C. Stanfill,
44, as our new President brings to this position three qualities that your Board believes will further assist the Company
in maintaining its leadership in the industry. These are
youth, experience and skill in the area of finance and cost
control.

There has been a major restructuring and realign-
ment of our executive personnel, giving younger
but experienced executives a greater voice in our
top management team. They include: our marketing group headed by Peter S. Myers, David Raphel
and Jonas Rosenfield, Jr., who in 1970 brought to
Fox the highest theatrical revenues in the history
of your Company; John P. Meehan, Controller, who
has been introducing financial controls for operations;
and Jerome Edwards, our General Counsel. We have
great confidence in this new team led by our new
president and in Elmo Williams, our new Vice Presi-
dent-Worldwide Production. In addition to all of
the above, the company continues to have available
the services of its Chairman, Darryl F. Zanuck. He
will now be in a position to devote his major efforts
to help in shaping our production program, having,
at his request, relinquished the responsibilities of
Chief Executive Officer. [2]

Ironically, Zanuck was never consulted, after being given
such flattering lipservice.

The management boasted that M*A*S*H, PATTON, TORA! TORA! TORA!, and THE GREAT WHITE HOPE had brought a total of 22 Academy nominations which would boost grosses. Of the 14 new films scheduled for 1971, six of which were in release, all but one was budgeted at $3 million or less. One was budgeted at approximately $5 million. A program was under way to cut costs by $20 million, and to further develop nine acres of land in Century City. The management encouraged shareholders to fill out white proxies.

The "blue proxy boys" were not impressed by the grandiose claims of management. After stating that Darryl Zanuck and current management suffered spectacular losses, that the book value of each share fell 62 percent in 1969, and that the market value of Fox stock fell from $41.75 in 1969 to $6.00 in 1970, they struck back.

> We believe that Darryl Zanuck predictions are un-reliable. After a loss of $36,804,000 in 1969--on March 3, 1970, Zanuck stated in a Fox release: "We face the future with great optimism...."
>
> On August 27, 1970, after an after-tax loss of $16,105,000 for the first six months of 1970, Mr. Zanuck--in a press release--said: "based on current estimates, it is expected that the next half-year will return the company to profitable operations."
>
> Result: For 1970, an after-tax loss of $77,355,000....
>
> Based on Fox's own estimates, as of November 19, 1970, of gain and loss on 33 feature pictures released in 1969 and 1970, only 9 pictures made a profit while 24 lost money.
>
> Remember: During this time Mr. Zanuck was Chairman and Chief Executive Officer and Mr. Stanfill, from October 1969, was Executive Vice President of Finance. Mr. Zanuck is still Chairman, now Mr. Stanfill is President and Fox does not have a Chief Executive Officer.
>
> We submit that your company is in desperate need of a change in management. We decided to seek out what we consider to be the most experienced and successful businessmen available--regardless of whether they were stockholders or not--to join with us to give Fox the new leadership we believe it so desperately needs.

These men would: impose financial responsibility; firmly limit the size of Fox film budgets to $2 million per picture; eliminate high fees and exhorbitant salaries to "name" stars; reduce overhead; reduce fixed production expenses; seek to modernize distribution; develop an environment which will attract to your company the most creative film talent and provide the most competent management available. [3]

Among the proposed board were two persons involved in film production, James B. Harris, who had produced some low-budget features, and Malcolm B. Kahn, president of Wylde Films Corp., a subsidiary of Fox which produced television commercials. Another was Alan V. Iselin, the president of Super 50 Theater Corp., which owned and operated drive-in theaters. The nine other directors had no relation to film in the least way. And their proposal was evidence of this, for their limitations of budget ran against everything Hollywood stood for. There had never been a workable low-budget figure for major studios since costs were always rising for top entertainment with money-making stars.

When the clouds of battle lifted, the Stanfill management was able to retain control and now could continue its reorganization. Gordon Stulberg was named president of Twentieth Century-Fox and Dennis C. Stanfill became chairman of the board. Stulberg had been an attorney for the Screen Writers Guild until he joined the Columbia Picture Corporation in 1956. In 1960, he was appointed vice-president and chief studio administration officer, and remained at Columbia until 1967, when he left to set up Cinema Center Films as a subsidiary of the Columbia Broadcasting System. Although Cinema Center released its first product in 1968, it very soon fell prey to the same excesses the majors had been practicing for many years. Productions such as LITTLE BIG MAN, FIGURES IN A LANDSCAPE, LE MANS, MONTE WALSH, and THE BOYS IN THE BAND ran up high costs, and huge losses. Cinema Center, releasing its films through the National General Corporation, had some successful films like A MAN CALLED HORSE and THE REIVERS but soon closed its production doors. In September 1971, Gordon Stulberg joined Fox at a salary of $150,000 per annum and $40,000 in guaranteed bonuses.

By the time Stulberg took over the production reins,

the roadshow era had ended with a thud; no company would
consider another in the immediate future. What lay ahead
for the major studios was a period of limited budgets and
a determination to stay away from any great risks.

This gave rise to co-productions with independent producers, in which the studio would finance a part of the
film; and negative pick-up deals, by which the company
would guarantee a set amount on the completion of production. This way a studio would not be responsible for cost
overruns. In a negative pick-up, it was the producer who
was at risk in overruns. Almost any variation of the standard deal would be made if it in some way benefitted the
studio. There were certainly enough independent producers
with projects to offer. Stars would now appear in movies
which they believed in for minimal salaries and a percentage
of the gross. This made lower budgets possible on certain
risky ventures perceived to have limited appeal.

The Fox studio, along with Paramount, Columbia, Warners,
and M-G-M, had become packagers picking and choosing
those deals which seemed to have the most potential, sometimes obliged to invest development funds up front. Universal remained the only studio with contract talent because
of its steady supply of television series and movies for
television. With the effective collapse of the "studio system"
in 1970 came the final death knell to a "house look." A
Paramount picture was now interchangeable with an M-G-M
picture or a Fox picture. Usually the film was made entirely
away from the studio, often without any studio financing,
and picked up for distribution after completion.

The motion pictures which were initiated by the Stulberg
regime included the average amount of successes and failures without any major breakaway hits. But there was one
great difference from the Zanuck years. Very few films
were high-budget product. Those which exceeded $3 mil-
lion were few and far between and the majority were in the
$1.5 million to $2 million range. Gordon Stulberg and his
board of directors decided that rather than going for the
$100 million market of THE SOUND OF MUSIC, inexpensive
films would be made to capture the more reliable $5 to $10
million market. Films like BATTLE FOR THE PLANET OF
THE APES, THE CULPEPPER CATTLE COMPANY, GORDON'S
WAR, TROUBLE MAN, THE HEARTBREAK KID, THE NEP-
TUNE FACTOR, and WHEN THE LEGENDS DIE were among

those designed for this particular market. Some achieved their goals; others did not.

Fox had realistically aligned its hopes for such motion pictures. From 1970 through 1973, one startling fact showed up at the end of each year. One runaway smash hit was produced every year, then several big hits, but the majority of films were in lower brackets. In 1970, the big runaway was Universal's AIRPORT ($45 million in domestic rentals) in 1971, Paramount's LOVE STORY ($50 million); and in 1972, the same company's THE GODFATHER ($86 million). Only in 1971 did Fox come anywhere near the runaway with THE FRENCH CONNECTION ($26.3 million). However, in 1973, Fox hit the top with THE POSEIDON ADVENTURE, a $5.5 million disaster epic which started a new trend in motion pictures and took in $42 million domestically. Unfortunately, Fox had only put up 50 percent of the cost and was entitled to only 50 percent of the profits, which on worldwide rentals of $75 million was substantial. Fox did receive its standard 35 percent distribution fee.

With the industry in such a topsy-turvy and unpredictable state, anyone might have been in the position of president at Fox and had the same showing. The law of averages was in effect more than any logical method of prediction and evaluation. The industry had become exactly what many producers had labelled it--a crap shoot. If every company could hold out long enough, they would have their share of hit pictures. Columbia had gone through a winning streak in 1968 and 1969; Paramount rose to the top in 1971; then came Warners in 1972; and Fox, to some extent, in 1973, with THE POSEIDON ADVENTURE. The industry had come to the point where an entire studio depended on the success of one GODFATHER or EXORCIST or POSEIDON ADVENTURE for survival.

However, Gordon Stulberg did bring a good deal of sanity to Fox, and not only in motion picture production. Since there were so few films being shot at the studio, which by 1971 was virtually deserted, Stulberg tried to bring others to the lot. Many movies for television were shot at Fox on the existing lots, using already-built sets, and although there was little profit in these features there was good reason for them. "The only 'carrot' I can see," says Stan Hough, "is that it sustains employment and it

keeps the juices running through your studio. It keeps
your stages occupied. It pays some tax money. It keeps
some important personnel on your lot and keeps some blood
running through the lot." 4

Stulberg also entered a co-production deal which probably never would have occurred had the industry's founding
fathers still been in control. Twentieth Century-Fox and
Warners both found themselves about to produce major films
based on similar properties, THE TOWER and THE GLASS
INFERNO. Rather than competing, the two studios joined
together for the first time in film history to co-produce a
feature. THE TOWERING INFERNO (1974) was distributed
in the North American markets by Fox, and in foreign countries by Warner Communications. The $14 million cost of the
film was shared by both companies as were the towering
world rentals of nearly $100 million.

The new Stanfill-Stulberg administration succeeded in
cutting costs and restoring Fox to a profitable position.
THE POSEIDON ADVENTURE and THE TOWERING INFERNO,
both from the "master of disaster" producer Irwin Allen,
helped contribute to that position. There were other optimistic signs. For the first time in several years, 1974's
results showed a greater spread of the wealth collected by
motion pictures, thus making many more pictures profitable
since the roadshow era. Fox had its share of successful
films--DIRTY MARY CRAZY LARRY ($12 million domestic),
THE THREE MUSKETEERS ($10 million), HARRY AND TONTO
($4.6 million)--and showed remarkable figures with the
reissue of BUTCH CASSIDY AND THE SUNDANCE KID ($13.8
million). Summer grosses for Fox product in 1974 reached
all-time record highs, along with the yearly tabulation for
the entire industry. Dollar volume equalled 1946, which
was the greatest year on record. In all the euphoria, no
one worried about the loss of dollar value through inflation.
Any upward dollar movement for the motion picture industry
was a bright sign in an otherwise clouded future.

Although Stulberg had succeeded in dragging Fox out
from the mire of red ink, Dennis Stanfill was not completely
satisfied. With the huge successes of THE TOWERING IN-
FERNO and YOUNG FRANKENSTEIN, Fox was not partaking
of enough of the profits. The deals Stulberg structured
had favored Mel Brooks more than was customary on the

latter and revenues from the former were split with Warners
and Irwin Allen. On an afternoon in December 1975, while
both pictures were breaking records, Stanfill reportedly
relieved Stulberg of his duties.

In January 1976, Dennis C. Stanfill took the title of
president in addition to his other posts with the intention
of becoming more involved in production and dealmaking.
Certainly, he had played his share in restoring Fox to profitability. Following the $103.8 million in losses in 1969 and
1970, Stanfill closed Fox's New York headquarters, cut studio
overhead, and sold off the 2,600 acre ranch in Malibu, with
a leaseback agreement for production when Fox needed it.
This resulted in profits each year of his administration. In
1974, with revenues of $281.9 million, Fox reported net
profits of $10.9 million. Coming from a business rather than
entertainment background, Stanfill wanted to run Fox more
like a corporation and less like the fly-by-the-seat-of-your-
pants operation motion picture production usually is. Asking
each department head to submit an annual plan, he would
go over the expenditure and growth projections constantly
for revisions. Stanfill immediately promoted Robert Sherman
and Jere Henshaw from vice-presidents of production to
senior vice-presidents. However, it was clear who would
make the final decisions.

Gordon Stulberg had left behind two annuities for the
company which were not apparent at the time of departure.
When Irwin Allen returned to feature production in 1972,
after seven years in television, Fox lost an important resource
in developing TV series. Allen had given Fox four years
of one of television's "all time favorite science-fiction series," [5] VOYAGE TO THE BOTTOM OF THE SEA (1964-1968),
which still runs in syndication, three years of LOST IN
SPACE (1965-1968), and two years of LAND OF THE GIANTS
(1968-1970). Of Fox's three series on the air in 1972, two
failed to last more than 13 episodes, THE NEW ADVENTURES
OF PERRY MASON and the expensive PLANET OF THE APES.
However, the third, initiated under the Stulberg administration debuted in the Fall season of 1972 and would run for
ten years. Spinning off the theatrical success of M*A*S*H
became a major profit center for Fox. Although the network
run of the show would be deficit-financed since television
production costs had outstripped the first-run license fees,
syndication would grow into a rich vein mined years later.

When M*A*S*H was finally sold to the syndicated stations (for runs during non-network hours or non-network-affiliated stations) revenues amounted to $200,000,000.

In the feature division, Stulberg's production deal for THE ROCKY HORROR PICTURE SHOW (1975) seemed like a disaster. The small-budget, British-made musical with a low-profile cast of Barry Bostwick and Susan Sarandon did absolutely no business. Almost simultaneously, though, was the growth of a small but steady market, the Saturday midnight show. Kids who had grown up with Saturday matinee shows were now staying up late enjoying cult favorites like THE NIGHT OF THE LIVING DEAD. With its irreverent blend of sexual satire, rock music and the ghoulish, THE ROCKY HORROR PICTURE SHOW fit the bill. It started playing and never stopped for almost a decade, netting grosses estimated at $50,000,000. This was from a movie the studio had initially written off as a loss.

Some of the other Stulberg projects were not as successful. One was AT LONG LAST LOVE, a compilation of Cole Porter's hit songs woven into a thin story line. Producer/director/writer Peter Bogdanovich, hot after the success of THE LAST PICTURE SHOW (1971), WHAT'S UP DOC? (1972), and PAPER MOON (1973)--with total domestic rentals of $58 million--starred Burt Reynolds, Cybill Shepherd, and Madeline Kahn to capture the style of the 1930's musicals in which numbers were recorded live. Unfortunately, none of his cast were musical or dancing stars and critics suggested the entire exercise was rather embarrassing. So were the grosses. AT LONG LAST LOVE opened and closed after a week in most engagements. The entire $5.5 million budget was lost.

When Stulberg finally assigned a large production budget, it was to LUCKY LADY which proved to be anything but lucky. Much of the money went to the high-powered talent involved. Liza Minnelli had won an Oscar for CABARET (1972) and was undisputedly a draw. Gene Hackman took home his Oscar for THE FRENCH CONNECTION (1971) and a pre-AT LONG LAST LOVE Burt Reynolds had starred in a series of successful potboilers and the outstanding DELIVERANCE (1970). Director Stanley Donen had been responsible for some of M-G-M's greatest musicals as well as the bright and entertaining CHARADE (1964). Scriptwriters Willard Huyck and

Gloria Katz were riding high on the hugely successful
AMERICAN GRAFFITI (1973). All in all, LUCKY LADY
looked like a big winner. Until it was released. Word got
out among critics that the movie was being shown with two
different endings. Three had actually been shot, including
a $1 million dollar spectacular shoot-out in which Hackman
and Reynolds met a grim death which was never seen by
the public. There was some doubt expressed in the reviews
that director Donen knew how to end the movie. Audiences
were generally lukewarm to LUCKY LADY even though rentals
amounted to $12.9 million on the $14 million negative. With
publicity and advertising, the net loss was estimated at $10
million. In short, Fox was not in good shape again and did
not have much of a slate for 1976. However, another production star was about to shine.

Alan Ladd, Jr. had joined Fox as a vice-president for
creative affairs in 1973. Son of the well-known actor, he
was unlike most Hollywood personalities. Almost withdrawn
and very low-key, he was characterized as speaking only
when necessary. Like many of the new generation of studio
executives, he had been an agent, then a producer in partnership with Jay Kanter and Elliott Kastner. The triumvirate
did not result in any very successful movies and was dis-
banded. At Fox, Ladd had been largely responsible for
bringing Mel Brooks aboard with YOUNG FRANKENSTEIN.
Columbia Pictures reportedly passed on the project because
the budget had gone from $1.7 to $1.8 million. Reminding
Ladd of the Saturday matinees of his youth, he pushed the
picture at Fox on a cost of $2.8 million. It brought domestic
rentals of $39 million. In January 1976, Dennis Stanfill
appointed Ladd as senior vice-president in charge of worldwide production. Ladd immediately brought along his former
partner Kanter, also an ex-agent, and a producer acquaintance from London, Gareth Wigan. This new triumvirate
would have better luck than the previous one.

Unfortunately, Ladd was off to a rocky start. LUCKY
LADY and AT LONG LAST LOVE had brought the studio
ridicule. A Russian co-production of a 1940 Shirley Temple
vehicle (the only one of her films to fail) THE BLUE BIRD
became another fiasco. More a political gesture of co-
existence, the George Cukor-helmed feature starred Elizabeth
Taylor, Jane Fonda, Ava Gardner, and Cicely Tyson in
cameo roles and went way over budget. An aging Cukor

was shooting very slowly and different Russian production methods were compounding the problems. The $10 million BLUE BIRD was without a doubt the turkey of the decade. Another blow to Ladd. By May of 1976, rumors spread around town that Stanfill was unhappy with Ladd and that there might be departure notices.

Ladd, Kanter, and Wigan were staking their hopes, and careers at Fox, on THE OMEN and Mel Brooks' latest laugh-fest, SILENT MOVIE. Both were iffy. OMEN had been turned down at Warners as a project for Oliver Reed. Gregory Peck replaced Reed when Ladd brought the movie to Fox. Peck, however, had not had a hit movie in years and meant little to the youth audience. SILENT MOVIE, starring Brooks, Marty Feldman and Dom DeLuise was completely without dialogue and relied on slapstick humor which had not found favor among American audiences since Jerry Lewis' heyday in the 1950's and 1960's. Nevertheless, by July 1976, Fox and Ladd were on their way to the top.

CHAPTER 17

■ STAR WARS AND BEYOND ■

THE OMEN opened to smash returns. SILENT MOVIE followed in the same pattern. After a losing streak a mile wide, Fox was recovering its reputation as a viable studio. More importantly, Alan Ladd, Jr. was solidifying his position and his ability to attract top talent to Twentieth Century-Fox. After the financial and critical embarrassments of THE BLUE BIRD, ALEX AND THE GYPSY, THE DUCHESS AND THE DIRTWATER FOX, SKY RIDERS, and THE LAST HARD MEN, Fox had cycled its way back to the position of winner.

Another example of Ladd's seeming astuteness was evidenced in the matter of a script entitled SUPER CHIEF, written by Colin Higgins. Producer Frank Yablans had been developing the project at Paramount where it was to star George Segal. When Paramount let its option lapse, Ladd moved in and brought the project to Fox for a record $400,000. Higgins, after all, was not a major writer even though his U.C.L.A. thesis script for HAROLD AND MAUDE had become a cult classic. Ladd starred Gene Wilder who had an ongoing relationship with Fox dating back to YOUNG FRANKENSTEIN (and THE ADVENTURES OF SHERLOCK HOLMES' SMARTER BROTHER [1976] which he wrote, directed, and starred in). With Wilder in the lead, Jill Clayburgh for romantic support, THE SILVER STREAK, as it was retitled, became Fox's Christmas release. It cost $5.5 million and took in $50 million in worldwide rentals.

Added to the more than $50 million returned by THE OMEN on a $2.8 million cost and nearly $40 million on SILENT MOVIE with a $4 million price tag, Fox was now known around Hollywood as a studio with the money to develop new properties.

It was no longer the repository for hand-me-downs and rejects from Paramount, Warners, and Columbia.

Fox had Gene Wilder and Mel Brooks working on new projects. Paul Mazursky, who hit his stride in 1968 with BOB AND CAROL AND TED AND ALICE but had later fallen prey to the excesses of 1970-style new-wave non-audience production, had a moderate success with NEXT STOP, GREENWICH VILLAGE in 1976 and stayed with Fox to develop AN UNMARRIED WOMAN for release in 1978. Herb Ross, a former dance director of FUNNY GIRL (1968), director of THE OWL AND THE PUSSYCAT (1970) and PLAY IT AGAIN, SAM, was readying THE TURNING POINT with Anne Bancroft and Shirley MacLaine. The legendary Fred Zinnemann, who directed FROM HERE TO ETERNITY (1953), A MAN FOR ALL SEASONS (1966) and THE DAY OF THE JACKAL (1973), was preparing the anxiously awaited JULIA, starring Jane Fonda and Vanessa Redgrave from an Alvin Sargent script based on Lillian Hellman's bestseller, Pentimento. But the biggest surprise was yet to come.

George Lucas, a 1967 graduate of the University of Southern California Cinema Department, had made AMERICAN GRAFFITI for Universal in 1973. Its budget of $900,000 was minuscule compared to the lofty $56 million in domestic rentals it grossed. Lucas, however, could not convince Universal to finance his $8.5 million homage to the Saturday matinee serials he saw as a child. STAR WARS struck the same chord with Alan Ladd, Jr. as YOUNG FRANKENSTEIN. Put into production in England with Lucas directing from his original script, STAR WARS eventually cost closer to $10 million. It was well worth it.

When STAR WARS was let out of its cage, it devoured the moviegoing audience. It produced weekly grosses at theaters that were absolutely unheard of. Released in limited engagements playing high-quality 70 mm prints with the new Dolby stereo sound systems, Fox marketing executives led by Ashley Boone had followed a policy of building a want-to-see movie. Rather than opening in 1,500 theaters at once to get maximum grosses, Fox let the picture build word-of-mouth. Endless lines in front of theaters only gave the movie more of a cachet. It became an "event." It didn't hurt that Time magazine had featured a story on STAR WARS or that the reviews were almost unanimously favorable.

STAR WARS shrewdly tapped into audiences of all ages--
those who were too young to remember BUCK ROGERS and
FLASH GORDON, and those who fondly recalled the serials
but had never seen an epic on such a scale before. With
a then little-known cast including Mark Hamill, Harrison
Ford and Carrie Fisher, it relied on special effects gimmickry
developed by Lucas and a talented team of artists. With a
credit roster longer than any in the history of movies, there
were innumerable names who would become integral to the
future of what would be known as the "special effects films."
A whole universe of filmmaking opened up with STAR WARS
and among the greatest beneficiaries would be Twentieth
Century-Fox. This was not a situation Wall Street overlooked. Fox's stock rose from a low of $6 per share in
June 1976, to nearly $27 after STAR WARS' release. After
only five months in release, STAR WARS' impact on Fox
earnings were clear. Revenues rose from $195 million in
1976 to $301 million in 1977. Ladd's salary rose accordingly
from $182,885 to $563,000, including bonuses.

STAR WARS included all kinds of high-profile spin-
offs for the company. Kenner Toys put out a hugely successful line of STAR WARS figures which would dominate the
toy market for years to come. John Williams' score for the
movie became a hit album and single and a disco version of
the theme became a number one disc on pop stations across
the country. Molded face masks of Darth Vader and Chew-
bacca were marketed for adults and became an instant novelty.
Fox Television, somewhat dormant except for M*A*S*H,
immediately prepared a STAR WARS Thanksgiving special
for C.B.S. and THE MAKING OF STAR WARS utilized behind-
the-scenes footage for another hour special. There was no
doubt that Fox had a phenomenon on its hands. The
next step was obviously a sequel. George Lucas even
announced that STAR WARS was really the fourth chapter
in an intermediate trilogy of his sprawling epic. It was to
eventually total nine complete features. Work immediately
began on the first sequel.

Aside from STAR WARS, Fox was doing well with other
products as well in 1977. Frank Yablans produced THE
OTHER SIDE OF MIDNIGHT, a pulpy Sidney Sheldon best-
seller which again reminded Ladd of movies of the 1930's
and 1940's--in this case, the woman's melodrama--and Fox
reaped hefty rentals of $18.4 million. Mel Brooks' spoof of

Alfred Hitchcock suspense thrillers, HIGH ANXIETY, brought
$19.1 million. JULIA and THE TURNING POINT both opened
to very favorable reviews and strong business even though
neither would be a blockbuster of STAR WARS' proportions.
JULIA ended up with $13 million and THE TURNING POINT
with $17 million. With foreign rentals, television and ancillary
markets, the pair would eventually each be profitable. The
only real disappointment of 1977 was DAMNATION ALLEY,
a more routine post-nuclear war, science-fiction adventure
which was a total loss on costs of $7.5 million. DAMNATION
ALLEY, released just before STAR WARS, was the final
fizzle to the standard sci-fi movie. Post STAR WARS audiences would demand much more sophisticated concepts in
set design, props and special effects. When Variety released its year-end list of big-rental films in the U.S.,
there were no surprises when STAR WARS weighed in with
$127 million, only $6 million away from the record established
by JAWS in 1975.

Further honors were to be bestowed on Ladd as the 1977
Oscars were announced in early 1978. STAR WARS, JULIA,
and THE TURNING POINT garnered 22 nominations, giving
Fox more nods than any other studio. Although only a
handful of the Oscars would be won, the laudatory effect
buttressed Alan Ladd, Jr.'s standing in the movie business.

The motion picture industry was already infected and
affected by STAR WARS. Suddenly, the big budget had
revitalized the near-defunct tradition of science-fiction.
Steven Spielberg and George Lucas had been friends before
their mega-grossing hits brought them into the rarefied
atmosphere of top producers. While Lucas was shooting
STAR WARS, Spielberg had been secretly filming CLOSE
ENCOUNTERS OF THE THIRD KIND.

Secrecy was also becoming an earmark of the major movie
since television was always standing by with ready crews to
adapt a notion which sounded appealing. Even before THE
TOWERING INFERNO was released in 1975, a TV movie
called TERROR ON THE 40TH FLOOR trapped people in a
burning highrise. From the timing, it seems clear TERROR
was inspired by announcements of the Fox-Warners co-
production.

CLOSE ENCOUNTERS OF THE THIRD KIND also relied
heavily on sophisticated special effects to make it successful,

elevating its budget to $21 million. Finally earning $82 million domestically with its 1980 reissue, it was an investment that paid off for Columbia Pictures. The danger with such expensive exercises in pyrotechnics was that eventually there would be losers--and at those elevated budgets, they could be deadly. METEOR was a $17 million sci-fi flop for American International Pictures which was trying to reach beyond exploitation movies. Renewed interest in STAR TREK, a television series which ran for 79 episodes from 1965-1967, prompted Paramount to spend $40 million on STAR TREK-THE MOTION PICTURE. It took in about $100 worldwide and barely broke even. Alexander Salkind produced SUPERMAN for Warner distribution for a reported $50 million. Warners only had a distribution deal with Salkind and collected 35 percent of its hefty $82.5 million take, but did not suffer the losses that resulted. Salkind would later amortize his costs over two SUPERMAN sequels. It was painfully clear that the lessions in excess suffered during the roadshow era were not heeded. With the exception of Steven Spielberg and George Lucas, the immediate future would bring forth some expensive failures.

With so many of its late 1977 releases (HIGH ANXIETY, JULIA, THE TURNING POINT, and STAR WARS) holding over into 1978, there were fewer new releases needed to fill up Fox's schedule. Ladd attracted more critical acclaim with Paul Mazursky's AN UNMARRIED WOMAN, starring Jill Clayburgh in an episodic drama about a woman whose husband leaves her for someone else. Along with the acclaim came $11 million in domestic rentals. Another Frank Yablans production, THE FURY, directed by Brian de Palma and based on a Stephen King novel brought in a disappointing $10 million domestically. OMEN II: DAMIEN did only slightly better with $12 million. But STAR WARS kept on going with $38 million in 1978. When the final count was in by 1980, STAR WARS totalled $193.5 million domestic, eclipsing JAWS' $129 million tally.

Ladd, Kanter, and Wigan also happily saw huge hikes in their salaries. With stock options and bonuses, Ladd took home $1,944,385; Kanter received $1,120,038; Wigan got $1,101,894. Dennis Stanfill, too, benefitted. In addition to his approximately $500,000 annual salary, he would receive in 1980 a $6 million bonus from the board of directors for increasing the value of Fox's stock.

As usually happens when grosses skyrocket and business increases, costs go up across the production board. Star salaries go the highest and the fastest. John Travolta who graduated from a TV series, WELCOME BACK, KOTTER, to SATURDAY NIGHT FEVER became an overnight sensation. His next movie, GREASE, took in $83 million in the U.S. and Canada. Suddenly, Travolta commanded multi-million dollar salaries. Sylvester Stallone put his career on the line and starred in his own script for ROCKY, costing $1 million. ROCKY was a hit with nearly $100 million in world rentals and spawned three sequels. Stallone's salary eventually rose to $15 million per movie. To be able to release a superstar's movies, a studio would make deals which allowed that star to develop and control all aspects of the production --from story to director. The audience allure of a big star name, after nearly a decade in eclipse, once again became that all-important insurance policy which studios felt could guarantee huge grosses. The casualty of this period would be the small films which major studios would shun since there was little "logic" in spending $3 million to make a picture which would cost $10 million to market. The independent producer would again fill the gap, supplying not only the property but the financing to make the movie, leaving the studio with only distribution rights and minimal risk.

Fortunately for the moment, Fox had its own releases to depend on. NORMA RAE won Sally Field an Oscar and $11 million on a $4.5 million budget. THE ROSE offered Bette Midler her first screen role and became a hit picture, continuing Ladd's trend towards dramas with solid, mature women's roles. BREAKING AWAY proved an exception to the studio rule of big is better. Its tiny $2.3 million cost resulted in a slow release to test the waters. In terms of cost, it broke away with $10 million in rentals and an Oscar for its writer Steve Tesich.

However, the year's big Fox hit proved to be ALIEN, a taut, horrific vision of man's most deadly enemy in space, with over $80 million worldwide. The unique approach to science-fiction again utilized advanced design in special effects and the added conceptual artistry of its Swiss set designer H.R. Giger. Ridley Scott, a British commercials director took his first screen assignment and richly invested it with skill and energy. Although its initial $9 million investment was more than covered, a lesson was to be learned from ALIEN. With early grosses equalling STAR WARS, ALIEN did not have the same staying power because it was rated "R," preventing anyone under 16 from attending without an adult. This cut down the youth crowd which had gone to see STAR WARS so many times over. Nor was there much of an ancillary market for the toy alien with its repulsive reptilian tail and movable projecting teeth, since children, the main market for toys, were less familiar with the creature.

By mid-1979, there were rumblings at Fox about executive shuffles. With his three-year contract ending in December, Alan Ladd, Jr. was campaigning for a bigger share of the company's profits. Dennis Stanfill tried negotiating with Ladd but the two could not agree. In June, Ladd announced that the Fox triumvirate would not be renewing their contracts with Fox. News of their imminent departure caused Fox stock to drop from $40.63 to $38.87 in one day.

Ladd's desire for more financial participation in the company was not unusual for an executive in his position. In January 1978, a group of chief executives at United Artists had departed to form Orion Pictures because they felt Transamerica's ownership of U.A. was diluting the importance of their contributions and ultimately, their remuneration. When they left, they attracted many long-term U.A. talents like Woody Allen who had worked with them for many years. Ironically, the new U.A. administration fared so poorly, Transamerica unloaded the company only three years later to financier and M-G-M owner, Kirk Kerkorian. Alan Ladd, Jr. certainly had made enough friends at Fox to allow him a roster of talents wherever he went.

Just before Ladd left Fox he had made a deal with Richard Zanuck and David Brown to return "home" as independent producers with their contract at Universal expiring. Having left that studio with its two highest grossing pictures, THE STING and JAWS, as well as THE EIGER SANCTION (1975) and JAWS II (1979), it looked like Ladd had pulled off a coup. However, with Ladd leaving both Zanuck and Brown expressed their doubts about the future. After all, they had signed the deal because they knew and trusted Ladd. As well, there was speculation that Zanuck might once again head the studio, a rumor quickly scotched by both Zanuck and Brown.

Ladd, Kanter and Wigan soon set up their own independent production unit with Warner Communications financing called The Ladd Company. They started out by acquiring the rights to be big winner which Fox turned down, CHARIOTS OF FIRE (1981) and were to continue their formula for prestigious picture-making, utilizing top talent in material that was less obviously commercial. Most of the subsequent projects were ambitious, like BODY HEAT (1981), but ultimately unsuccessful at the box office.

LOVE CHILD (1982) starring Beau Bridges and Amy Madigan was a $5 million tear-jerker which played a short run to empty houses. FIVE DAYS ONE SUMMER (1983) starring Sean Connery and directed by Fred Zinnemann cost $15 million and was a complete write-off. ONCE UPON A TIME IN AMERICA (1984), Sergio Leone's four-hour gangster epic, co-financed by Arnon Milchan to the tune of $30 million was also a disaster.

After several releases The Ladd Company was staking its survival on THE RIGHT STUFF, a $27 million epic about the founding of the American space program directed by Philip Kaufman, who had displayed great talent but had never been able to nail down a commercial success in a 15-year career. With a great deal of publicity and critical acclaim, including a feature story in Time magazine, THE RIGHT STUFF, the most eagerly anticipated picture of the year, opened to mild business. Its domestic rentals would only total $10.3 million.

Ironically, after announcing that The Ladd Company would be closing its doors, Warner Bros. released the young unit's biggest-grossing picture. Not only was it atypical of Ladd's choice in subjects, it was everything his pictures were not. POLICE ACADEMY (1984) was vulgar, crass, ridiculous--and wildly successful, grossing nearly $100 million at the box office on a $4.5 million investment. In Hollywood nothing succeeds like excess and POLICE ACADEMY was followed by three money-making sequels. Alan Ladd, Jr., still a valued member of the production community, was later appointed head of production at M-G-M.

At various times in their history, studios go through periods of instability. Fox was in for a bout of executive musical chairs which would become almost legendary. In August 1979, Sandy Lieberson was appointed president of Twentieth Century-Fox Productions and Ashley Boone was promoted to president of Distribution and Marketing. Both activities were newly created divisions of Fox.

Lieberson had been with the company since 1977, was previously vice-president of European production where he had supervised such productions as the German NOSFERATU (1979) and the British-made ALIEN.

Boone, with Fox since 1972, had been in sales and marketing and was largely credited with exhibiting early enthusiasm for STAR WARS and masterminding its promotion.

A recent scandal at Columbia Pictures in which its production chief, David Begelman, had been caught in a check-forging scheme had brought a major executive shake-up that would ultimately affect the entire Fox organization. Alan J. Hirschfield had been at Columbia since 1973 and worked his way up to the presidency by helping rebuild that studio after some financial problems in the early 1970's. However, Hirschfield opposed the powerful Columbia board of directors when they wanted to rehire Begelman after the scandal and was fired. A strong studio executive, his background included an early career on Wall Street, similar to Dennis Stanfill's. Both men understood the need for fiscal responsibility in producing motion pictures. It appeared to be a marriage made in heaven. Hirschfield became vice-chairman and chief operating officer in October 1979. And so began the Columbia-ization of Fox.

Michael Nolin, who served as vice-president and executive assistant to vice-chairman, Norman Levy, during this period, recalled:

> They would've liked Sandy Lieberson to stay initially and Sandy left on his own. Hirschfield had had this really rocky time at Columbia but there were a number of people who had supported him there. Dan Melnick who was in charge of production and Norm Levy in distribution. So Hirschfield, having lived through this very painful period at Columbia, wanted to ensure that didn't happen again at Fox. And he thought the way to ensure that was to pick

> people who were loyal to him. Dan Melnick did not
> want to be an executive anymore and, the way I
> understand it, he wanted to position himself sort of
> like the crown prince on the lot the way Ray Stark
> was at Columbia. He didn't like the day to day
> responsibilities, so he pushed his protegee Sherry
> Lansing to be head of production. [1]

Sherry Lansing was made president of Twentieth Century-Fox Productions, a position created only a few months earlier for Sandy Lieberson. A former school teacher and actress, Lansing had been a production executive at Columbia where she was reportedly responsible for developing such hits as THE CHINA SYNDROME (1979, domestic rentals, $25.5 million) and KRAMER VS. KRAMER (1979, domestic rentals, $60 million). Norman Levy was brought in as head of distribution, replacing Ashley Boone who promptly went on to a marketing position at George Lucas' Marin County-based concern, Lucasfilm. Daniel Melnick was invited to bring his IndieProd company to develop projects for Fox. Along the ladder of responsibility Columbia people replaced Fox people.

> There is incredible enthusiasm [Nolin recalls of the
> initial atmosphere]. There's a sense that things
> are going to be very, very successful. Sherry, I
> think, was given pretty much a free rein to do
> what she wants, although there's a certain degree
> of competetiveness between her and Norm Levy.
> Sherry puts a number of pictures into production--
> all of which have a kind of stamp to them--they're
> all relationship movies. [2]

In the feature divison, with six months of turmoil, there were very few features resulting for 1980. Luckily, one holdover from the Ladd regime, NINE TO FIVE, starring Jane Fonda, Lily Tomlin and introducing Dolly Parton to the screen, was a huge hit. A $10 million budget brought $59 million domestically.

Only BRUBAKER, starring Robert Redford as an innovative and fair-minded prison warden, would shine among the other three homebased Fox productions with rentals of $19 million. The rest of the release slate was filled with pickups, making Norm Levy's distribution department more important to the company than ever.

Levy was able to structure several profitable deals for Fox.

> Norman knew what he was doing [Mike Nolin con-
> cluded]. Production would basically say, "We're
> going to roll the dice and out of the ten movies
> we're going to make, we'll need to have a big hit."
> Norman's philosophy was to acquire ten movies which
> would give away the upside, but protect the down-
> side, so he'd have no huge losers and make a bit
> of money on everything. 3

One of the deals made was with Melvin Simon Productions. Having made a fortune in construction, Simon decided to become a movie producer. Keeping his average budget around $5 million, he would make modest entertainments with well-known talent. Levy arranged to get worldwide distribution rights for approximately a 25 percent investment in the package. The first two releases, SCAVENGER HUNT, a zany multi-starred action comedy, and THE RUNNER STUMBLES, a controversial drama starring Dick Van Dyke and directed by Stanley Kramer, did not fare well. However, MY BODYGUARD returned rentals of $9.5 million and, along with THE STUNT MAN, received considerable critical acclaim.

A straight distribution deal with no up-front investment was made with Time-Life Productions for LOVING COUPLES, a mix-and-match romance with Shirley MacLaine and James Coburn, and a similarly-themed picture, A CHANGE OF SEASONS, also starring MacLaine, Anthony Hopkins, and Bo Derek was acquired. MIDDLE AGE CRAZY, another contemporary romantic drama with sex produced in Canada with Toronto substituting for Houston, starring Ann-Margret and Bruce Dern became a Fox release. Most notable among the pick-ups was ALL THAT JAZZ, co-financed and released in Europe by Columbia Pictures, a deal arranged by Alan Ladd, Jr. The Bob Fosse-directed $12 million semi-autobiographical drama with music drew in a healthy, but not overwhelming $20 million in domestic rentals. The only undisputed box-office champion of 1980 was Fox's sequel to STAR WARS, THE EMPIRE STRIKES BACK.

Between the production and release of STAR WARS, George Lucas acquired a great deal of independence.

Through his company, Lucasfilm, he was able to realize
enormous profits on the movie and retain a major percentage
of ancillary marketing. This became Lucas' cash cow. Kenner
reportedly paid Lucasfilm nearly $70 million for its share in
toy sales. With this autonomy and copyright ownership of
STAR WARS, Lucas was able to finance sequels on his own
and have Fox participate only as distributor. Although
the final deal for THE EMPIRE STRIKES BACK was never
revealed to the public, industry sources placed Fox's distribution percentage at somewhat lower than its usual 35
percent fee. Nevertheless, even its smaller percentage
brought approximately $60 million into the company.

Reissued every year until THE EMPIRE STRIKES BACK
was released, STAR WARS was bringing in so much cash
to the company, Dennis Stanfill decided other areas of
investment should be explored to alleviate Fox's dependence
on cyclical profits. Stanfill purchased three television stations (the Federal Communications Commission only allowed
a company to own a total of five), luxury resorts in Aspen,
Colorado and Pebble Beach, California, and a very profitable
Coca-Cola Bottling Midwest. In the days of steep and still-
rising interest rates, a company like Fox having a cash
horde of $100 million was a major asset.

Fox's television department, almost dormant, and with
M*A*S*H* producers announcing that the tenth season of its
critically acclaimed run was to be the last, Stanfill and
Hirschfield looked around for a strong leader to head this
division. Another Columbia alumnus, Harris Katleman, took
over the underexploited Fox Television. Katleman had
aggressively pursued series, movies-for-TV, and mini-series
at Columbia and had a good working relationship with executives at all three networks. Fox Television had lacked
a strong boss since William Self's departure in the 1960's.
With money pouring in from STAR WARS, a natural funnel
for that money would be to make Fox a powerhouse in the
potentially lucrative television market.

One of the most commercially successful of the Universal
Studios' producers for nearly seven years was snared by
Katleman. Glen A. Larson had created such long-running
hit shows as SWITCH (1975-1978), THE SIX MILLION DOLLAR
MAN (1974-1978), THE BIONIC WOMAN (1976-1978), QUINCY,
M.E. (1976-1984), MAGNUM, P.I. (1980-1987), KNIGHT RIDER

(1981-1985) as well as the highly publicized (and budgeted) BATTLESTAR GALACTICA and BUCK ROGERS IN THE 25TH CENTURY, which immediately followed the release of STAR WARS. Larson, given his own million-dollar office facility near the television building, immediately started making series deals. THE FALL GUY (1982-1986), starring Lee Majors, was the first and most successful of his Fox series.

Having come from careers on Wall Street, both Stanfill and Hirschfield realized that the cost of Fox's stock was low considering its assets and would eventually make the company a likely takeover target for a corporate raider. To fend off an unfriendly takeover which could lose them their positions, Stanfill and Hirschfield sought to protect themselves by announcing a plan to make Fox a private company by selling it to a few management officials and other investors.

Stanfill's management purchase plan failed. There was dissension between Stanfill, Hirschfield and each one's loyal executives. Fox had still not been able to get a steady stream of successful productions since Alan Ladd, Jr.'s departure. Most importantly though, profits were down in 1980 to $54,567,000 from $57,303,000 in 1979, despite a hefty jump in revenues to $865,236,000.

Indeed, Fox's stock was being acquired. Chris-Craft Industries, Inc. wanted Fox's three TV stations--KMSP-TV in Minneapolis-St. Paul, KTVX in Salt Lake City, and KMOL-TV in San Antonio--to add to its KCOP in Los Angeles and KPTV in Portland, fulfilling its maximum complement of five. Chris-Craft had purchased 22 percent of the company's shares and there was the distinct possibility that it would use that leverage to ally with another company in a takeover attempt. Fearing the worst, Stanfill and company battened down for a battle. But on the horizon, a white knight appeared. Marvin Davis, an oil billionaire from Denver, would soon be the first individual since Howard Hughes to own a major Hollywood studio.

CHAPTER 18

■ A PRIVATE COMPANY ■

Marvin Harold Davis was born August 28, 1925, in Newark, New Jersey. His father became wealthy manufacturing women's dresses. In his teens he was a partner in the family's Jay-Day Dress Company. Although there was a gap of several generations, Marvin Davis would eventually own the motion picture company founded by another garment manufacturer, William Fox.

Davis' father also invested in oil wells through a friend. Marvin spent the summers of his youth learning the oil business and later began to explore the Denver Basin for his own wells. After several years of bad luck, he struck it rich in the late 1960's with finds in the Wyoming Powder River Basin. When gasoline shortages plagued the United States in the 1970's, sending the cost of crude soaring, Davis became one of the most powerful men in the American oil industry.

Engaging in the riskiest of oil searches, Davis was a wildcatter, knowing that only one well in fifty would be a winner. So, he decided to sink as many wells as possible. During the first six months of 1980, the Davis Oil Company was the 17th most active in the country. Davis' investments in oil wells, real estate, and business holdings ranked him in the class of billionaire.

The six-foot-four-inch, three-hundred-pound Davis developed an appetite for a good investment which would be "fun." Two previous "fun" investments which were never consummated would have led to the acquisition of the Oakland A's baseball team and the Denver Post. But now, there was

Twentieth Century-Fox, a company whose management had been trying to take it private.

Davis allied with Herbert J. Siegel, chairman and president of Chris-Craft, then proposed to buy all of Fox's stock at $60 a share, well above the $45 price Stanfill would have offered in his deal with management and more than the $53 market price. Stanfill and the board of directors were immediately encouraged by the offer because it appeared Davis would keep a "hands off" approach to the company and pledged not to make any major changes in its operations. Davis appeared to be exactly the rescuer Stanfill needed to keep Fox out of hostile hands which might loot the company and sell off its assets for a quick profit. As well, Stanfill stood to make an estimated $6.67 million profit on the options and stock he owned. Alan Hirschfield, who had been with Fox a little more than a year, would earn a $2.8 million profit. Certainly, the shareholders of the company would come out well since the stock had appreciated 709 percent since Stanfill took over on September 16, 1971.

On June 8, 1981, a formal merger agreement was presented to stockholders for approval. Fox would be merged into a company called TCF holdings, principally owned by Davis and members of his family. Chris-Craft would get a strong position on the board of directors of United Television (Fox's stations) and may have at some point applied to the F.C.C. for control of the three stations.

Using techniques for financing acquired in his oil business, Davis relied heavily on outside investors to raise money for the $722 million deal. Aetna Life & Casualty Company would raise nearly $200 million to repay part of the debt and would receive a 50 percent ownership in real estate and non-entertainment assets of Fox. Another partner named Richco of the Netherlands Antilles, headed by the secretive financier Marc Rich, an associate of Davis, would help him raise $550 million from a syndicate of banks and receive an equal amount of non-voting stock as Davis and family. In all, Davis would sell off pieces of the pie to acquire Fox. His personal investment would amount to only $50 million for which he would get control of a company estimated at $800 million.

There were celebrations at Fox when the deal was

approved. It looked like the company was safe. But when
Davis appeared at his first Fox executive meeting with Stanfill two weeks later on June 23, his intentions were clear.
The company was now his and he would not be the "absentee
landlord" Stanfill had anticipated.

A particularly thorny point of contention surrounded
Harris Katleman. The Los Angeles Times alleged that
Katleman had abused his expense account privileges and
that a police investigation was under way. Stanfill, concerned about the air of scandal because of the Begelman
affair at Columbia, was not satisfied with Katleman's explana-
tions and wanted his resignation. Davis, on the other hand,
countermanded Stanfill's orders, infuriating the chairman.
Stanfill realized the relationship between him and Davis had
become untenable. On June 29, 1981, Stanfill handed Davis
his resignation. Alan Hirschfield, who had waged a tug of
war with Stanfill after the merger for Fox's top position
and had sided with his Columbia alumnus Katleman, now
emerged as heir-apparent for chairman and chief executive
officer.

In his newly-elevated position, Hirschfield would have
to supply Marvin Davis with an adequate cash flow to make
the investment of $724,620,000 pay off. Meanwhile, Davis
had his own ideas about the movie business and considered
running a studio like running an oil company. "They're
all creative people, and they're all dealing with the unknown.
Failure is the rule and success comes rarely." But he also
acknowledged differences.

"This is the first time in my life I've ever had to go
out for public acceptance. If I get a dry hole in the oil
business, I lick my wounds and go home, and that's the end
of it." [1]

Davis would soon learn that the public, and industry
leaders in particular, would be watching his company's every
move. Critics and filmmakers alike would be quick to pounce
on failure. Fox's initial Davis offerings were also those of
Sherry Lansing, the first woman to hold a major studio
presidency. The 38-year-old executive announced that Fox
was making films that were "fiscally responsible." TAPS
(1981) and MODERN PROBLEMS (1981) performed adequately
at the box office with rentals of $20.5 and $15.5 million,
respectively.

Yet, it was two distribution pickups which yielded the company's highest grossing pictures. One, CANNONBALL RUN, was an independently financed slapstick action comedy starring Burt Reynolds, Farrah Fawcett, Dom DeLuise, Dean Martin, and Sammy Davis, Jr. and directed by former stuntman Hal Needham. Producer Albert S. Ruddy, initiator of such smashes as THE GODFATHER (1972) and THE LONGEST YARD (1975) raised the $18 million to make CANNONBALL RUN, which then returned $38.5 million in the domestic market controlled by Fox.

The other was a more unlikely hit, made on location in Florida for only $5 million, starring unknowns, written and directed by a Canadian with investment from Montreal's Astral-Bellevue-Pathe unit under the banner of Melvin Simon Productions which had never come up with a major hit. "I think the triumph of PORKY'S is that it was marketed extremely well," remarks Mike Nolin. "That was Norman. I think his genius was the 'looking through the peep-hole' campaign. They didn't know exactly what they had. They took two markets in Utah and South Carolina and they marketed it there and the picture did great. Virtually after that, it booked itself." [2] PORKY'S was so successful it ended up with a domestic gross of over $100 million and rentals of $53.5 million. Added to moderate grossing pickups like FORT APACHE, THE BRONX and Mel Brooks' HISTORY OF THE WORLD--PART I, it was becoming evident that Norman Levy's distribution arm was contributing more to the profitable operation of Fox than production.

Lansing's slate of 1982 releases was not only unencouraging, it was downright depressing. The deals might have looked good on paper but somehow when they got to the screen most met scathing critical reviews and dismal box office. AUTHOR! AUTHOR! starring Al Pacino and Dyan Cannon performed well below expectations. KISS ME GOODBYE, starring Academy-Award winner Sally Field with James Caan and Jeff Bridges in a romantic comedy with a touch of BLITHE SPIRIT, was roundly lambasted by critics and audiences alike. Neil Simon could always be counted on for some box-office punch but I OUGHT TO BE IN PICTURES starring Walter Matthau was kayoed on release. The controversial MAKING LOVE, about a doctor who leaves his wife for another man, was another flop.

Even independent producers who had deals with Fox were experiencing bad luck. Frank Yablans who had contributed SILVER STREAK and THE OTHER SIDE OF MIDNIGHT, produced MONSIGNOR, based on a best-selling novel starring Christopher Reeve and Genevieve Bujold, which never even made back its production costs. SIX PACK, a low-brow family comedy starring Kenny Rogers had gotten all of Marvin Davis' support and just about broke even. And that was among the best performers of Fox's year.

In Mike Nolin's estimation,

> There was all this pressure. There was a new owner and everyone was looking for a winning combination. I think Sherry started out thinking she would be completely autonomous--which probably never materialized for her the way she wanted it to. And as her pictures didn't perform, her autonomy got eroded more and more.

As usual, there were also studio politics at play.

> There were certain loyalties. Sherry had a strong loyalty to Dan Melnick and also Stanley Jaffe. There was also a certain sense of politeness. Alan and Norman and Sherry all liked each other. As a consequence, there wasn't any kind of mogul. There wasn't a Thalberg or a Cohn. There was this committee and the feeling that everybody should have some input. Alan's theory was "I've got these people and they'll be able to sort it out." But they never were able to. Alan put together a very capable team in terms of each individual person, but it never quite gelled. It's like having great players on a baseball team and a manager who doesn't quite know how to motivate them. [3]

Richard Zanuck and David Brown had been at Fox since 1979 and yet no projects had resulted. Reports of creative disagreements between Z/B Productions and Sherry Lansing began to surface. Their first Fox project was supposed to be NEIGHBORS, based on the darkly comedic novel by Thomas Berger. The budget was set at $8.5 million and several drafts of the script had been completed by the M*A*S*H television series creator Larry Gelbart. To

Zanuck/Brown's chagrin, Lansing decided to pass on the project which was then taken to Columbia where John Belushi and Dan Aykroyd were cast. When Columbia released the final product, it brought in rentals of $17.5 million--not a blockbuster, but with the exception of TAPS, it was more successful than anything Lansing had initiated that year.

The next picture Richard Zanuck and David Brown produced under their agreement with Fox was THE VERDICT, starring Paul Newman. Released as Fox's Christmas attraction of 1982, the Sidney Lumet-directed drama reaped world rentals of close to $50 million. Stung by their experience on NEIGHBORS, Zanuck and Brown soon decided to leave Fox once more.

But Marvin Davis was not disappointed by the results of the feature division. Coca-Cola Bottling, for which Fox paid $28 million in 1977, was sold for $70 million, and the motion picture library was a constantly appreciating asset. Also, the latest technology was beginning to be felt in the industry and Davis aggressively positioned his company to take advantage of recent developments in pay-cable and home video. With approximately 1,500 sound releases and thousands of episodes of television series, Fox was in a perfect position to benefit from the "video revolution." Referring to the television rights, Davis boasted, "We're sitting here with a library we undervalued by 50%. Countries you would not think of need product. We just sold STAR WARS to Australia for $2 million, THE SOUND OF MUSIC was sold in England for $10 million, and M*A*S*H is unbelievable." Even though Fox lost $16.9 million in 1982, a good deal of earnings were used to service the debt load needed to acquire the company. Davis still felt Fox was the "steal of the year." [4]

In December, 1982, after two years of disappointing results in the presidency, Sherry Lansing was replaced by Joe Wizan, a one-time agent and long-time producer whose credits included such films as the very successful JEREMIAH JOHNSON (1972), and the not-very-successful JUNIOR BONNER (1972), AUDREY ROSE (1977), ... AND JUSTICE FOR ALL (1979), and BEST FRIENDS (1982). Wizan was currently in the process of producing TWO OF A KIND starring John Travolta and Olivia Newton-John. It would not be a hit--nor would Wizan's tenure.

Entering 1983 with a production expenditure earmarked at $200 million, increased 66 percent over 1982, including productions like a remake of UNFAITHFULLY YOURS, starring Dudley Moore and Nastassia Kinski, and Mel Brooks' remake of TO BE OR NOT TO BE. Other 1983 releases were largely controlled by strong producers who had brought their pictures to Fox, like Frank Yablans (THE STAR CHAMBER), ABC Motion Pictures (SILKWOOD, MR. MOM), and Melvin Simon-Astral-Bellevue-Pathe (PORKY'S II - THE NEXT DAY). One other independently financed picture would again bring attention to Fox.

It had been three years since a Fox release scored a direct bulls-eye hit like THE EMPIRE STRIKES BACK. Paramount began a record-breaking series of hits, scoring repeatedly with AIRPLANE (1980--$38 million domestic rentals on a $3.5 million negative cost), the George Lucas/Steven Spielberg RAIDERS OF THE LOST ARK (1981--$175 million world rentals), AN OFFICER AND A GENTLEMAN (1982--$52 million domestic rentals on a $6 million negative), STAR TREK II: THE WRATH OF KHAN (1982--domestic rentals, $40 million), the FRIDAY, THE 13TH series, TRADING PLACES (1983--$41 million domestic rentals), FLASHDANCE (1983--$36 million domestic rentals), STAYING ALIVE (1983--$34 million domestic rentals), 48 HRS. (1983--$31 million domestically). Universal, of course, held the unequalled record of E.T.--THE EXTRATERRESTRIAL (world rentals of nearly $300 million on a $10 million investment). Columbia had TOOTSIE (1983--rentals of $95 million), and M-G-M./United Artists had the ROCKY and the James Bond series which always turned over hefty amounts as well as POLTERGEIST (1982) and WAR GAMES (1983). Warners had the SUPERMAN series, RISKY BUSINESS (1982) and NATIONAL LAMPOON'S VACATION (1983).

Although more a morale booster than profit-maker because of a further reduced distribution percentage, RETURN OF THE JEDI, also financed by Lucasfilm to the tune of $32.5 million, brought Fox back into a high-profile position in the industry. With its astronomical domestic rentals of $168 million, it became the third highest grossing motion picture of all time. Twentieth Century-Fox now released three of the top-six all-time grossing motion pictures. More importantly, of the six pictures (E.T., STAR WARS, RETURN OF THE JEDI, THE EMPIRE STRIKES BACK, JAWS, RAIDERS OF

TABLE XIII

1984 RELEASES

TITLE	COST (millions)	DOMESTIC RENTALS (millions)
The Cotton Club (Orion)	$51.0	$12.9
Dune (Univ.)	$42.0	$16.0
Greystoke, the Legend of Tarzan (W.B.)	$33.0	$23.0
Supergirl (W.B.)	$30.0	$ 6.0
The Natural (Tri-Star)	$28.0	$25.0
2010 (M-G-M/UA)	$28.0	$20.1
Sheena, Queen of the Jungle (Col.)	$26.0	$ 2.9
The Bounty (Orion)	$25.0	$ 4.5
The River (Univ.)	$21.0	$ 4.9
Streets of Fire (Univ.)	$19.5	$ 4.2
Body Double (Col.)	$19.0	$ 3.7
Mrs. Soffel (M-G-M/U.A.)	$14.0	$ 1.7

THE LOST ARK) three were directed by Steven Spielberg and four were produced by George Lucas. Two young men had, in less than a decade, become the most popular film-makers in the history of movies.

Because of audiences returning to see the final install-ment of George Lucas' STAR WARS trilogy, a $200 million sale of M*A*S*H to syndication, and increased pay-television fees, Fox's earnings soared to $776.5 million compared to $554.9 million in 1982.

It was to be an important year. George Orwell had made it a catchphrase decades earlier, but finally 1984 had arrived. At Fox, Marvin Davis and Alan Hirschfield were determined to develop and finance more movies in-house to partake more substantially of the hits. It was also a year in which escalating costs had again gotten out of control. A prime example was RHINESTONE. Budgeted at $18 million, the Sylvester Stallone-Dolly Parton vehicle was a quasi-musical which ended up costing $28 million--and almost half went to pay for the star talent. Domestic rentals barely hit $12 million. GIMME AN "F," another raunchy teen comedy, cost $17 million and was never even given a full release. Fox began preproduction on a feature called SEA TRIAL with William (THE FRENCH CONNECTION, THE EXORCIST) Friedkin and soon abandoned it at a cost of $6 million. Then there was ENEMY MINE, a science-fiction drama which had begun shooting and then was shut down with $10 million in expenditures so far. It would eventually reach $33 million. JOHNNY DANGEROUSLY, a spoof of gangster movies starring Michael Keaton, cost $9 million and was released but only returned $9.1 million domestically. Considering about $10 million for prints and advertising, the picture was an almost total loss. There definitely seemed to be a lack of adequate control over production.

However, Fox was not alone in runaway costs as shown by the list of unsuccessful releases on Table XIII (p. 199).

Of Fox's three most successful releases of 1984, two were studio-financed, ROMANCING THE STONE, with world rentals of $80 million, and BACHELOR PARTY, a zany teenage-oriented comedy with Tom Hanks with rentals of $19 million. REVENGE OF THE NERDS, a co-finance venture, took in $19.5 million domestically.

With losing pictures outnumbering winners, it was time for another executive change. Lawrence Gordon, an independent producer who had been responsible for action melodramas like THE DRIVER, and Eddie Murphy's successful debut feature, 48 HRS., took over the production reins in August, 1984. Just one month later, Alan J. Hirschfield "resigned." The Los Angeles Times reported on September 11, that a studio observer noted "The word was out on the street that after Labor Day there would be some major changes at Fox, and I guess this is it. I guess Davis had just had it." Another observer noted Hirschfield "was clearly fired. There's only one chief executive and his name is Marvin Davis." [5]

Barry Diller had become a star in the executive world. After high school he almost immediately dropped out of UCLA and started working in the mail room of the powerful William Morris talent agency. In 1966, he was hired by the ABC network and there created the Movie-of-the-Week (or M.O.W. as it is now called). Placed in charge of the network's programming, he became experienced in all facets of production and in 1974 was made head of production at Paramount. He was only 32 but had almost ten years' experience in the business. Recruiting another ABC executive he had worked with, Diller brought Michael Eisner to Paramount where the pair fashioned a release program which consistently captured a large portion of the moviegoing audience. As mentioned earlier, their high ratio of hits in 1983 suddenly brought them to the attention of the industry. They were not depending on a George Lucas or Steven Spielberg to supply them with one massive mega-hit. They were creating their own smashes in-house. Even though Columbia topped out with GHOSTBUSTERS (domestic rentals of $128 million), Paramount's slate included INDIANA JONES AND THE TEMPLE OF DOOM ($109 million), BEVERLY HILLS COP ($108 million), TERMS OF ENDEARMENT ($50 million), STAR TREK III ($39 million), FOOTLOOSE ($34 million), and FRIDAY THE 13TH--THE FINAL CHAPTER ($16 million). Excluding INDIANA JONES, which was financed by Lucasfilm, the four other titles represented production costs of approximately $50 million. Domestic rentals alone totalled $247 million-- almost a 500 percent return on investment.

Marvin Davis immediately cast a line out to Barry Diller reportedly offering a $3 million annual salary as well as a 25 percent stake in the company--worth upwards of $50 million. Diller was still bemoaning the 1983 death of his mentor at Paramount, Gulf and Western founder Charles Bludhorn, and felt he'd "lost any rudder that kept me." [6] Accepting Davis' offer, Diller became Chairman and Chief Executive Officer of Twentieth Century-Fox.

However, Fox still had to ride out a rocky release schedule for 1985, partially initiated by Larry Gordon. MOVING VIOLATIONS was a follow-up slapstick comedy from the team which produced BACHELOR PARTY. It only returned $4.9 million in rentals, less than its promotion and release costs. TURK 182 came from the director of PORKY'S and the producer of REVENGE OF THE NERDS. The results--a paltry $1.9 million in rentals. Another low-budget location-produced MISCHIEF brought in only $4.1 million. The summer's anticipated big comedy was THE MAN WITH ONE RED SHOE, with the very popular Tom Hanks heading an all-star cast including Dabney Coleman, Carrie Fisher, and Jim Belushi, was directed by Stan Dragoti who had done the tremendously successful LOVE AT FIRST BITE (1979). The combination of cast and director as well as the farcical plot line of the 1972 French comedy THE TALL BLOND MAN WITH ONE BLACK SHOE seemed to have all the ingredients for success. But the picture laid an egg with only $4.3 million--on a $16 million budget!

Finally, the summer brought a hit. Zanuck/Brown had brought Fox a project called COCOON, an unusual science-fiction fantasy. Fox exercised its right with Z/B and passed on the script but then revived it when Z/B was about to go elsewhere. Although expensive for a Zanuck/Brown project at $17.5 million it returned world rentals of close to $100 million.

COCOON is an excellent example of the vagaries of the movie industry and the prognosticatory abilities of studio executives. It was originally set to be directed by a graduate of the University of Southern California Cinema Department who had become a protege of Steven Spielberg. Robert Zemeckis had directed a pair of unsuccessful comedies, I WANNA HOLD YOUR HAND (1978) and USED CARS (1980). Finally, in 1983, he was assigned to a major project by producer-actor Michael Douglas. Douglas had bought a script from a former waitress who dreamed of becoming a screenwriter, Diane Thomas. Optioned at various studios over a five-year period, the script finally ended up at Fox. RO-MANCING THE STONE was to be made on a fairly tight $9.5 million in Mexico. Douglas would star along with Kathleen Turner. An adult comedy adventure, the movie was a surefire hit when it opened. However, Fox executives and producer Richard Zanuck in particular, did not feel the rough footage they saw was very encouraging. As a result, Zemeckis was replaced on COCOON by Ron Howard, who had proven his commercial ability with SPLASH. Zemeckis had

written a script with his partner, Robert Gale, which Steven
Spielberg wanted to produce for some time, but Zemeckis
never felt he was ready. Now, he knew he had to shoot it.
While ROMANCING THE STONE became Fox's highest grossing
picture of 1983, Zemeckis directed BACK TO THE FUTURE
which was 1985's blockbuster, grossing about $250 million
at the world's box offices. Hollywood is not without irony.

"This company will never be sold as long as I'm alive," [7]
declared Marvin Davis to <u>Business Week</u> in April of 1982.
That was before his financial partner, Marc Rich, was involved in a government investigation into an oil price scandal.
As the scandal intensified, Rich sought refuge in Switzerland and in late 1983 a federal grand jury indicted him on
charges of evading $100 million in U.S. income taxes. The
cloud surrounding Rich left a half ownership in Fox up for
grabs. Within three years of a declaration of his intentions,
Marvin Davis would sell all his ownership in Twentieth
Century-Fox.

CHAPTER 19

■ AFTER DAVIS ■

From the moment Marvin Davis entered the picture at Fox, critics and long-time employees feared that he would loot the studio. After all, he had no background in the movies, no sense of history or attachment. The film library was a matter of dollars and cents to him--lots of them--not the accumulated creative work and record of generations past. It was a commodity like oil. That library could be spun off as a separate company as Warner Bros. had sold its pre-1948 movies to United Artists in the 1960's. The remaining sixty acres of prime land the Fox studio was situated on in Century City could be developed for high-rises or pricey condominiums.

After Davis left, it became evident that, as Barry Diller stated, "Aside from its financial status, which was some sort of electric shock to the brain, there was very little of a real company ... with any kind of thoughtful rationale and any kind of integration working for it." 1 Fox had been looted, perhaps not as insidiously as in 1930, but it had been through the ringer.

Since there never was an abundance of hits under Davis' ownership, the oilman had liquidated much of the studio's non-film assets to not only provide cash, but to also pay off $550 million in financing for his $720 million purchase of the studio. All the while, Fox was incurring greater debt with interest costs being paid out of revenues. For the fiscal year ending August 25, 1984, a loss of $89 million was disclosed. Stockholder equity in the company had dwindled from $301 million a year earlier to $67 million. Long-term debt, meanwhile, nearly tripled to $392 million. Another change, more historical than financial, was the dropping of a hyphen from the fifty year old trademark of Twentieth Century-Fox.

Finally, in early 1985, Marvin Davis sold the 50 percent ownership he retrieved from Marc Rich to the reclusive Australian-born international newspaper magnate, Rupert Murdoch for $162.5 million plus an $88 million advance to the Davis family holding company. Six months later, Murdoch agreed to pay $325 million more for Davis' share. Davis retained ownership of the Pebble Beach golf course near Monterey, California, a Colorado skiing resort in Aspen, and the land under a high-rise constructed on the Fox lot. It was estimated that Marvin Davis came away with $500 million and several hundreds of millions in profits.

Rupert Murdoch, with Barry Diller's help, saw Twentieth Century Fox as more than just a producer of motion pictures and television entertainment. After purchasing Marvin Davis' interests in the Company for $575 million, Murdoch spent an additional $1.6 billion to acquire the Metromedia group of television stations. With five strong major-city stations as a core group, Fox would attract other satellites to its proposed fourth network. All combined under the new Fox, Inc. banner, Fox Broadcasting Co. would finally challenge the three major networks. Through his News Corp., Murdoch would have the capital to spend on Fox.

"This is a long-term investment," Barry Diller reported, "We're not going to be jumping out of any windows if we don't show a profit in six months." [2] Certainly, with losses projected at $50 million for the first year of operation, Murdoch and Diller meant business. Fortunately, the studio turned out some successful movies. JEWEL OF THE NILE, a sequel to ROMANCING THE STONE, yielded about $100 million in world rentals. ALIENS, a sequel to ALIEN, performed almost as well. The non-remake of THE FLY in which very little save the initial concept of the 1958 "B" classic was used turned out to be a surprise financial and critical hit as well with $17.5 million in domestic rentals.

However, there was to be more executive shuffling. Leonard Goldberg, a successful television producer and Barry Diller's former boss at ABC, was brought on as president and chief operating officer, replacing Alan Horn whose tenure had

lasted only months. Horn could not bide by the amount of
involvement Diller wanted to partake in. Scott Rudin, the
chief production executive who was credited with initiating
such off-beat hits as ALIENS and THE FLY, would now report to Goldberg instead of waiting for Diller to respond.

By April 1987, the Los Angeles Times business section
announced on a full-page that "Diller's Hands-On Efforts Pull
Firm Off the Critical List." Most important for Fox was the
emergence of its television division and Fox Broadcasting.
For the first time in thirty years, there was an ongoing
competitor for the traditional bastions of TV power, the
networks. Fox announced a slate of original first-run
programs from producers like Gene Reynolds of M*A*S*H,
Ed Weinberger of THE MARY TYLER MOORE SHOW and THE
COSBY SHOW, and Stephen Cannell of THE A-TEAM and THE
ROCKFORD FILES. With a first-year production budget of
$110 million and a loosely-knit group of 100 stations, Fox
could offer advertisers an alternative to the ultra-high rates
of the networks.

Only time will tell how it will work. Fox could become
a television power, controlling more and more viewer time,
or it could be relegated to a drab fourth place for a financially debilitating period of time.

No matter what important technologies the future holds
for the entertainment industry, whether in theatrical entertainment, cable or satellite broadcasting, high-definition
home video, or over-the-air transmission, Twentieth Century
Fox through Rupert Murdoch's Fox, Inc. will most likely be
an important player in the race for the billions spent each
year in moviegoing and televiewing dollars. But producers
will always be on the edge of their seats wondering whether
their brainchild will hit the Variety All-Time Blockbuster
chart, or will sink into oblivion. Stan Hough, a long-
time industry member and observer stated succinctly, "That's
the agony of this business. If there's one reality, it's the
fact there is no reality. It's mind-boggling. There's nothing
in this industry you can put in a bottle and say, 'This is
it!' You just can't do it." [3]

■ CHAPTER NOTES ■

Chapter 1

1. Benjamin B. Hampton, A History of the Movies (New York: Covici Friede Publishers, 1931), p. 335.
2. Ibid., p. 337.
3. Bosley Crowther, The Lion's Share (New York: Dutton, 1957), p. 141.
4. New York Times Film Reviews, 1913–1931, (New York: New York Times and Arno Press, 1970).

Chapter 2

1. "Grosses in 1933 and 1934," Variety, January 1, 1935.
2. Sol Lesser, interviewed by Aubrey Solomon, December 18, 1974.
3. Samuel G. Engel, interviewed by Aubrey Solomon, December 16, 1974.
4. Ibid.
5. Fortune, December 1935, p. 90.
6. Mae D. Huettig, Economic Control of the Motion Picture Industry, A Dissertation in Industry (Philadelphia: University of Pennsylvania, 1944), p. 110.

Chapter 3

1. Samuel G. Engel, interviewed by Aubrey Solomon, December 8, 1976.
2. Ibid.
3. Ibid.
4. Nunnally Johnson, interviewed by Aubrey Solomon, May 30, 1973.

Chapter 3 (cont.)

5. Fortune, pp. 130-132.
6. Ibid., pp. 136-138.
7. The New York Times Film Reviews, 1932-1938, p. 1421.
8. Samuel G. Engel, December 16, 1974.
9. Ibid.
10. Huettig, p. 89.

Chapter 4

1. Norman Zierold, The Moguls, (New York: Coward, McCann, 1969), p. 257.
2. Time, June 12, 1950, p. 64.
3. Nunnally Johnson.
4. J.P. McEvoy, "He's Got Something," Saturday Evening Post, July 1, 1939, pp. 66-67.
5. Nunnally Johnson.
6. Philip Dunne, self-interview, tape, Special Collections, University of Southern California, Los Angeles.
7. Samuel G. Engel, December 8, 1976.
8. Leonard Mosley, Zanuck (Boston: Little, Brown, 1984), p. 145.
9. Time, June 12, 1950, p. 64
10. Nunnally Johnson.
11. Samuel G. Engel, December 16, 1974.
12. Ibid.
13. Delmer Daves, interviewed by Aubrey Solomon, March 6, 1973.
14. Darryl Zanuck, memo to Michael Curtiz, April 29, 1954, Philip Dunne Collection, Special Collections, University of Southern California, uncatalogued.
15. Darryl Zanuck, Memo to Philip Dunne, January 21, 1954, Philip Dunne Collection.
16. Darryl Zanuck, memo to Philip Dunne, August 3, 1953, Philip Dunne Collection.
17. Mel Gussow, Don't Say Yes Until I Finish Talking (New York: Doubleday, 1971), p. 75.
18. Ibid., p. 99.
19. Ibid., p. 100.
20. Time, June 12, 1950, p. 64.
21. Nunnally Johnson.

Chapter 5

1. Sol Lesser.
2. Ibid.
3. Huettig, p. 61.
4. Ibid., p. 136.
5. Ibid., p. 139.
6. Ibid., p. 140.
7. "Movie Surrender?," Business Week, November 17, 1945, p. 55.
8. Ibid., p. 56.
9. "Movie Makers Fear the Worst," Business Week, May 15, 1948, p. 28.

Chapter 6

1. "Retake for War," Business Week, July 25, 1942, p. 42.
2. "Nelson in Movies," Business Week, June 30, 1945, p. 28.
3. "Movies Worry," Business Week, March 16, 1946, p. 86.
4. Variety, January 5, 1949, p. 6.
5. "Boxoffice Pinch," Business Week, October 4, 1947.
6. Stan Hough, interviewed by Aubrey Solomon, December 16, 1974.

Chapter 7

1. Darryl Zanuck, memo to Philip Dunne, May 7, 1953, Philip Dunne Collection.
2. Ibid.
3. Darryl Zanuck, memo to Philip Dunne, August 1, 1953, Philip Dunne Collection.
4. Darryl Zanuck, memo to Philip Dunne, May 7, 1953, Philip Dunne Collection.
5. Variety, January 3, 1953.

Chapter 8

1. Life, July 20, 1953, p. 92.
2. "CinemaScope--What It Is; How It Works," American Cinematographer, Volume 34, Number 3, March 1953, p. 112.

Chapter 8 (cont.)

3. Ibid., p. 113.
4. Ibid., p. 132.
5. Delmer Daves.
6. Darryl Zanuck, memo to staff, March 12, 1953, Philip Dunne Collection.
7. Daily Variety, March 15, 1954, p. 1.

Chapter 9

1. Daily Variety, January 10, 1955, p. 1.
2. Ibid., March 3, 1954, p. 6.
3. Darryl Zanuck, memo to Philip Dunne, August 20, 1953, Philip Dunne Collection.
4. Ibid.
5. Darryl Zanuck, memo to Philip Dunne, August 26, 1953, Philip Dunne Collection.
6. Darryl Zanuck, memo to Philip Dunne, December 17, 1953, Philip Dunne Collection.
7. Sid Rogell, memo to Darryl Zanuck, October 27, 1954, Philip Dunne Collection.
8. Darryl Zanuck, memo to staff, October 26, 1955, Philip Dunne Collection.
9. Geoffrey Shurlock, letter to Frank McCarthy, June 27, 1955, Philip Dunne Collection.
10. Nunnally Johnson.
11. Philip Dunne, interviewed by Tom Stempel, Louis B. Mayer Foundation, American Film Institute, Los Angeles, 1971, p. 169.
12. Ibid., pp. 169–170.

Chapter 10

1. Stan Hough.
2. Samuel G. Engel.
3. Nunnally Johnson.
4. Samuel G. Engel.
5. Philip Dunne, interviewed by Tom Stempel, p. 134.
6. Stan Hough.
7. Ibid.
8. Samuel G. Engel.
9. Ibid.

Chapter 11

1. Nunnally Johnson.
2. Samuel G. Engel.
3. Tom Stempel, letter to Aubrey Solomon, August 2, 1973.
4. Nunnally Johnson.
5. Ibid.
6. Ibid.
7. Samuel G. Engel.
8. Philip Dunne, interviewed by Tom Stempel, p. 128.
9. Ibid., p. 172.
10. Ibid., p. 177.
11. Ibid., p. 180.
12. Stan Hough.
13. Op cit., p. 118.
14. Ibid., p. 170.
15. Samuel G. Engel.
16. Nunnally Johnson.
17. Daily Variety, July 25, 1957, p. 1.
18. Samuel G. Engel.
19. Philip Dunne, letter to Darryl Zanuck, February 16, 1961, Philip Dunne Collection.

Chapter 12

1. Daily Variety, March 20, 1957, p. 1.

Chapter 13

1. Jerry Wald, interviewed by Arthur Knight, T.V. Odyssey--The Liveliest Arts, tape, Special Collections, University of Southern California, September 13, 1961.

Chapter 14

1. Stan Hough.
2. Ibid.

Chapter 15

1. Stan Hough.

Chapter 15 (cont.)

2. Ibid.
3. Ibid.

Chapter 16

1. The Wall Street Journal, New York, April 22, 1971, p. 17.
2. Ibid.
3. Ibid., April 30, 1971, p. 7.
4. Stan Hough.
5. Tim Brooks and Earle Marsh, The Complete Directory to Prime Time Network TV Shows (New York: Ballantine, 1979), p. 662.

Chapter 17

1. Michael Nolin, interviewed by Aubrey Solomon, May 26, 1987.
2. Ibid.
3. Ibid.

Chapter 18

1. "Marvin Davis' script for 20th Century-Fox," Business Week, April 19, 1982, p. 93.
2. Michael Nolin.
3. Ibid.
4. Business Week, April 19, 1982.
5. "Hirschfield Resigns as Chairman of Fox," Los Angeles Times, September 11, 1984, Part IV, p. 93.
6. "Diller's Hands-On Efforts Pull Firm Off the Critical List," Los Angeles Times, April 19, 1987, Business Section, p. 1.
7. Business Week, April 19, 1982.

Chapter 19

1. Los Angeles Times, April 19, 1987.
2. Ibid.
3. Stan Hough.

■ BIBLIOGRAPHY ■

Allvine, Glendon. The Greatest Fox of Them All. New
York: Lyle Stuart, Inc., 1969.

American Cinematographer, Hollywood, California.

Boxoffice, Kansas City.

Business Week, New York.

Crowther, Bosley. The Lion's Share. New York: Dutton,
1957.

Daily Variety, Los Angeles.

Daves, Delmer. Interviewed by Aubrey Solomon, Los
Angeles: March 6, 1973.

Philip Dunne Collection, Los Angeles: USC Cinema Library.

Dunne, Philip. Interviewed by Tom Stempel, The American
Film Institute, The Louis B. Mayer Foundation, Los
Angeles: 1971.

Dunne, Philip. Self-interview, USC Cinema Library.

Engel, Samuel G. Interviewed by Aubrey Solomon, Los
Angeles: December 16, 1974.

Engel, Samuel G. Interviewed by Aubrey Solomon, Los
Angeles: December 8, 1976.

Fortune, New York: Time-Fortune Corporation.

Griffith, Richard, and Arthur L. Mayer. The Movies. New
York: Simon & Schuster, 1957.

Guild, Leo. Zanuck, Hollywood's Last Tycoon. Los Angeles: Holloway House Publishing Company, 1970.

Gussow, Mel. Don't Say Yes Until I Finish Talking. New York: Doubleday, 1971.

Hampton, Benjamin B. A History of the Movies. New York: Covici Friede Publishers, 1931.

Hough, Stan. Interviewed by Aubrey Solomon, Los Angeles: December 16, 1974.

Huettig, Mae D. Economic Control of the Motion Picture Industry, A Dissertation in Industry. Philadelphia: University of Pennsylvania, 1944.

Johnson, Nunnally. Interviewed by Aubrey Solomon, Los Angeles: May 28, 1973.

Knight, Arthur. The Liveliest Art. New York: Mentor Books, 1959.

Lesser, Sol. Interviewed by Aubrey Solomon, Los Angeles: December 18, 1974.

Life, New York.

Los Angeles Times, Los Angeles: Times-Mirror Publishing.

MacGowan, Kenneth, Behind the Screen. New York: Dell, 1965.

Mosley, Leonard, Zanuck. Boston: Little, Brown, 1984.

New York Times Film Reviews, 1913-1968. New York: New York Times and Arno Press, 1970.

Nolin, Michael. Interviewed by Aubrey Solomon, Los Angeles: May 26, 1987.

Sarris, Andrew. The American Cinema. New York: Dutton, 1968.

Sinclair, Upton. Upton Sinclair Presents William Fox. Los Angeles: (personally published) 1933.

<u>Time</u>. New York.

Thomas, Tony, and Aubrey Solomon, <u>The Films of 20th Century-Fox</u>. Secaucus, NJ: Citadel Press, 1985.

<u>T.V. Movies</u>, edited by Leonard Maltin. New York: Signet Books, 1969.

<u>Variety</u>, New York.

<u>The Wall Street Journal</u>, New York.

Wanger, Walter, and Joe Hyams. <u>My Life with Cleopatra</u>. New York: Bantam, 1963.

Zierold, Norman. <u>The Moguls</u>. New York: Coward, McCann, 1968.

■ APPENDIXES ■

These appendixes have been prepared as reference sources for the domestic rentals and costs of motion pictures produced and/or released by Twentieth Century-Fox. There are no complete listings of rentals but Variety started keeping a tally in 1946. Their figures are fairly accurate and serve as a good yardstick. For the purposes of these appendixes, the years 1935 through 1945 were reconstructed by figuring out a dollar equivalent to Boxoffice magazine's listing of percentages of normal business. These figures have been confirmed whenever possible from other industry papers such as The Motion Picture Almanac.

In the area of cost, there was little public information until Variety began routinely publishing reported budgets in the mid-1970's. For the costs of films before that, sources at the Fox studio have been helpful in assembling these appendixes.

In both cases, discrepancies may be found, but they are unintentional. There are also many features not included in the production cost listings due to a lack of information on some titles.

A. DOMESTIC RENTALS OF FILMS RELEASED BY ■ TWENTIETH CENTURY-FOX ■

1935	IN MILLIONS
Steamboat Round the Bend	1.5
In Old Kentucky	1.4
The Littlest Rebel	1.3
The Little Colonel	1.2
Curly Top	1.1
King of Burlesque	1.1

1936	
Lloyds of London	2.0
The Country Doctor	1.4
Poor Little Rich Girl	1.4
Captain January	1.3
Stowaway	1.0
Dimples	1.0
Ramona	1.0
Sing, Baby, Sing	1.0
The Road to Glory	1.0
Girls' Dormitory	1.0
Pigskin Parade	.9
Pepper	.5

1937	
In Old Chicago	2.5
Life Begins in College	1.5
Thin Ice	1.3
One in a Million	1.3
On the Avenue	1.3

Wake Up and Live	1.25
Slave Ship	1.1
This Is My Affair	1.0
Love Is News	1.0
Wife, Doctor, and Nurse	1.0
Heidi	1.0
Banjo on My Knee	.9
Cafe Metropole	.75
Seventh Heaven	.7

1938

Jesse James	3.0
Alexander's Ragtime Band	3.0
Suez	2.0
Happy Landing	2.0
Little Miss Broadway	1.75
Kentucky	1.75
My Lucky Star	1.75
Rebecca of Sunnybrook Farm	1.25
Five of a Kind	1.0
Just Around the Corner	1.0
Submarine Patrol	.95
Second Honeymoon	.85
Love and Hisses	.8
Susannah of the Mounties	.8

1939

The Rains Came	2.5
Drums Along the Mohawk	2.2
Stanley and Livingstone	2.0
Rose of Washington Square	1.5
Swanee River	1.25
The Little Princess	1.2
Second Fiddle	1.2
Hollywood Cavalcade	1.0
The Story of Alexander Graham Bell	.95
Young Mr. Lincoln	.75

1940

The Grapes of Wrath	2.5

Tin Pan Alley	2.0
Down Argentine Way	2.0
The Mark of Zorro	2.0
Brigham Young	1.5
The Return of Frank James	1.3
Chad Hanna	1.25
Lillian Russell	1.0
Johnny Apollo	1.0
Little Old New York	.9
Maryland	.9

1941

How Green Was My Valley	3.0
A Yank in the RAF	2.75
Charley's Aunt	2.4
Sun Valley Serenade	2.25
Blood and Sand	1.75
Weekend in Havana	1.75
Tobacco Road	1.65
That Night in Rio	1.6
Belle Starr	1.5
Swamp Water	1.5
Man Hunt	1.4
I Wake Up Screaming	1.25

1942

The Black Swan	3.5
Springtime in the Rockies	3.5
To the Shores of Tripoli	3.0
Footlight Serenade	2.5
My Gal Sal	2.5
Tales of Manhattan	2.5
Iceland	2.25
This Above All	2.2
Son of Fury	2.1
The Pied Piper	2.0
Orchestra Wives	2.0
Song of the Islands	1.75
Thunder Birds	1.75
Roxie Hart	1.5
The Magnificent Dope	1.25
Rings on Her Fingers	1.0

1943

Sweet Rosie O'Grady	3.5
Guadalcanal Diary	3.0
The Gang's All Here	2.5
Heaven Can Wait	2.5
Immortal Sergeant	2.5
My Friend Flicka	2.4
Claudia	2.25
The Lodger	2.0
Buffalo Bill	2.0
Home in Indiana	1.75
Jane Eyre	1.75
The Purple Heart	1.5
The Happy Land	1.5
Holy Matrimony	1.5
Lifeboat	1.0
The Sullivans	1.0
The Ox-Bow Incident	.75

1944

The Song of Bernadette	4.7
Winged Victory	4.0
A Tree Grows in Brooklyn	3.0
Diamond Horseshoe	3.0
The Keys of the Kingdom	2.4
Nob Hill	2.3
Thunderhead--Son of Flicka	2.25
A Wing and a Prayer	2.25
Irish Eyes Are Smiling	2.25
Laura	2.0
Sunday Dinner For a Soldier	2.0
Pin-Up Girl	2.0
Greenwich Village	1.85
Where Do We Go From Here?	1.75
A Royal Scandal	1.5
Sweet and Low Down	1.25
Something for the Boys	1.25
Take It or Leave It	1.1
Don Juan Quilligan	1.0
The Fighting Lady	.9
Hangover Square	.85
The Big Noise	.75

1945

The Dolly Sisters	4.0
State Fair	4.0
The House on 92nd Street	2.5
A Bell for Adano	2.5
A Walk in the Sun	2.25
Wilson	2.0
Junior Miss	1.75
Fallen Angel	1.5
Somewhere in the Night	1.5
Captain Eddy	1.0
A Yank in London	1.0
And Then There Were None	1.0

1946

Leave Her to Heaven	5.75
Margie	4.0
Smoky	4.0
Anna and the King of Siam	3.5
Centennial Summer	3.0
Do You Love Me?	3.0
Dragonwyk	3.0
Sentimental Journey	3.0
Three Little Girls in Blue	3.0
My Darling Clementine	2.75
Doll Face	2.5
Claudia and David	1.65
The Dark Corner	1.0
Cluny Brown	1.0
Black Beauty	.9
Wake Up and Dream	.9
Shock	.8
It Shouldn't Happen to a Dog	.8

1947

Forever Amber	6.0
The Razor's Edge	5.0
Mother Wore Tights	4.15
I Wonder Who's Kissing Her Now	3.2
The Foxes of Harrow	3.15

13 Rue Madeleine	2.75
Miracle on 34th Street	2.65
The Homestretch	2.35
Boomerang	2.25
The Shocking Miss Pilgrim	2.25
The Late George Apley	1.0
Carnival in Costa Rica	1.0
The Ghost and Mrs. Muir	.9

1948

Gentleman's Agreement	3.9
Captain From Castile	3.65
Sitting Pretty	3.55
When My Baby Smiles at Me	3.4
Apartment for Peggy	2.7
Call Northside 777	2.7
Road House	2.35
The Street With No Name	2.35
Give My Regards to Broadway	2.1
Green Grass of Wyoming	2.1
The Iron Curtain	2.0
Scudda Hoo Scudda Hay	2.0
You Were Meant for Me	2.0
Daisy Kenyon	1.75
Walls of Jericho	1.75
Kiss of Death	1.65
That Lady in Ermine	1.5

1949

Pinky	4.2
I Was a Male War Bride	4.1
The Snake Pit	4.1
Mr. Belvedere Goes to College	3.65
Come to the Stable	3.0
Yellow Sky	2.8
A Letter to Three Wives	2.75
Mother Is a Freshman	2.45
You're My Everything	2.4
House of Strangers	2.0
It Happens Every Spring	1.85
Father Was A Fullback	1.8

Down to the Sea in Ships	1.65
Slattery's Hurricane	1.65
That Wonderful Urge	1.65
Everybody Does It	1.6
Thieves' Highway	1.5
Sand	1.5

1950

Cheaper by the Dozen	4.3
Broken Arrow	3.5
12 O'Clock High	3.2
All About Eve	2.9
The Black Rose	2.65
Prince of Foxes	2.5
I'll Get By	2.45
American Guerilla in the Philippines	2.28
My Blue Heaven	2.28
Wabash Avenue	2.1
The Gunfighter	1.95
Oh, You Beautiful Doll	1.95
Three Came Home	1.9
Mister 880	1.75
When Willie Comes Marching Home	1.75
The Jackpot	1.53
No Way Out	1.3
Ticket to Tomahawk	1.3
The Big Lift	1.3
Dancing in the Dark	1.3
Where the Sidewalk Ends	1.0

1951

David and Bathsheba	7.0
Halls of Montezuma	2.65
On the Riviera	2.5
The Desert Fox	2.4
Call Me Mister	2.2
I'd Climb the Highest Mountain	2.15
Frogmen	2.1
People Will Talk	2.1
Elopement	2.0
Meet Me After the Show	2.0

Rawhide	1.95
The Day the Earth Stood Still	1.85
Take Care of My Little Girl	1.85
I'll Never Forget You	1.75
Mr. Belvedere Rings the Bell	1.75
For Heaven's Sake	1.7
Bird of Paradise	1.6
You're in the Navy Now	1.6
Anne of the Indies	1.55
Golden Girl	1.5
Half Angel	1.5
Fixed Bayonets	1.45
I Can Get It for You Wholesale	1.4
The Secret of Convict Lake	1.35
Let's Make It Legal	1.25
Follow the Sun	1.15
No Highway in the Sky	1.15
Millionaire for Christy	1.0
The Mudlark	1.0

1952

The Snows of Kilimanjaro	6.5
With a Song in My Heart	3.25
Stars and Stripes Forever	3.0
Belles on Their Toes	2.0
Bloodhounds of Broadway	2.0
Dreamboat	2.0
Lure of the Wilderness	2.0
Monkey Business	2.0
We're not Married	2.0
What Price Glory	2.0
Viva Zapata	1.9
Lydia Bailey	1.75
Pony Soldier	1.65
Pride of St. Louis	1.65
Decision Before Dawn	1.5
Don't Bother to Knock	1.5
Diplomatic Courier	1.4
Way of a Gaucho	1.4
Five Fingers	1.35
Phone Call From a Stanger	1.35
Deadline U.S.A.	1.25
Kangaroo	1.25

Red Skies of Montana	1.25
Wait 'Til the Sun Shines Nellie	1.25
The Model and the Marriage Broker	1.15
Les Miserables	1.1
My Pal Gus	1.0
O'Henry's Full House	1.0

1953

The Robe	17.5
How to Marry a Millionaire	7.3
Gentlemen Prefer Blondes	5.1
Call Me Madam	2.85
Niagara	2.35
Titanic	2.25
White Witch Doctor	2.0
Pickup on South Street	1.9
Ruby Gentry	1.75
Mr. Scoutmaster	1.6
The President's Lady	1.35
My Cousin Rachel	1.3
The "I Don't Care" Girl	1.25
Destination Gobi	1.2
The Girl Next Door	1.2
Treasure of the Golden Condor	1.2
The Farmer Takes a Wife	1.15
The Desert Rats	1.1
Powder River	1.0
The Star	1.0

1954

Three Coins in the Fountain	5.0
Desiree	4.5
Demetrius and the Gladiators	4.25
The Egyptian	4.25
River of No Return	3.8
Broken Lance	3.8
Beneath the 12-Mile Reef	3.6
Garden of Evil	3.1
Woman's World	3.0
Hell and High Water	2.7
King of the Khyber Rifles	2.6

Prince Valiant	2.6
Black Widow	2.5
Night People	2.15

1955

The Seven Year Itch	5.0
A Man Called Peter	4.5
There's No Business Like Show Business	4.5
The Tall Men	4.25
The Left Hand of God	4.0
Love Is a Many-Splendored Thing	4.0
Soldier of Fortune	2.75
Carmen Jones	2.5
Daddy Long Legs	2.5
Untamed	2.5
The Racers	1.75
House of Bamboo	1.7
How To Be Very, Very Popular	1.65
White Feather	1.65
The View From Pompey's Head	1.5
The Girl in the Red Velvet Swing	1.3
Violent Saturday	1.25

1956

The King and I	8.5
Anastasia	5.0
Love Me Tender	4.5
The Man in the Grey Flannel Suit	4.35
Bus Stop	4.25
Carousel	3.75
The Rains of Ranchipur	2.6
The Best Things in Life Are Free	2.25
Between Heaven and Hell	2.0
The Revolt of Mamie Stover	2.0
D-Day, the 6th of June	1.95
Teenage Rebel	1.75
The Last Wagon	1.5
The Proud Ones	1.4
On the Threshold of Space	1.15
The Bottom of the Bottle	1.12

Hilda Crane	1.0
23 Paces to Baker Street	1.0

1957

Island in the Sun	5.0
Heaven Knows, Mr. Allison	4.2
April Love	4.0
An Affair to Remember	3.8
Bernardine	3.75
The Sun Also Rises	3.5
Boy on a Dolphin	2.8
The Girl Can't Help It	2.8
Kiss Them For Me	1.8
The Wayward Bus	1.75
Desk Set	1.7
The True Story of Jesse James	1.5
A Hatful of Rain	1.5
Will Success Spoil Rock Hunter?	1.4
The Three Faces of Eve	1.4
Stopover Tokyo	1.35
No Down Payment	1.2

1958

South Pacific	17.5
Peyton Place	11.5
A Farewell to Arms	5.0
The Young Lions	4.5
The Inn of the Sixth Happiness	4.4
The Long, Hot Summer	3.5
The Roots of Heaven	3.0
The Barbarian and the Geisha	2.5
In Love and War	2.5
Mardi Gras	2.5
The Bravados	2.2
The Hunters	2.1
Ten North Frederick	2.0
The Fly	1.7
A Certain Smile	1.3

1959

Journey to the Center of the Earth	5.0
Say One for Me	3.6
Rally Round the Flag, Boys	3.4
The Best of Everything	3.0
Blue Denim	2.5
The Diary of Anne Frank	2.3
Compulsion	1.8
The Sound and the Fury	1.7
Warlock	1.7
A Private Affair	1.5
The Blue Angel	1.4
The Remarkable Mr. Pennypacker	1.3
Woman Obsessed	1.3
Holiday for Lovers	1.1

1960

From the Terrace	5.2
North to Alaska	5.0
Can-Can	4.2
The Story of Ruth	3.0
Sink the Bismark	3.0
High Time	2.5
The Lost World	2.5
Wake Me When It's Over	2.0
Wild River	1.5
Sons and Lovers	1.5
Crack in the Mirror	1.0
Masters of the Congo Jungle	1.0

1961

Return to Peyton Place	4.5
The Hustler	2.8
Voyage to the Bottom of the Sea	2.3
Flaming Star	2.0
Francis of Assisi	1.8
Snow White and the Three Stooges	1.5
All Hands on Deck	1.5
The Marriage-Go-Round	1.3

1962

The Longest Day	17.5
Mr. Hobbs Takes a Vacation	4.0
State Fair	3.5
Gigot	1.6
The Stripper	1.3
The Lion	1.3
Tender Is the Night	1.25
Satan Never Sleeps	1.2
Bachelor Flat	1.2
Five Weeks in a Balloon	1.2
The Innocents	1.2

1963

Cleopatra	26.0
Move Over, Darling	6.0
Take Her, She's Mine	3.4
Sodom and Gomorrah	2.3
The Leopard	1.8
The Condemned of Altona	1.1
Nine Hours to Rama	1.0

1964

What A Way to Go!	6.1
Goodbye Charlie	3.7
Rio Conchos	2.5
The Visit	1.1
The Man in the Middle	1.0
Fate Is the Hunter	1.0

1965

The Sound of Music (including reissue)	83.9
Those Magnificent Men in Their Flying Machines	14.0
Von Ryan's Express	7.7
Zorba the Greek	4.4
Hush, Hush Sweet Charlotte	4.0

The Agony and the Ecstasy	4.0
John Goldfarb, Please Come Home	3.0
Dear Brigitte	2.2
The Nanny	2.0

1966

The Bible	15.0
The Blue Max	8.4
Our Man Flint	7.2
Fantastic Voyage	5.5
How to Steal A Million	4.4
Stagecoach	4.0
Do Not Disturb	4.0
Flight of the Phoenix	3.0
Modesty Blaise	2.0
Way, Way Out	2.0
Batman	1.8

1967

Valley of the Dolls	20.0
The Sand Pebbles	13.5
Hombre	6.5
In Like Flint	5.0
A Guide for the Married Man	5.0
Tony Rome	4.0
Two For the Road	3.0
One Million Years, B.C.	2.5
Caprice	2.0
The Quiller Memorandum	1.5
The Flim-Flam Man	1.2
Fathom	1.0

1968

Planet of the Apes	15.0
The Boston Strangler	8.0
The Detective	6.5
Doctor Dolittle	6.2
Bandolero	5.5
Prudence and the Pill	4.5

The Secret Life of an American Wife	3.0
Bedazzled	1.5
The Sweet Ride	1.3

1969

Butch Cassidy and the Sundance Kid (including reissue)	44.0
The Undefeated	4.5
Star	4.2
100 Rifles	3.5
The Prime of Miss Jean Brodie	3.0
Che	2.5
The Chairman	2.5
Justine	2.2
Staircase	1.85
Hard Contract	1.75
Joanna	1.25
The Magus	1.0

1970

M*A*S*H (including reissue)	40.5
Patton (including reissue)	28.1
Hello Dolly	15.2
Tora! Tora! Tora!	14.5
Beneath the Planet of the Apes	8.45
Beyond the Valley of the Dolls	6.8
John and Mary	4.1
Myra Breckinridge	4.0
The Only Game in Town	1.5
The Sicilian Clan	1.0

1971

The French Connection	27.5
Escape From the Planet of the Apes	5.5
Vanishing Point	4.25
The Great White Hope	2.8
Little Murders	1.5

1972

Conquest of the Planet of the Apes	4.5
The Other	3.5
The Hot Rock	3.5
Concert for Bangladesh	2.5
Made for Each Other	1.5
The Culpepper Cattle Company	1.25

1973

The Poseidon Adventure (including reissue)	42.5
The Sound of Music (reissue)	11.0
Sounder	9.0
Sleuth	5.75
The Heartbreak Kid	5.6
Battle for the Planet of the Apes	4.0
The Neptune Factor	2.75
The Legend of Hell House	2.5
Emperor of the North	2.0
Gordon's War	1.25
The Last American Hero	1.25

1974

Butch Cassidy and the Sundance Kid (reissue)	13.8
Dirty Mary and Crazy Larry	12.1
The Three Musketeers	10.1
The Poseidon Adventure (reissue)	4.75
SPYS	4.55
Harry and Tonto	4.5
The Seven-Ups	4.1
M*A*S*H (reissue)	4.0
Cinderella Liberty	3.7
The Paper Chase	3.6
Claudine	3.0
Conrack	2.0
Zardoz	1.8
The Laughing Policeman	1.75

1975

The Towering Inferno	52.0
Young Frankenstein (including reissues)	38.8
The Rocky Horror Picture Show	26.0
The Four Musketeers	8.76
W.W. and the Dixie Dancekings	8.0
Race With the Devil	5.8
French Connection II	5.6
Capone	2.0
At Long Last Love	2.5

1976

The Omen	27.85
Silent Movie	21.24
Lucky Lady	12.1
Adventures of Sherlock Holmes' Smarter Brother	9.4
Mother, Jugs & Speed	7.63
The Duchess and the Dirtwater Fox	4.12
The Blue Bird	3.5
I Will, I Will ... For Now	1.74
Sky Riders	1.73
Alex and the Gypsy	1.06
Next Stop, Greenwich Village	1.06

1977

Star Wars (including reissues)	193.5
Silver Streak	30.0
The Other Side of Midnight	18.4
Young Frankenstein (reissue)	8.0
Damnation Alley	4.0
Wizards	3.3
Suspiria	1.8
Raggedy Ann and Andy	1.35
Mr. Billion	1.3

1978

High Anxiety	19.1
The Turning Point	17.06
Julia	13.05
Omen II: Damien	12.05
An Unmarried Woman	12.0
The Fury	11.1
The World's Greatest Lover	9.9
The Boys From Brazil	7.98
A Wedding	3.6
The Driver	2.25

1979

Alien (including reissues)	40.3
The Rose	19.1
Magic	13.08
Star Wars (reissue)	11.54
Breaking Away	10.3
Norma Rae	10.0
Young Frankenstein (reissue)	4.29
Butch and Sundance: The Early Years	2.26

1980

The Empire Strikes Back (including reissues)	141.6
All That Jazz	20.03
Brubaker	19.3
My Bodyguard	9.5
A Change of Seasons	7.27
Middle Age Crazy	6.0
Terror Train	3.5
The Stunt Man	3.0

1981

9 to 5	59.1
The Cannonball Run	36.8
The Empire Strikes Back	14.15

History of the World--Part I	14.4
Fort Apache--The Bronx	13.65
The Final Conflict	10.0
Hardly Working	8.86
On the Right Track	5.9
Zorro, the Gay Blade	5.1
Eyewitness	4.5
Tribute	4.0
Death Hunt	3.05
Southern Comfort	1.76

1982

Porky's	54.0
Taps	20.5
Young Doctors in Love	15.2
Modern Problems	14.8
Quest For Fire	12.2
Six Pack	10.7
Star Wars (reissue)	8.36
Author! Author!	7.5
Monsignor	6.5
Visiting Hours	6.4
Making Love	6.1
The Empire Strikes Back (reissue)	5.79
Alien (reissue)	5.1
National Lampoon's Class Reunion	5.0
Brubaker (reissue)	5.0
The Pirate Movie	4.0
I Ought to Be in Pictures	4.2
The Amateur	4.0
All That Jazz (reissue)	3.75
Megaforce	3.5
My Bodyguard (reissue)	3.5

1983

Return of the Jedi	168.0
Mr. Mom	31.5
The Verdict	27.3
Porky's II: The Next Day	17.2
Man From Snowy River	9.25
Max Dugan Returns	8.8

All the Right Moves	8.1
Kiss Me Goodbye	7.6
Star Chamber	2.8
The Osterman Weekend	2.5
Betrayal	1.8
Heaven	1.75
The Empire Strikes Back	1.6
Eating Raoul	1.6
Tough Enough	1.3
The King of Comedy	1.2

1984

Romancing the Stone	36.0
Revenge of the Nerds	19.5
Bachelor Party	19.0
Silkwood	17.83
The Gods Must Be Crazy	13.0
Rhinestone	12.25
Two of a Kind	12.0
The Flamingo Kid	11.6
Unfaithfully Yours	10.0
Blame It on Rio	9.75
Johnny Dangerously	9.1
To Be or Not to Be	6.0
Dreamscape	5.4
The Adventures of Buckaroo Banzai	3.0
Reuben, Reuben	1.1

1985

Cocoon	40.0
Jewel of the Nile	36.5
Commando	17.0
Prizzi's Honor	13.0
Porky's Revenge	10.2
Enemy Mine	5.6
Moving Violations	4.9
The Man With One Red Shoe	4.3
Mischief	4.1
Plenty	3.0
Turk 182	1.9
Bad Medicine	1.0

1986

Aliens	42.5
The Fly	17.5
Jewel of the Nile	16.5
Jumpin' Jack Flash	11.0
The Morning After	8.5
Big Trouble in Little China	6.0
Space Camp	5.0
Lucas	3.3
The Boy Who Could Fly	2.85
The Name of the Rose	2.5
The Manhattan Project	2.0

B. PRODUCTION COSTS OF FILMS RELEASED BY
▪ TWENTIETH CENTURY-FOX ▪

C/S denotes CinemaScope   P/V denotes Panavision

1929

Sunnyside Up	$805,000
The Cock-Eyed World	$765,000

1930

The Big Trail	$1,900,000
Just Imagine	$1,100,000
Renegades	$570,000
Wild Company	$240,000

1931

Delicious	$690,000
The Yellow Ticket	$470,000
Quick Millions	$208,000

1932

Call Her Savage	$545,000
Down to Earth	$545,000
Sherlock Holmes	$395,000
Chandu the Magician	$395,000
Six Hours to Live	$380,000
Me and My Gal	$355,000

The Golden West	$300,000
Silent Witness	$200,000

1933

Cavalcade	$1,300,000
State Fair	$705,000
Zoo in Budapest	$485,000
Hot Pepper	$420,000
Pilgrimage	$415,000
Doctor Bull	$415,000
Mr. Skitch	$415,000
The Power and the Glory	$405,000
Hello Sister	$395,000
The Worst Woman in Paris	$290,000
Sailor's Luck	$285,000
Pleasure Cruise	$275,000
Broadway Bad	$275,000
The Devil's in Love	$265,000
Walls of Gold	$186,000
The Man Who Dared	$180,000
Jimmy and Sally	$170,000
Arizona to Broadway	$135,000

1934

The World Moves On	$835,000
Music in the Air	$675,000
Change of Heart	$495,000
The Coming Out Party	$360,000
She Learned About Sailors	$230,000
Wild Gold	$215,000

1935

George White's 1935 Scandals	$995,000
Clive of India	$650,000
Thanks a Million	$647,000
Charlie Chan in Paris	$125,000
Hard Rock Harrigan	$125,000

1936

Lloyds of London	$1,000,000
The Country Doctor	$650,000
Ramona (Technicolor)	$600,000
Stowaway	$500,000

1937

On the Avenue	$1,000,000
Wings of the Morning (Technicolor)	$850,000
We're Going to Be Rich	$500,000

1938

In Old Chicago	$1,550,000
Alexander's Ragtime Band	$1,300,000
Kentucky (Technicolor)	$1,000,000
Heidi	$600,000
Five of a Kind	$500,000

1939

Drums Along the Mohawk (Tech-nicolor)	$1,400,000
Stanley and Livingstone	$1,340,000
Jesse James (Technicolor)	$1,165,000
Swanee River (Technicolor)	$1,000,000
The Little Princess (Tech-nicolor)	$700,000

1940

Brigham Young, Frontiersman	$1,485,000
The Blue Bird (Technicolor)	$1,000,000
The Mark of Zorro	$1,000,000
The Return of Frank James (Technicolor)	$950,000
The Grapes of Wrath	$800,000
Down Argentine Way (Technicolor)	$800,000

1941

Blood and Sand (Technicolor)	$1,200,000
Moon Over Miami (Technicolor)	$950,000
How Green Was My Valley	$800,000
Charley's Aunt	$650,000

1942

The Black Swan (Technicolor)	$1,500,000
Iceland	$1,120,000
Springtime in the Rockies (Technicolor)	$1,050,000
To the Shores of Tripoli (Technicolor)	$1,000,000
China Girl	$900,000
The Pied Piper	$650,000
Manila Calling	$280,000
Berlin Correspondent	$205,000

1943

The Gang's All Here	$2,085,000
Buffalo Bill	$2,040,000
Song of the Islands (Technicolor)	$2,010,000
Jane Eyre	$1,705,000
Hello, Frisco, Hello (Technicolor)	$1,665,000
Wintertime	$1,650,000
Coney Island (Technicolor)	$1,620,000
Crash Dive (Technicolor)	$1,565,000
The Moon Is Down	$1,195,000
Sweet Rosie O'Grady (Technicolor)	$1,185,000
Guadalcanal Diary	$1,135,000
Heaven Can Wait (Technicolor)	$1,115,000
Claudia	$1,095,000
The Immortal Sergeant	$1,025,000
The Meanest Man in the World	$915,000
Stormy Weather	$910,000
My Friend Flicka (Technicolor)	$760,000
Happy Land	$710,000
Holy Matrimony	$705,000

The Ox-Bow Incident	$565,000
Life Begins at 8:30	$505,000
Tonight We Raid Calais	$415,000

1944

Wilson (Technicolor)	$2,995,000
Keys of the Kingdom	$2,680,000
Something For the Boys (Technicolor)	$2,005,000
Wing and a Prayer	$1,895,000
Greenwich Village (Technicolor	$1,830,000
A Tree Grows in Brooklyn	$1,820,000
Irish Eyes Are Smiling (Technicolor)	$1,635,000
Pin-Up Girl (Technicolor)	$1,615,000
Lifeboat	$1,590,000
Winged Victory	$1,530,000
Sweet and Low Down	$1,295,000
Home in Indiana (Technicolor)	$1,285,000
The Eve of St. Mark	$1,255,000
Four Jills in a Jeep	$1,125,000
Thunderhead--Son of Flicka (Technicolor)	$1,090,000
Sunday Dinner for a Soldier	$1,085,000
Laura	$1,020,000
The Sullivans	$955,000
The Lodger	$870,000
The Purple Heart	$840,000

1945

Diamond Horseshoe (Technicolor)	$2,535,000
The Dolly Sisters (Technicolor)	$2,510,000
Captain Eddie	$2,465,000
Where Do We Go From Here? (Technicolor)	$2,445,000
Do You Love Me? (Technicolor)	$2,245,000
Nob Hill (Technicolor)	$2,235,000
State Fair (Technicolor)	$2,075,000
A Bell For Adano	$1,995,000
Dragonwyck	$1,920,000
A Royal Scandal	$1,755,000

Junior Miss	$1,325,000
Hangover Square	$1,155,000
Fallen Angel	$1,075,000
Colonel Effingham's Raid	$1,050,000
The House on 92nd Street	$965,000

1946

The Razor's Edge	$3,355,000
Carnival in Costa Rica (Technicolor)	$3,215,000
The Shocking Miss Pilgrim (Technicolor)	$2,595,000
Three Little Girls in Blue (Technicolor)	$2,335,000
Centennial Summer (Technicolor)	$2,275,000
My Darling Clementine	$2,235,000
Anna and the King of Siam	$2,210,000
Thirteen Rue Madeleine	$2,005,000
Margie (Technicolor)	$1,635,000
If I'm Lucky	$1,615,000
Cluny Brown	$1,600,000
Wake Up and Dream (Technicolor)	$1,590,000
Smoky (Technicolor)	$1,380,000
Claudia and David	$1,265,000
The Dark Corner	$1,225,000
Doll Face	$1,120,000
Home Sweet Homicide	$1,110,000
Sentimental Journey	$1,015,000
Somewhere in the Night	$915,000

1947

Forever Amber (Technicolor)	$6,375,000
The Foxes of Harrow	$2,905,000
Mother Wore Tights (Technicolor)	$2,725,000
The Homestretch (Technicolor)	$2,650,000
I Wonder Who's Kissing Her Now (Technicolor)	$2,650,000
The Late George Apley	$2,070,000
Moss Rose	$2,020,000
The Ghose and Mrs. Muir	$1,965,000
Nightmare Alley	$1,915,000

Scudda Hoo Scudda Hay (Technicolor)	$1,685,000
Miracle on 34th Street	$1,570,000
Kiss of Death	$1,525,000
Boomerang	$1,140,000
The Brasher Doubloon	$1,000,000

1948

Captain From Castile (Technicolor)	$4,500,000
The Snake Pit	$2,640,000
That Lady in Ermine	$2,485,000
When My Baby Smiles at Me (Technicolor)	$2,360,000
Beautiful Blonde From Bashful Bend (Technicolor)	$2,260,000
Gentleman's Agreement	$1,985,000
Green Grass of Wyoming (Technicolor)	$1,970,000
Walls of Jericho	$1,945,000
Unfaithfully Yours	$1,925,000
Daisy Kenyon	$1,850,000
The Iron Curtain	$1,785,000
Luck of the Irish	$1,785,000
The Street With No Name	$1,660,000
Give My Regards to Broadway (Technicolor)	$1,650,000
Apartment For Peggy (Technicolor)	$1,595,000
Fury At Furnace Creek	$1,520,000
Deep Waters	$1,500,000
Road House	$1,440,000
Call Northside 777	$1,440,000
Sitting Pretty	$1,320,000
You Were Meant For Me	$1,265,000

1949

I Was A Male War Bride	$3,330,000
Prince of Foxes	$2,600,000
Down to the Sea in Ships	$2,490,000
Oh, You Beautiful Doll (Technicolor)	$1,965,000

Chicken Every Sunday	$1,935,000
You're My Everything (Technicolor)	$1,920,000
The Forbidden Street	$1,790,000
That Wonderful Urge	$1,670,000
A Letter to Three Wives	$1,665,000
Dancing in the Dark (Technicolor)	$1,640,000
Slattery's Hurricane	$1,625,000
House of Strangers	$1,610,000
Come to the Stable	$1,590,000
Pinky	$1,585,000
Mother Is a Freshman (Technicolor)	$1,560,000
Yellow Sky	$1,500,000
Everybody Does It	$1,460,000
Father Was a Fullback	$1,430,000
The Fan	$1,420,000
Sand (Technicolor)	$1,400,000
Mr. Belvedere Goes to College	$1,330,000
It Happens Every Spring	$1,330,000
Thieves' Highway	$1,300,000

1950

The Black Rose (Technicolor)	$3,735,000
My Blue Heaven (Technicolor)	$2,135,000
Wabash Avenue (Technicolor)	$2,115,000
Broken Arrow (Technicolor)	$2,025,000
A Ticket to Tomahawk (Technicolor)	$1,910,000
Twelve O'Clock High	$1,875,000
Cheaper By the Dozen (Technicolor)	$1,700,000
American Guerilla in the Philippines (Technicolor)	$1,655,000
Under My Skin	$1,635,000
Three Came Home	$1,635,000
The Big Lift	$1,570,000
I'll Get By (Technicolor)	$1,545,000
Halls of Montezuma (Technicolor)	$1,500,000
Where the Sidewalk Ends	$1,475,000
Night and the City	$1,460,000
The Gunfighter	$1,420,000
All About Eve	$1,400,000
When Willie Comes Marching Home	$1,390,000
Panic in the Streets	$1,370,000

Whirlpool	$1,295,000
No Way Out	$1,290,000
Mr. 880	$1,200,000
Love That Brute	$1,065,000

1951

David and Bathsheba (Technicolor)	$2,170,000
No Highway in the Sky	$2,165,000
On the Riviera (Technicolor)	$2,090,000
Kangaroo (Technicolor)	$2,035,000
Decision Before Dawn	$2,000,000
Two Flags West	$1,900,000
Call Me Mister (Technicolor)	$1,900,000
The Mudlark	$1,875,000
Meet Me After the Show (Technocolor)	$1,825,000
Lydia Bailey	$1,775,000
Bird of Paradise (Technicolor)	$1,600,000
I'll Never Forget You (Technicolor)	$1,600,000
Down Among the Sheltering Palms (Technicolor)	$1,570,000
The House on Telegraph Hill	$1,500,000
You're in the Navy Now	$1,475,000
Follow the Sun	$1,450,000
Anne of the Indies (Technicolor)	$1,420,000
Mr. Belvedere Rings the Bell	$1,415,000
The Desert Fox	$1,400,000
Fourteen Hours	$1,360,000
The Frogmen	$1,350,000
Rawhide	$1,305,000
Stella	$1,280,000
Half Angel (Technicolor)	$1,250,000
For Heaven's Sake	$1,220,000
Take Care of My Little Girl (Technicolor)	$1,200,000
I'd Climb the Highest Mountain (Technicolor)	$1,190,000
I Can Get It For You Wholesale	$1,150,000
The Jackpot	$1,150,000
The Thirteenth Letter	$1,075,000
Day the Earth Stood Still	$995,000
Love Nest	$765,000

1952

The Snows of Kilimanjaro (Technicolor)	$2,615,000
Way of a Gaucho (Technicolor)	$2,240,000
Tonight We Sing (Technicolor)	$2,070,000
The Farmer Takes a Wife (Technicolor)	$1,860,000
The I Don't Care Girl (Technicolor)	$1,810,000
Stars and Stripes Forever (Technicolor)	$1,805,000
Viva Zapata	$1,800,000
What Price Glory? (Technicolor)	$1,790,000
Pony Soldier (Technicolor)	$1,690,000
With A Song in My Heart (Technicolor)	$1,665,000
The Girl Next Door (Technicolor)	$1,620,000
Monkey Business	$1,615,000
People Will Talk	$1,480,000
Les Miserables	$1,425,000
Diplomatic Courier	$1,350,000
Wait Til the Sun Shines Nellie (Technicolor)	$1,305,000
Red Skies of Montana (Technicolor)	$1,290,000
Dreamboat	$1,220,000
We're Not Married	$1,170,000
Belles on Their Toes (Technicolor)	$1,130,000
Five Fingers	$1,110,800
Lure of the Wilderness (Technicolor)	$1,095,000
Model and the Marriage Broker	$1,020,000
Elopement	$960,000
O. Henry's Full House	$945,000
Bloodhounds of Broadway (Technicolor)	$875,000
Let's Make It Legal	$835,000
Phone Call From a Stranger	$800,000
Return of the Texan	$765,000
Something For the Birds	$760,000
The Pride of St. Louis	$725,000
Night Without Sleep	$705,000
Fixed Bayonets	$685,000
Don't Bother to Knock	$555,000

1953

The Robe (C/S, color)	$4,100,000
Call Me Madam (Technicolor)	$2,460,000
Gentlemen Prefer Blondes (Technicolor)	$2,260,000
White Witch Doctor (Technicolor)	$2,020,000
How to Marry a Millionaire (C/S, color)	$1,870,000
Titanic	$1,805,000
Niagara (Technicolor)	$1,670,000
Beneath the 12-Mile Reef (C/S, color)	$1,560,000
The President's Lady	$1,475,000
Down Among the Sheltering Palms (Technicolor)	$1,400,000
Destination Gobi (Technicolor)	$1,340,000
The Desert Rats	$1,320,000
Treasure of the Golden Condor (Technicolor)	$1,220,000
Sailor of the King	$1,220,000
Man On a Tightrope	$1,200,000
My Cousin Rachel	$1,200,000
Inferno (Technicolor, 3-D)	$1,055,000
Powder River (Technicolor)	$985,000
The Glory Brigade	$850,000
Taxi	$820,000
Mr. Scoutmaster	$795,000
Pickup on South Street	$780,000
City of Bad Men (Technicolor)	$740,000
My Pal Gus	$725,000
The Kid From Left Field	$670,000
Vicki	$560,000
The Silver Whip	$560,000

1954

There's No Business Like Show Business (C/S, color)	$4,340,000
The Egyptian (C/S, color)	$3,900,000
Prince Valiant (C/S, color)	$2,970,000
Desiree (C/S, color)	$2,720,000
River of No Return (C/S, color)	$2,195,000
King of the Khyber Rifles (C/S, color)	$2,190,000

Garden of Evil (C/S, color)	$2,070,000
Woman's World (C/S, color)	$2,010,000
Demetrius and the Gladiators (C/S, color)	$1,990,000
Hell and High Water (C/S, color)	$1,870,000
Three Coins in the Fountain (C/S, color)	$1,700,000
Broken Lance (C/S, color)	$1,685,000
Night People (C/S, color)	$1,250,000
Black Widow (C/S, color)	$1,095,000
The Raid (Technicolor)	$650,000
Three Young Texans (Technicolor)	$505,000
Princess of the Nile (Technicolor)	$475,000
Gorilla At Large (Technicolor, 3-D)	$400,000

1955

Untamed (C/S, color)	$3,560,000
The Tall Men (C/S, color)	$3,115,000
The Racers (C/S, color)	$2,730,000
Daddy Long Legs (C/S, color)	$2,600,000
Soldier of Fortune (C/S, color)	$2,515,000
The Left Hand of God (C/S, color)	$1,785,000
Love Is a Many Splendored Thing (C/S, color)	$1,780,000
A Man Called Peter (C/S, color)	$1,740,000
The Girl in the Red Velvet Swing (C/S, color)	$1,700,000
The Virgin Queen (C/S, color)	$1,600,000
Prince of Players (C/S, color)	$1,570,000
How to Be Very, Very Popular (C/S, color)	$1,565,000
Seven Cities of Gold (C/S, color)	$1,545,000
Good Morning, Miss Dove (C/S, color)	$1,470,000
House of Bamboo (C/S, color)	$1,380,000
The View From Pompey's Head (C/S, color)	$1,230,000
White Feather (C/S, color)	$1,125,000
Violent Saturday (C/S, color)	$955,000

1956

The King and I (C/S, color)	$4,550,000

Anastasia (C/S, color)	$3,520,000
Carousel (C/S, color)	$3,380,000
The Rains of Ranchipur (C/S, color)	$2,900,000
The Best Things in Life Are Free C/S, color)	$2,710,000
Man in the Gray Flannel Suit (C/S, color)	$2,670,000
Bus Stop (C/S, color)	$2,200,000
D-Day, the 6th of June (C/S, color)	$2,075,000
The Revolt of Mamie Stover (C/S, color)	$2,000,000
The Bottom of the Bottle (C/S, color)	$1,695,000
The Last Wagon (C/S, color)	$1,670,000
Between Heaven and Hell (C/S, color)	$1,520,000
On the Threshold of Space (C/S, color)	$1,505,000
The Proud Ones (C/S, color)	$1,400,000
Twenty Three Paces to Baker Street (C/S, color)	$1,375,000
Love Me Tender (C/S)	$1,250,000
Hilda Crane (C/S, color)	$1,140,000
Bigger Than Life (C/S, color)	$1,000,000
Teenage Rebel (C/S)	$985,000
The Lieutenant Wore Skirts (C/S, color)	$970,000
Stagecoach to Fury (C/S)	$125,000

1957

The Sun Also Rises (C/S, color)	$3,815,000
Boy On A Dolphin (C/S, color)	$3,300,000
Heaven Knows, Mr. Allison (C/S, color)	$2,905,000
Island in the Sun (C/S, color)	$2,250,000
An Affair to Remember (C/S, color)	$2,120,000
Kiss Them For Me (C/S, color)	$1,945,000
The Enemy Below (C/S, color)	$1,910,000
Desk Set (C/S, color)	$1,865,000
A Hatful of Rain (C/S)	$1,820,000

Oh Men, Oh Women (C/S, color)	$1,780,000
The True Story of Jesse James (C/S, color)	$1,585,000
The Wayward Bus (C/S)	$1,465,000
April Love (C/S, color)	$1,425,000
The Girl Can't Help It (C/S, color)	$1,310,000
Bernardine (C/S, color)	$1,230,000
Stopover: Tokyo (C/S, color)	$1,055,000
Three Brave Men (C/S)	$1,050,000
Will Success Spoil Rock Hunter? (C/S, color)	$1,050,000
No Down Payment (C/S)	$995,000
The Three Faces of Eve (C/S)	$965,000
The Way to the Gold (C/S)	$920,000
Forty Guns (C/S)	$300,000
China Gate (C/S)	$150,000

1958

South Pacific (Todd-AO, color)	$5,610,000
A Farewell to Arms (C/S, color)	$4,100,000
The Inn of the 6th Happiness (C/S, color)	$3,570,000
The Young Lions (C/S)	$3,550,000
The Barbarian and the Geisha (C/S, color)	$3,495,000
The Roots of Heaven (C/S, color)	$3,300,000
The Hunters (C/S, color)	$2,440,000
A Certain Smile (C/S, color)	$2,330,000
Peyton Place (C/S, color)	$2,200,000
Rally Round the Flag, Boys (C/S, color)	$1,870,000
The Blue Angel (C/S, color)	$1,700,000
Mardi Gras (C/S, color)	$1,690,000
The Long, Hot Summer (C/S, color)	$1,645,000
These Thousand Hills (C/S, color)	$1,645,000
In Love and War (C/S, color)	$1,590,000
Ten North Frederick (C/S)	$1,550,000
Fraulein (C/S, color)	$1,400,000
The Gift of Love (C/S, color)	$1,215,000
Sing, Boy, Sing (C/S)	$860,000
The Fiend Who Walked the West C/S)	$850,000
The Fly (C/S, color)	$495,000

1959

The Diary of Anne Frank (C/S)	$3,800,000
Journey to the Center of the Earth (C/S, color)	$3,440,000
Warlock (C/S, color)	$2,400,000
Beloved Infidel (C/S, color)	$2,340,000
Say One For Me (C/S, color)	$1,990,000
Holiday for Lovers (C/S, color)	$1,970,000
The Best of Everything (C/S, color)	$1,965,000
The Man Who Understood Women (C/S, color)	$1,775,000
Woman Obsessed (C/S, color)	$1,730,000
The Sound and the Fury (C/S, color)	$1,710,000
The Remarkable Mr. Pennypacker (C/S, color)	$1,475,000
Compulsion (C/S)	$1,345,000
A Private's Affair (C/S, color)	$1,200,000
Hound Dog Man (C/S, color)	$1,045,000
Blue Denim (C/S)	$980,000

1960

Can-Can (Todd-AO, color)	$4,995,000
North to Alaska (C/S, color)	$3,800,000
Let's Make Love (C/S, color)	$3,585,000
From the Terrace (C/S, color)	$3,035,000
The Story of Ruth (C/S, color)	$2,930,000
High Time (C/S, color)	$2,815,000
Wild River (C/S, color)	$1,595,000
The Story on Page One (C/S)	$1,748,000
Flaming Star (C/S, color)	$1,700,000
Seven Thieves (C/S)	$1,650,000
The Lost World (C/S, color)	$1,515,000
Sink the Bismark (C/S)	$1,330,000
One Foot in Hell (C/S, color)	$1,090,000
Sons and Lovers (C/S)	$805,000
A Dog of Flanders (C/S, color)	$600,000

1961

The Comancheros (C/S, color)	$4,260,000

Wild in the Country (C/S, color)	$2,975,000
Snow White and the 3 Stooges (C/S, color)	$2,285,000
The Hustler (C/S)	$2,125,000
Francis of Assisi (C/S, color)	$2,015,000
Sanctuary (C/S)	$1,915,000
Return to Peyton Place (C/S, color)	$1,785.000
Marines, Let's Go (C/S, color)	$1,665,000
Voyage to the Bottom of the Sea (C/S, color)	$1,580,000
All Hands on Deck (C/S, color)	$1,115,000
The Right Approach (C/S)	$920,000
The Fiercest Heart (C/S, color)	$745,000
Misty (C/S, color)	$705,000
The Pirates of Tortuga (C/S, color)	$675,000
Wizard of Baghdad (C/S, color)	$575,000
Seven Women from Hell (C/S)	$300,000

1962

The Longest Day (C/S)	$7,750,000
State Fair (C/S, color)	$4,410,000
Mr. Hobbs Takes a Vacation (C/S, color)	$4,105,000
Adventures of a Young Man (C/S, color)	$4,100,000
Tender Is the Night (C/S, color)	$3,900,000
Five Weeks in a Balloon (C/S, color)	$2,340,000
The Stripper (C/S)	$2,175,000
Bachelor Flat (C/S, color)	$1,495,000

1963

Cleopatra (Todd-AO, color)	$42,000,000
The Lion (C/S, color)	$4,345,000
Nine Hours to Rama (C/S, color)	$3,610,000
Move Over, Darling (C/S, color)	$3,350,000
Satan Never Sleeps (C/S, color)	$2,885,000
Take Her, She's Mine (C/S, color)	$2,435,000

1964

What a Way to Go (C/S, color)	$3,750,000
Goodbye, Charlie (C/S, color)	$3,500,000
Fate Is the Hunter (C/S)	$2,525,000
The Pleasure Seekers (C/S, color)	$2,100,000
Shock Treatment (C/S)	$1,285,000

1965

The Sound of Music (Todd-AO, color)	$8,020,000
The Agony and the Ecstasy (Todd-AO, color)	$7,175,000
Those Magnificent Men in Their Flying Machines (Todd-AO, color)	$6,500,000
Morituri	$6,290,000
Von Ryan's Express (C/S, color)	$5,760,000
The Blue Max (C/S, color)	$5,000,000
Do Not Disturb (C/S, color)	$3,890,000
John Goldfarb, Please Come Home (C/S, color)	$3,705,000
The Reward (C/S, color)	$2,685.000
Dear Brigitte (C/S, color)	$2,470,000
Hush, Hush Sweet Charlotte	$2,235,000

1966

The Bible (Dimension 150, color)	$15,000,000
The Sand Pebbles (Todd-AO, color)	$12,110,000
How To Steal a Million (P/V, color)	$6,480,000
Flight of the Phoenix (color)	$5,355,000
Fantastic Voyage (C/S, color)	$5,115,000
Our Man Flint (C/S, color)	$3,525,000
Stagecoach (C/S, color)	$3,500,000
Way, Way Out (C/S, color)	$2,955,000
Batman (color)	$1,540,000

1967

Doctor Dolittle (Todd-AO, color)	$17,015,000

Hombre (P/V, color)	$5,860,000
Two for the Road (P/V, color)	$5,080,000
Valley of the Dolls (P/V, color)	$4,690,000
Caprice (C/S, color)	$4,595,000
The Detective (P/V, color)	$4,490,000
The Flim-Flam Man (P/V, color)	$3,845,000
In Like Flint (C/S, color)	$3,775,000
Tony Rome (P/V, color)	$3,480,000
A Guide for the Married Man (P/V, color)	#3,325,000
Fathom (C/S, color)	$2,225,000
St. Valentine's Day Massacre (P/V, color)	$2,175,000
The Incident	$1,050,000
The Day the Fish Came Out (color)	$875,000
Bedazzled (P/V, color)	$770,000

All releases after 1967 are in color

1968

Star! (Todd-AO)	$14,320,000
Planet of the Apes (P/V)	$5,800,000
A Flea in Her Ear (P/V)	$4,950,000
Bandolero (P/V)	$4,450,000
The Boston Strangler (P/V)	$4,100,000
The Magus (P/V)	$3,775,000
Prudence and the Pill	$3,570,000
Decline and Fall of a Bird Watcher	$1,970,000
The Sweet Ride (P/V)	$1,935,000
The Touchables	$1,215,000

1969

Justine (P/V)	$7,870,000
The Undefeated (P/V)	$7,115,000
Butch Cassidy and the Sundance Kid (P/V)	$6,825,000
Staircase (P/V)	$6,370,000
Che (P/V)	$5,160,000
The Chairman (P/V)	$4,915,000
Hard Contract (P/V)	$4,070,000
One Hundred Rifles	$3,920,000
Lady in Cement (P/V)	$3,585,000

The Prime of Miss Jean Brodie	$2,760,000
Joanna (P/V)	$1,195,000
The Guru	$970,000

1970

Tora! Tora! Tora! (P/V)	$25,485,000
Hello, Dolly (Todd-AO)	$25,335,000
Patton (Dimension 150)	$12,625,000
The Only Game in Town	$10,235,000
The Great White Hope (P/V)	$9,870,000
The Kremlin Letter (P/V)	$6,095,000
Myra Breckinridge (P/V)	$5,385,000
The Games (P/V)	$4,895,000
Beneath the Planet of the Apes (P/V)	$4,675,000
Hello, Goodbye	$4,400,000
The Sicilian Clan (P/V)	$4,170,000
M*A*S*H (P/V)	$3,025,000
MOVE (P/V)	$2,785,000
A Walk With Love and Death	$2,410,000
Run, Shadow, Run	$2,140,000
Beyond the Valley of the Dolls (P/V)	$2,090,000

1971

The Hot Rock (P/V)	$4,895,000
The French Connection	$3,300,000
The Seven Minutes	$2,415,000
Marriage of a Young Stockbroker	$2,230,000
Escape From the Planet of the Apes (P/V)	$2,060,000
Panic in Needle Park	$1,645,000
Vanishing Point	$1,585,000
Little Murders	$1,340,000
The Culpepper Cattle Company	$1,000,000

1972

The Poseidon Adventure (P/V)	$4,700,000
The Other	$2,250,000

The Salzburg Connection	$1,955,000
Conquest of the Planet of the Apes (P/V)	$1,595,000
When Legends Die (P/V)	$1,520,000
Sounder (P/V)	$900,000

1973

Emperor of the North	$3,705,000
Ace Eli and Rodgers of the Skies (P/V)	$3,350,000
The Neptune Factor (P/V)	$2,500,000
Cinderella Liberty (P/V)	$2,465,000
The Seven-Ups	$2,425,000
The Laughing Policeman (P/V)	$2,280,000
The Last American Hero (P/V)	$2,130,000
Kid Blue (P/V)	$2,000,000
Battle for the Planet of the Apes (P/V)	$1,710,000
Gordon's War	$1,600,000
Hex	$980,000

1974

The Towering Inferno (P/V)	$14,265,000
Young Frankenstein (black & white)	$2,780,000
Conrack (P/V)	$2,370,000
Crazy World of Julius Vrooder (P/V)	$1,700,000
Zardoz (P/V)	$1,570,000
Dirty Mary and Crazy Larry	$1,140,000

1975

At Long Last, Love	$5,140,000
French Connection II	$4,340,000
Royal Flash (P/V)	$4,040,000
The Adventures of Sherlock Holmes' Smarter Brother	$2,895,000
W.W. and the Dixie Dancekings	$2,805,000
Peeper (P/V)	$2,325,000

The Long, Hard Ride (P/V)	$2,140,000
Race With the Devil	$1,745,000
The Nickel Ride	$1,400,000
The Rocky Horror Picture Show	$1,400,000
Capone	$970,000

1976

Damnation Alley (P/V)	$8,000,000
Silver Streak	$6,500,000
The Duchess and the Dirtwater Fox (P/V)	$4,590,000
Silent Movie	$4,055,000
Mother, Jugs, and Speed (P/V)	$3,220,000
The Omen (P/V)	$2,800,000
Alex and the Gypsy	$2,260,000
Wizards	$2,000,000
All This and World War II	$1,300,000

1977

Star Wars (P/V)	$9,500,000
The Other Side of Midnight	$9,000,000
Julia	$7,840,000
The World's Greatest Lover	$4,800,000
Mr. Billion	$4,590,000
High Anxiety	$4,015,000
Raid On Entebbe (Made for TV)	$3,500,000
Fire Sale	$1,500,000

1978

Avalanche Express (P/V)	$12,000,000
The Boys From Brazil	$12,000,000
The Fury	$7,500,000
Damien: Omen II (P/V)	$6,800,000
The Driver	$4,000,000
An Unmarried Woman	$2,515,000

1979

All That Jazz	$12,000,000

The Rose	$9,250,000
Butch and Sundance: The Early Years	$9,000,000
Luna	$5,000,000
Norma Rae (P/V)	$4,500,000
Breaking Away	$2,300,000
A Perfect Couple (P/V)	$1,900,000

1980

The Empire Strikes Back (P/V)	$25,000,000
Nine to Five	$10,000,000
Tribute	$8,000,000
Kagemusha	$7,500,000
Scavenger Hunt	$7,000,000
A Change of Seasons	$6,000,000
Willie and Phil	$5,500,000
Health (P/V)	$5,200,000
Middle Age Crazy	$5,100,000
Terror Train	$4,200,000
My Bodyguard	$3,000,000
The Man with Bogart's Face	$2,000,000

1981

Cannonball Run	$18,000,000
Taps	$14,000,000
Zorro, the Gay Blade	$12,600,000
Quest For Fire (P/V)	$12,000,000
The Amateur	$10,000,000
Death Hunt	$10,000,000
History of the World--Part I (P/V)	$10,000,000
Eyewitness	$8,500,000
Southern Comfort	$8,000,000
Chu Chu and the Philly Flash	$7,000,000
The Final Conflict (P/V)	$5,000,000
Porky's	$5,000,000
Tattoo	$5,000,000

1982

Megaforce	$20,000,000

The Verdict	$16,000,000
Making Love	$14,000,000
Monsignor	$10,000,000
The Entity (P/V)	$9,000,000

1983

Return of the Jedi (P/V)	$32,500,000
King of Comedy	$19,000,000
Star Chamber (P/V)	$8,000,000
One Night in Heaven	$6,000,000

1984

Rhinestone	$28,000,000
Adventures of Buckaroo Banzai (P/V)	$17,000,000
Romancing the Stone (P/V)	$9,500,000
Johnny Dangerously	$9,000,000
To Be or Not to Be	$9,000,000
Dreamscape	$6,000,000
Revenge of the Nerds	$6,000,000

1985

Enemy Mine (P/V)	$33,000,000
Jewel of the Nile (P/V)	$25,000,000
Cocoon	$21,000,000
The Man With One Red Shoe	$16,000,000
Prizzi's Honor	$16,000,000
Turk 182	$15,000,000

1986

Big Trouble in Little China	$20,000,000
The Name of the Rose	$18,500,000
Space Camp	$18,000,000
Aliens	$18,000,000
The Boy Who Could Fly	$9,000,000
The Fly	$9,000,000
Lucas	$6,000,000

DATE DUE

FE 21 '95			

DEMCO 38-297